THE REVELS PLAYS

General Editor: Clifford Leech

PHILASTER
OR, LOVE LIES A-BLEEDING

PHYLASTER.

Or, Loue lyes a Bleeding.

Acted at the Globe by his Maiesties Seruants.

Written by { *Francis Baymont* and *Iohn Fletcher* } Gent.

Printed at *London* for *Thomas walkley*, and are to be sold at his

Title-page of the 1620 Quarto (*Reproduced by courtesy of the Trustees of the British Museum*)

Philaster

or

Love Lies a-Bleeding

FRANCIS BEAUMONT
& JOHN FLETCHER

EDITED BY

ANDREW GURR

THE REVELS PLAYS

METHUEN & CO LTD
11 NEW FETTER LANE · LONDON EC4

This edition first published 1969
Introduction, Apparatus Criticus, etc.
© 1969 Andrew Gurr
Printed in Great Britain by
The Broadwater Press Ltd, Welwyn Garden City, Herts
SBN 416 13630 3

Distributed in the USA by Barnes & Noble, Inc.

General Editor's Preface

The Revels Plays began to appear in 1958, and in the General Editor's Preface included in the first few volumes the plan of the series was briefly sketched. All those concerned in the undertaking recognized that no rigid pattern could be proposed in advance: to some extent the collective experience of the editors would affect the series as it developed, and the textual situation was by no means uniform among the plays that we hoped to include. The need for flexibility is still recognized, and each editor indicates in his introduction the procedures that have seemed best in relation to his particular play.

Nevertheless, we were fairly convinced that in some matters our policy would remain constant, and no major change in any of these respects has been made. The introduction to each volume includes a discussion of the provenance of the text, the play's stage-history and reputation, its significance as a contribution to dramatic literature, and its place within the work of its author. The text is based on a fresh examination of the early editions. Modern spelling is used, archaic forms being preserved only when rhyme or metre demands them or when a modernized form would not give the required sense or would obscure a play upon words. The procedure adopted in punctuation varies to some extent according to the degree of authority which an editor can attribute to the punctuation of the copy-text, but in every instance it is intended that the punctuation used in a Revels volume should not obscure a dramatic or rhetorical suggestiveness which may be discerned in the copy. Editorial stage-directions are enclosed in square brackets. The collation aims at making clear the grounds for an editor's choice wherever the original or a frequently accepted modern reading has been departed from. Annotations attempt to explain difficult passages and to provide such comments and illustrations of usage as the editor considers desirable.

When the series was planned, it was intended that each volume should include a glossary. At an early stage, however, it was realized that this would mean either an arbitrary distribution of material between the glossary and the annotations or a duplication of material. It has therefore become our practice to dispense with a glossary but to include an index to the annotations, which avoids duplication and facilitates reference.

Act-divisions are employed if they appear in the copy-text or if the structure of the play clearly points to a five-act division. In other instances, only scene-numbers are inserted. All act- and scene-indications which do not derive from the copy-text are given unobtrusively in square brackets. In no instance is an editorial indication of locality introduced into a scene-heading. When an editor finds it necessary to comment on the location of a scene, this is done in the annotations.

The series continues to use the innovation in line-numbering that was introduced in the first volume. Stage-directions which occur on lines separate from the text are given the number of the immediately preceding line followed by a decimal point and 1, 2, 3, etc. Thus 163.5 indicates the fifth line of a stage-direction following line 163 of the scene. At the beginning of a scene the lines of a stage-direction are numbered 0.1, 0.2, etc.

The Revels Plays have begun with the re-editing of a number of the best-known tragedies and comedies of the later Elizabethan and Jacobean years, and there are many such plays to which the techniques of modern editing need to be applied. It is hoped, however, that the series will be able to include certain lesser-known plays which remain in general neglect despite the lively interest that an acquaintance with them can arouse.

The present volume is the second in which a new procedure is followed in the handling of '-ed' verbal terminations. Previously we used '-ed' in past tenses and past participles when the termination was probably syllabic, and '-'d' elsewhere. Now we use '-ed' for non-syllabic terminations and '-èd' for syllabic. This seems in line with our attempt to give the reader an edition with modernized spelling while at the same time indicating the metrical pattern. It follows that in such a form as 'studied' we now imply a probably dissyllabic pronunciation, and have dropped the form 'study'd'. Moreover, in verbs and adjectives ending in '-e', the second person singular and the superlative are given as '-est', whether or not the termination appears to be syllabic. In prose passages only '-ed' and '-est' are used.

It has always been in the forefront of attention that the plays included should be such as deserve and indeed demand performance. The editors have therefore given a record (necessarily incomplete) of modern productions; in the annotations there is, moreover, occasional conjecture on the way in which a scene or a piece of stage-business was done on the original stage. Perhaps, too, the absence of indications of locality and of editorial scene-headings will suggest the advantage of achieving in a modern theatre some approach to the characteristic fluidity of scene and the neutrality of acting-space that Shakespeare's fellows knew.

CLIFFORD LEECH

Toronto, 1969

Contents

Preface

It will be obvious to the reader that for this edition I owe irredeemable debts to the textual labours of Robert K. Turner jr and to the critical views of J. F. Danby and Clifford Leech. Professor Turner's work, like that of his fellow editors in the new series of critical textual editions of the Beaumont and Fletcher plays under the general editorship of Fredson Bowers, is a perch from which students of the texts will only hesitantly fly, and I must express my gratitude for Professor Turner's kindness in correspondence on matters about which I was hesitant.

In addition to my recognizable debts to the published work of Professor Danby and Professor Leech on the Beaumont and Fletcher plays, I should like to record my more private gratitude to my colleagues Charles Barber and Geoffrey Hill, who have continued to listen to me on matters concerning Jacobean drama and who have given me the benefit of their own ideas. I should also like to thank Professor S. Musgrove of the University of Auckland for detailed assistance on certain points, and Dorothy L. Swerdlove of the Theatre Collection at the Lincoln Center, New York, and Helen D. Willard of the Harvard College Library Theatre Collection for their ready replies to my distanced queries about *Philaster*'s theatre history. In the same connection I should like to thank Adam O'Riordan, who produced *Philaster* at Oxford in 1947, and whose reply to my inquiry was splendidly informative.

I owe by far the greatest debt, of course, to the General Editor of the Revels Series, the ghost in the editorial cellarage, whose presence has supplied any steadiness this edifice may possess.

ANDREW GURR

Leeds, 1969

Abbreviations

Bentley   G. E. Bentley, *The Jacobean and Caroline Stage*,
                 7 vols. (Oxford, 1941–68).

Boas   *Philaster*, ed. by F. S. Boas (London, 1898).

Brooke   *English Drama 1580–1642*, ed. by C. F. Tucker
                 Brooke and Nathaniel Burton Paradise (New
                 York, 1933).

Chambers, *E.S.*   E. K. Chambers, *The Elizabethan Stage*, 4 vols.
                 (Oxford, 1923).

Chambers, *W.S.*   E. K. Chambers, *William Shakespeare*, 2 vols.
                 (Oxford, 1930).

Colman   *The Dramatic Works of Beaumont and Fletcher*,
                 ed. by G. Colman, 10 vols. (London, 1778).

D.A.   *Dissertation Abstracts.*

Daniel   *The Works of Francis Beaumont and John
                 Fletcher*, ed. by A. H. Bullen, P. A. Daniel, etc.,
                 4 vols. (unfinished) (London, 1904–12).

Dyce   *The Works of Beaumont and Fletcher*, ed. by
                 Alexander Dyce, 11 vols. (London, 1843–6).

ELH   *E[nglish] L[iterary] H[istory].*

E.S.   *English Studies.*

Langbaine   *The Works of Beaumont and Fletcher*, 7 vols.
                 (London, 1711).

Mason   J. Monck Mason, *Comments on the Plays of
                 Beaumont and Fletcher* (London, 1798).

M.L.N.   *Modern Language Notes.*

M.L.R.   *Modern Language Review.*

O.E.D.   *The Oxford English Dictionary.*

P.M.L.A.   *Publications of the Modern Language Association of America.*

P.Q.   *Philological Quarterly.*

R.E.S.   *Review of English Studies.*

S.B.   *Studies in Bibliography.*

Sh.S.   *Shakespeare Survey.*

S.P.   *Studies in Philology.*

S.Q.   *Shakespeare Quarterly.*

Spencer   *Elizabethan Plays,* ed. by Hazelton Spencer (Boston, 1933).

Theobald   *The Works of Beaumont and Fletcher,* ed. by L. Theobald, T. Seward, and J. Sympson, 15 vols. (London, 1750).

Thorndike   *'Philaster' and 'The Maid's Tragedy',* ed. by Ashley H. Thorndike (Boston, 1906).

Turner   *Philaster,* ed. by R. K. Turner jr, in *The Dramatic Works in the Beaumont and Fletcher Canon,* gen. ed. Fredson Bowers, vol. 1 (Cambridge, 1966).

Weber   *The Works of Beaumont and Fletcher,* ed. by Henry Weber, 14 vols. (Edinburgh, 1812).

Quotations and line-numbers for Shakespeare are taken from the Tudor Shakespeare, ed. by P. Alexander. Quotations and line-numbers for plays of Beaumont and Fletcher apart from *Philaster* where possible are taken from *The Dramatic Works in the Beaumont and Fletcher Canon,* gen. ed. Fredson Bowers (i.e., for *The Knight of the Burning Pestle* and *The Coxcomb*). Quotations and line-numbers from plays and poems not printed in the first Bowers volume are taken from Dyce. References to plays of dramatists other than Beaumont and Fletcher or Shakespeare where not separately noted are taken from the following editions:

Jonson   *Ben Jonson,* ed. by C. H. Herford, P. and E. Simpson, 11 vols. (Oxford, 1925–52).

Marston   *The Works of John Marston*, ed. by A. H. Bullen,
                   3 vols. (London, 1887).

Massinger   *The Plays of Philip Massinger*, ed. by F. Cun-
                   ningham (London, [1871]).

Chronology

This conjectural chronology is based on Chambers, *E.S.*, III, 219–35; Baldwin Maxwell, *Studies in Beaumont, Fletcher and Massinger*, Chapel Hill, 1939; and J. E. Savage, 'The Date of Beaumont and Fletcher's *Cupid's Revenge*', *ELH*, XV (1948), 286–94. See also Richard Proudfoot, 'Shakespeare and the New Dramatists of the King's Men, 1608–1613', *Later Shakespeare*, Stratford-upon-Avon Studies 8, pp. 234–61.

Introduction

There is little external evidence to prove that Beaumont and Fletcher collaborated in the writing of *Philaster*. Certainly when first published in 1620, four years after Beaumont's death, the play had both names on the title-page; but by then the linked names of Beaumont and Fletcher were so famous that every product of Fletcher and the later collaborators such as Massinger was credited to the original partnership. In 1610, soon after the play was written, John Davies of Hereford, one of the few contemporaries whom we know to have been an acquaintance of both authors, ascribed it to Fletcher alone. In the commendatory verses to the first Beaumont and Fletcher Folio of 1647 four writers, Herrick, Lovelace, Howard, and Thomas Stanley, all address Fletcher as the sole author, three of them giving him credit for *The Maid's Tragedy* and *A King and No King* as well. On the other hand John Earle, in verses in the same Folio, which were said to have been written 'thirty yeares since, presently after his [i.e., Beaumont's] death', attributed all three plays to Beaumont. Only Dryden unhesitatingly ascribed it to both authors, in his *Essay of Dramatic Poesy* written nearly half a century after both playwrights were dead.

Neither can we turn with much confidence to the various versification and linguistic tests which have been used in the attempt to distinguish the different authors of the so-called Beaumont and Fletcher canon. On the whole they have established Fletcher's and Massinger's shares with some precision in the plays written after about 1615, but Beaumont is linguistically an altogether more shadowy figure than the longer-lived playwright, and if it were not that his name figures as a founder of the partnership there might be reason to doubt whether he existed in it at all. His linguistic practices in the two plays he wrote unaided (if indeed we can even be sure he did that) are hardly consistent enough for us to make a reliable identification of his share in others. He was enough of a chameleon to make the spelling and verse tests of even the latest and most careful disintegrator of the canon misleading, to the extent of attributing *The Faithful Shepherdess*, one of the few plays certainly all Fletcher's, rather to Beaumont than Fletcher.[1] Only the fact that the two names did get the credit for all the plays suggests that they were the original pair, and that therefore they most likely did jointly write the plays which made the collaboration famous; otherwise it would be tempting to see Beaumont as no more than a disintegrator's explanation why the first plays are, as they are traditionally thought to be, the best in the canon.

We know relatively little of Beaumont's and Fletcher's lives, and still less of their collaboration. Like Shakespeare, they became legendary in their lifetimes, and being almost as famous as their older contemporary their legend is almost as misty. The actual concept of collaboration became an essential part of the legend. Aubrey's notorious jotting, made several decades after both authors were dead, retails some of the gossip: 'They lived together on the Banke side [i.e., Southwark], not far from the Play-house, both batchelors; lay together—from Sir John Hales, etc.; had one wench in the house between them, which they did so admire; the same cloathes and cloake, &c., betweene them.'[2] It can be weighed more as a contribution to a legend than as a testimonial, though there must have been a basis of truth in it. We can see the collaborators and the collaboration more clearly by looking at their respective backgrounds.

Fletcher was born in 1579, one of nine children; in 1591 he probably attended Bene't (Corpus Christi) College, Cambridge, where his father had been President. His father was made Bishop of London in 1595, but died in the following year heavily in debt and under the royal displeasure. Fletcher was thus not only a younger son of a father who was unable to provide him with either money

---

[1] Cyrus Hoy, 'The Shares of Fletcher and his Collaborators in the Beaumont and Fletcher Canon (III)', *S.B.*, XI (1958), 85–106; and cf. Clifford Leech, *The John Fletcher Plays*, London, 1962, p. 25.

[2] *Brief Lives*, ed. Andrew Clark, Oxford, 1898, I, 96.

or preferment but actually had his chances of making his own way hindered by his parentage. We know nothing of him through the crucial years from eighteen to twenty-eight. In 1607 he joined Beaumont in writing commendatory verses for Jonson's *Volpone*, and he may have revised Beaumont's *The Woman Hater* before its publication in the same year. His own first published play, *The Faithful Shepherdess*, written in 1608, was prefaced like *The Woman Hater* by a commendation from Jonson. His regular collaboration with Beaumont probably began in 1608 when he was twenty-seven and Beaumont twenty-two. Their first joint play, *Cupid's Revenge*, was written, like the other early plays, for a boys' company, and they went on to write *Philaster* in 1609 for Shakespeare's company, the King's Men, who were more or less their sole employers thereafter. Aubrey's jotting relates to this and the next few years, which produced altogether about six joint plays. From about 1613, when Beaumont dropped out, Fletcher collaborated successively with Shakespeare, Massinger, Field, and Rowley, until his death in 1625, by which time he and his various collaborators had raised the total number of plays in the canon to over fifty. He was buried in St Mary Overy's (now St Saviour's) in Southwark, where he had probably lived since he began writing with Beaumont. He may be the John Fletcher whose marriage to Joan Herring is recorded in the St Saviour's register, 3 November 1612.

Beaumont was the third son of a Justice of Common Pleas, born 1584–5 in Leicestershire. He went to Oxford in 1597, and taking no degree proceeded to the Inner Temple in 1600. The anonymous *Salmacis and Hermaphroditus*, an Ovidian poem published in 1602, was probably his, and we have a manuscript dating from about the same time of a burlesque grammar lecture he gave before the students of the Inner Temple.[1] His first known play, *The Woman Hater*, was performed by Paul's Boys in about 1605. His comic masterpiece, *The Knight of the Burning Pestle*, was given a single performance by the Revels Children in 1607, and he probably then joined Fletcher, whose *Faithful Shepherdess* for the same company

[1] Reprinted by Mark Eccles, 'Francis Beaumont's Grammar Lecture', *R.E.S.*, XVI (1940), 402–14.

had been similarly unsuccessful,[1] in writing *Cupid's Revenge*. His collaboration with Fletcher lasted till 1612 or early 1613, when he married profitably and retired to the country. He died on 6 March 1616, and was buried in Westminster Abbey.

He was five years younger than Fletcher, and, to judge by his success in marrying an heiress and by his burial place, his social connections were a little higher. There is familiarity if not intimacy in the tone of his verse epistle to the Countess of Rutland, Sidney's daughter, and the elegy written within three days of her death in 1612 is genuinely emotional. Both he and Fletcher are usually regarded as socially superior to their fellow playwrights, and they did have rather more respectable backgrounds than, say, Jonson or Shakespeare. But both were younger sons, and while they were bachelors in London they both attached themselves most closely to the circle of their literary peers, and mainly the circle which fed on Jonson. Beaumont wrote prefatory verses for *Volpone*, *The Silent Woman*, and *Catiline*, and Fletcher for *Volpone* and *Catiline*, while Beaumont and Jonson wrote for Fletcher's *Faithful Shepherdess*. Jonson himself showed a great affection for Fletcher in his outpourings to Drummond of Hawthornden in 1619, and a more qualified regard for Beaumont,[2] who wrote nostalgically in his turn in the famous epistle to Jonson from the country of their witty meetings at the Mermaid.[3] They evidently read each other's plays, since Jonson's *Alchemist* (1610) has distinct echoes of *The Knight of the Burning Pestle*, which had only been staged on the one unhappy occasion three years before,[4] and they mainly exchanged their

[1] The circumstances of the sole original performance of *The Knight of the Burning Pestle* are given by the publisher of the 1613 quarto in his preface. Fletcher tells of his play's failure in his own preface to the 1609/10 edition of his play.

[2] 'xi his acquaintance & Behaviour with poets Living with him... Francis Beaumont loved too much himself & his own Verses... Chapman and Fletcher were loved of him.' William Drummond of Hawthornden, *Notes of Conversations with Ben Jonson, 1619*, ed. G. B. Harrison, Bodley Head Quartos, London, 1923, p. 8.

[3] Cf. I. A. Shapiro, 'The "Mermaid Club"', *M.L.R.*, XLV (1950), 6–17, and subsequent correspondence, *M.L.R.*, XLVI (1951), 58–63, 435–6.

[4] *The Alchemist*'s reference in IV. iv to a 'Knight o' the curious cockscomb' is taken by Herford and Simpson to refer to *The Coxcomb*, but is very probably a conflated allusion to the two plays, since coxcomb and

comedies, judging by the fact that the only recognizable echoes are of comedies—Jonson echoes *The Burning Pestle* and *The Coxcomb* (1610) in *The Alchemist*, and Beaumont and Fletcher echo his *Silent Woman* (1609) and *Alchemist* in *The Scornful Lady* (1610) and *The Woman's Prize* (1611).[1] Other friends besides Jonson received manuscripts of other plays. The publisher of *A King and No King* in 1619 acknowledged his receipt of the manuscript used to print the play from Sir Henry Neville, a familiar of the playwrights; and the publisher of the 1647 Folio went so far as to claim, with only partial truth, that all his manuscripts had been obtained from 'such as received them from the *Authours* themselves'.

The processes of collaboration inspired a good deal of contemporary curiosity. Aubrey noted of Beaumont that 'I have heard Dr. John Earles (since Bishop of Sarum), who knew them, say that his maine businesse was to correct the overflowings of Mr. Fletcher's witt',[2] a view reiterated in verse by William Cartwright in the 1647 Folio. Sir John Birkenhead offered a modified view in the same volume:

> *Some thinke Your Witts of two Complexions fram'd,*
> *That One the Sock, th'Other the Buskin claim'd;*
> *That should the Stage embattaile all it's Force,*
> FLETCHER *would lead the Foot,* BEAUMONT *the Horse.*
> *But, you were Both for Both: not Semi-witts,*
> *Each Piece is wholly Two, yet never splits:*

The first disintegrators of the canon at the end of last century were on the whole inclined to endorse the view that Beaumont's was the tragic buskin and Fletcher's the comic sock, though usually with some of Birkenhead's qualifications. Boyle, for instance, thought

---

pestle were both common terms for a phallus. A reference in v. i to a six-year-old 'with the great thing' is paralleled by an allusion in *The Knight of the Burning Pestle*, III. ii; 'fire-drake' and 'lungs' describing Face on successive lines in II. i of *The Alchemist* are probably an unconscious memory of 'fire-drake' and 'Lungeis' fourteen lines apart in II. iv of the *Burning Pestle*, referring to Jasper; and I. iii. 4 'Free of the Grocers' and I. ii. 61 'velvet head' in *The Alchemist* may also be memories of Beaumont's comedy.

[1] Cf. C. M. Gayley, *Francis Beaumont, Dramatist*, London, 1914, p. 369, and Baldwin Maxwell, *Studies in Beaumont, Fletcher and Massinger*, Chapel Hill, 1939, p. 18.

[2] *Brief Lives*, I, 95–6.

Philaster to be all Beaumont's except for the scenes concerning the comic citizens, v. iii. 127–70 and v. iv. Fleay further attributed the opening scene with its social satire to Fletcher, and Oliphant also gave him the bawdy prose scenes in II. ii and iv. Oliphant and after him Thorndike and Gayley did suggest that the satirical prose of the opening scene was Beaumont's and the verse after the King's entry Fletcher's, but the general tendency is apparent in Gayley's pervasive desire to attribute the credit in the collaboration to Beaumont and the blame to Fletcher. He divides even short passages inside the scenes between the authors with a disarming over-confidence.[1] The most recent disintegrator, Cyrus Hoy,[2] has used spelling and linguistic tests which on the whole avoid the difficulties the earlier scholars using verse tests had in attributing prose, but still lack a basis of consistent practice in Beaumont. He finds that Fletcher probably wrote all of I. i, II. ii, II. iv after Pharamond's entrance, IV. i–ii (the hunting scenes of bawdy prose), v. iii after the King's exit, and v. iv. This would give Fletcher the buskin in the opening scene and a snippet of v. iii only, and Beaumont no comedy at all, which seems a little odd, since Beaumont's two plays before he started collaborating with Fletcher were brilliant comedies, and Fletcher's one play was a serious and erudite pastoral drama. If, as Hoy believes, Beaumont's was the controlling hand to the extent that he copied out the final draft and so laid his orthographic characteristics over the whole play, then evidently to be confident in attributing any line in the play to one or other of the authors is to stretch the available evidence beyond its breaking-point.

Nonetheless, despite the lack of contemporary testimony to the play's dual authorship and the insufficiency of the disintegration tests, it is probable that the play was Beaumont's and Fletcher's in fairly equal shares. The circumstantial evidence associates one or

---

[1] F. G. Fleay, *On Metrical Tests as applied to Dramatic Poetry: Part II, Beaumont, Fletcher and Massinger*, London, 1886; E. H. C. Oliphant, 'The Works of Beaumont and Fletcher', *E.S.*, XIV (1890), 53, XV (1891), 321, XVI (1892), 180; reiterated with slight modifications in *The Plays of Beaumont and Fletcher*, New Haven, 1927; Gayley, *op. cit.*

[2] Cyrus Hoy, 'The Shares of Fletcher and his Collaborators in the Beaumont and Fletcher Canon', seven articles, *S.B.*, VIII–IX, XI–XV (1956–62).

the other writer, or both together, with the play, and there is no real reason for refusing to accept the consensus. More importantly in the long run, there are also various pieces of internal evidence suggesting some of the specific interests each author might have contributed to the making of the play; though it is impossible to fix much more than a division of initial interests. The collaboration was so close and efficient that no loose ends, no incongruities between one scene and another or variations in the treatment of theme or character can be established in any of the major plays.

Philaster is one of the most ambitious works of literary collaboration ever written. Its aim was no less than the translation of the high literary and educational designs of Sidney's *Arcadia* into commercial drama, and the aim was directed by not one but a pair of authors, at a time when only the lowest potboiling third of the dramatic repertory was produced by multiple authorship. It was, moreover, a hybrid work not only as a collaborated play but as a new type of tragicomedy. The aim hit a mark of sorts in creating a fashion which Stuart audiences appreciated for thirty years, and which made Beaumont and Fletcher the only authors besides Shakespeare and Jonson to be granted the accolade of a posthumous collection of their plays in Folio. It is a minor quirk of fate that the success with this target has to some extent obscured the success in hitting the other, the imitation of the *Arcadia*, and left *Philaster* to be considered as a harbinger of the major play of the collaboration, *The Maid's Tragedy*, and the many plays in the canon which followed, and as a rarity of literary history, a self-consciously new work in a hybrid genre, and no more. It is perhaps the inevitable undergrowth of its fame. More than anything else, however, the play is the end-product of an extraordinarily ingenious exploitation of the collaborative process, almost an exploitation of its limitations, in the course of which Beaumont and Fletcher found a form of drama of unprecedented literary pretensions, and one with inherent in it a considerable degree of theatrical effectiveness. Because it was a success its total novelty at the time has been obscured to some extent, and it is our misfortune that so much undergrowth has to be burrowed through before the kind of ingenuity it displays can be properly inspected.

2. THE DATE

John Davies of Hereford, a friend of Fletcher and acquaintance of
Beaumont,[1] saw *Philaster*, probably in manuscript, by about mid-
1610. He wrote commending it in his *Scourge of Folly* (entered on
the Stationers' Register 8 October 1610), Epigram 206:

> To the well deserving Mr. John Fletcher.
>
> *Love lies ableeding*, if it should not prove
> Her uttmost art to shew why it doth love.
> Thou being the *Subject* (now) It raignes upon;
> Raign'st in *Arte, Judgement, and Invention*:
> *For this* I *love thee: and can doe no lesse*
> *For thine as faire, as faithful* Sheepheardesse.

Since the reference is to the play's second title, which would not
have been apparent on stage, Davies probably either saw or was
presented with a copy of the play in manuscript by Fletcher, which
would explain his attribution of it to the older collaborator alone.
It was not unknown for the collaborators to give copies of their
plays to friends. He probably met Fletcher's *Faithful Shepherdess*
in the same way, since it was unsuccessful when first performed in
1608, before its publication in late 1609–10. On the other hand, of
course, Davies might have learned of *Philaster*'s second title from
the players' advertisement for the play's performance. All the epigram certainly tells us is that the play must have been completed,
whether performed or not, by the summer of 1610.

Davies is not likely to have written an epigram on a play which
was not new. He assumes it was newer than *The Faithful Shepherdess*, an assumption confirmed by the switch in the acting companies for which the two plays were written. The Blackfriars children owned *The Faithful Shepherdess, Cupid's Revenge*, and *The
Coxcomb*, all of which can be dated in 1609 or earlier, and the King's
Men owned *Philaster* together with *The Maid's Tragedy, A King
and No King*, and almost all the other plays which can be dated in
1610 or later. The Blackfriars children were involved in prohibition
troubles stemming initially from Chapman's *Byron* in 1608, and in

---

[1] Davies' epigram on Beaumont in *The Scourge of Folly* is phrased in
markedly less intimate terms than those he uses to Fletcher.

that year lost their theatre to the King's Men; either of these happenings may have given sufficient reason for Beaumont and Fletcher to change their employers.[1] James E. Savage[2] has shown that *Cupid's Revenge* very probably preceded *Philaster* and was written in late 1607–8. *Philaster* must therefore have been written between late 1608 and early 1610.

Most scholars have agreed in assigning the play to the limits of these two years, putting it at one extreme or the other according to whether they believe it preceded or followed *Cymbeline*, which is generally dated in or about 1609. One piece of internal evidence, however, suggests it was written precisely in the middle between the agreed limits. The reference to 'the new platform' (v. iii. 3) is difficult to make sense of if it does not mean the 'great platform' (i.e., a model of the main deck, the waist) of Prince Henry's lavishly constructed new ship, the *Prince Royal*. The building of the ship was the occasion of a series of charges laid by the Earl of Northampton and others against the Lord Admiral, the Earl of Nottingham, who was responsible for its construction. James himself heard the evidence of both sides at the yard where the ship was being built, in Woolwich, on 8 May 1609. The builder, Phineas Pette, subsequently (and thankfully, since the judgment was in the Lord Admiral's and therefore his favour) reported that

> one main point of proportion was mainly insisted upon, and with much violence and eagerness urged on both sides, which was the square of the ship's flat in the midships, they offering constantly upon their oaths that it was full 13 feet, we as constantly insisting that it was 11 feet 8 inches. But, because this difference was long, and could not be tried upon the small plats, his Majesty referred the trial to be made on the great platform, which was purposely framed of planks to the full scale of the ship.[3]

There are doubts about this identification: first, it is said in the play to be in the city; and secondly as a full-scale mock-up of a ship

---

[1] See below, p. xliii.

[2] James E. Savage, 'Beaumont and Fletcher's *Philaster* and Sidney's *Arcadia*', *ELH*, XIV (1947), 194–206; and 'The Date of Beaumont and Fletcher's *Cupid's Revenge*', *ELH*, XV (1948), 286–94.

[3] J. B. Nichols, *The Progresses, Processions and Magnificent Festivities of King James the First*, 3 vols., London, 1828, II, 252.

set up in the yard where the ship was being constructed it would hardly qualify for distinction as 'the new' platform. On the other hand, as the deciding point in a quarrel between my Lords of Nottingham and Northampton, it would have made talk, and in the play, as the phenomenon which Pharamond goes sightseeing after, it had to be located in the City, since Pharamond had to be captured by the citizens. In the absence of any other suggestion of what the new platform was, it seems that *Philaster* was being composed in and after May 1609.[1]

There are three possible echoes in the play of Shakespeare's *Cymbeline*,[2] which is dated in 1609 mainly on the ground that it preceded *The Winter's Tale*, which was seen by Simon Forman at the Globe early in 1611. The fact that they are merely verbal echoes and that they are so slight, coupled with the further rather surprising fact that apart from the mutual dependence of the two plays on the romance tradition there is little structural resemblance, suggests if anything that each play was written in ignorance of the other, at least till very late in the composition of the indebted play, whichever that was. *Philaster* developed naturally enough from *Cupid's Revenge*, in the same way that *Cymbeline* developed from *Pericles*, so there is no need to presume anything more than a parallel progression in the processes of composition of the two plays. Their resemblance is more important to their dramatic genre than to their dating.

The placing of *Philaster* in its sequence amongst the Beaumont and Fletcher plays is conjectural. Apart from Savage's evidence for the priority of *Cupid's Revenge*, there is only Dryden's statement in the *Essay of Dramatic Poesy* that 'the first play that brought Fletcher and [Beaumont] in esteem was their *Philaster*: for before that they had written two or three very unsuccessfully',[3] to support the presumption which most scholars have made, that *Philaster*

---

[1] Savage has a further piece of dating evidence in 'The "Gaping Wounds" in the text of *Philaster*', *P.Q.*, xxviii (1949), 455, suggesting that the reference in v. iv to 'a man of war' relates to the failure to launch the same *Prince Royal* on 24 September 1610. This is based on a misunderstanding of the text. See note to v. iv. 19–21.

[2] See below, p. xlv.

[3] *The Essays of John Dryden*, ed. W. P. Ker, I, 81.

preceded the other major plays of the collaboration written for the King's Company, *The Maid's Tragedy* and *A King and No King*. It was nearly ten years before any of them edged into print, though they were all popular enough to be played at Court by 1612. Apart from the evidence for dating *Philaster* in 1609, which leaves little time for the composition of the other major plays before then, there is only the internal evidence of the development from specific political concerns in *Philaster* to more theoretical constructions in the other plays. The cumulative evidence is slight but consistent for the dating of the plays written for the Blackfriars children in 1607–8, followed by *Philaster* for the King's Men in 1609 and *The Maid's Tragedy* and *A King and No King* in 1610–11, before Beaumont withdrew from the partnership in 1612 or 1613.

3. SOURCES

There is no obvious single source for *Philaster*. Few of the earlier Beaumont and Fletcher plays are concerned to give dramatized renderings of old stories in the Shakespearean manner. Beaumont and Fletcher were dramatizing not a story but a whole genre, the traditional prose romance, and the basic requirement of the genre was originality of plot. Instead of a plot serving as vehicle for the 'personation' of character in splendid verse, the characters are set in patterns to serve the plot. The conventions are those of prose romance literature, not of Shakespearean drama. There are no sources in the usual sense because the first necessity is a well-made and therefore original plot.

This is a point with important implications for the critical evaluation of *Philaster*. One would not wish to say that the Beaumont and Fletcher plays are simply that mockery of literary standards the 'well-made play', but their characters do function on a similar, fairly elementary dramatic level. They are dramatizations rather than dramas if one views them in terms of characterization. The important thing is not to do so. The 'well-made play' can be a literary vehicle in its own right provided it is seen to draw its conventions from an idealized world and not from any sort of familiar reality of the kind we expect in Shakespeare. The collaborators copied Sidney in utilizing the conventions of a popular genre to figure their golden world. The conventions of the prose romance accordingly provided the material sources of the play, while Sidney's example gave the essential formula. The first priority of these sources is a carefully designed story which will operate as a vast and complex metaphor or moral paradigm, a construction of situations exemplifying various moral desiderata in a way which is necessarily complex though ultimately unambiguous. The subtleties of characterization and poetic expression in verbal metaphor remain subordinate to the exemplification by means of the situation. It was a priority which lent itself more happily to collaborative writing than other kinds of drama, since it meant labouring first at the carpentry of an intricate and original story, with the actual cladding of words a subsequent matter to be divided in alternating stints once the essential plot metaphor was properly understood.

Sources for *Philaster* are to be found, then, in the *Arcadia* and in the conventions of the prose romances. E. M. Waith[1] has categorized the latter as, first, an imitation of the manners of the familiar world with an actual remoteness from it, intricacy of plot, an 'improbable hypothesis' on which the plot is based (the Sidneian testing situation designed to illuminate a moral question), an atmosphere of evil, protean characters, lively passions, and the language of emotion. All of these *Philaster* in varying degrees possesses. It is based not on the retelling of a historical or pseudo-historical story essentially displaying a single famous historical character, as was almost all the tragic drama before it, but on the invention of a story designed to present a problematical situation within which a pattern of characters moves to demonstrate the implications of the situation. As in the *Arcadia*, the individuality of the situation overrides in importance the individuality of the characters in it.

With a play of this kind the usual virtues of source-hunting for the purpose of seeing how the author modifies his given material disappear, and the value of sources for criticism becomes a question of recognizing what are conventions and what is being done through them. This can best be performed in *Philaster*'s case by analysing its authors' use of three specific sources, Montemayor's *Diana*, the

---

[1] E. M. Waith, *The Pattern of Tragicomedy in Beaumont and Fletcher*, Yale Studies in English No. 120, New Haven, 1952, pp. 36–42.

Arcadia, and *Hamlet*, in relation to the new kind of play which came out of the conjunction of the sources.

The basic story-situation in *Philaster* is anticipated in Alonso Perez's novella in Books VII and VIII of his continuation of Montemayor's romance.[1] Perez's continuation of the *Diana* was available in Bartholomew Yong's translation published in 1598, though Beaumont and Fletcher were evidently familiar with several Spanish pastoral romances in the original, and may have been with the *Diana*. In Perez, Rotindus King of Aeolia favours the head of one of the two great houses in his kingdom, Sagastes, over the other, Disteus, who is less wealthy but far surpasses him 'in vertue, wherewith his minde was bountifully enriched'.[2] Disteus, like Philaster, is hated by the King and loved by the people, while the reverse is true of Sagastes. Disteus loves Dardanea, Sagastes' sister, who like Arethusa returns his love secretly, though because of the enmity of the two houses she has in despair taken another husband, who has recently died at the outset of the story. The equivalent of Bellario in Perez is Disteus' old nurse Palna, who is stolen from Disteus by Sagastes to serve Dardanea, and who goes willingly in the hope of acting as go-between for the lovers. Among the incidents before the lovers gain each other which bear a resemblance to *Philaster* are Disteus' outburst of misanthropy at his discovery of Palna's desertion (equivalent to Philaster's speeches in III. i when he is told Bellario and Arethusa are false to him), Sagastes' nocturnal courting of a lady Marthea, a parallel of sorts to Pharamond's pursuit of Megra, and Disteus' subsequent rescue of Sagastes when he is attacked by a rival lover, which broadly corresponds to Philaster's rescue of Pharamond from the citizens. The situation at the beginning of Perez's story is closer than at the end, and there are numerous incidents which bear no resemblance to Beaumont and Fletcher's version at all. They took the basic elements from Perez and elaborated them for their own different purposes.

Sidney used the structural outline and the pastoral tradition of

---

[1] T. P. Harrison, 'A Probable Source of Beaumont and Fletcher's *Philaster*', *P.M.L.A.*, XLI (1926), 294–303.

[2] *Diana of George of Montemayor, translated out of Spanish into English by Bartholomew Yong*, London, 1598, p. 331.

the *Diana* for his own *Arcadia*, and up to a point Beaumont and
Fletcher followed his lead in using the structure and traditional
characterization of Perez's story for *Philaster*. They also transformed the Perez story as Sidney transformed his pastoral material,
and with the same underlying intention. If the view is correct that
Philaster is a reconstruction of the materials in *Cupid's Revenge*,
which in its turn is a conflation of two stories from the *Arcadia*,[1]
then it can be said that the essentials, if not of the story then of what
the story is designed to do, come from the *Arcadia* and not the
Diana. The four character-types of Perez, the noble hero Disteus,
the love-lorn maiden Dardanea, the lecherous antagonist Sagastes,
and the faithful go-between Palna, all types which appear in the
Arcadia, are presented in *Cupid's Revenge* with the addition of the
further Arcadian types of lecherous woman, stupid King, and girl
disguised as page to the hero. In *Cupid's Revenge*, the King is a
conflation of *Arcadia*'s King of Lycia with the King of Iberia, and
their stories are similarly conflated. Hidaspes, the King's daughter,
is Erona, daughter of the Lycian King, led by love into an unfortunate marriage which results in the deaths of the lovers. His son
Leucippus is Plangus, son of the Iberian King who becomes in-
fatuated with his son's mistress and marries her. When the new
Queen seeks to resume her relationship with the son, the youth
repulses her and in revenge she poisons the King's mind against
him. The stories of the two Kings and their unfortunate children
from Sidney are conflated so that Cupid's revenge is visited on one
family, the gullible father and his two erring children. Characteristics of the conflated King in his aspect as foolish lover of his son's
mistress are taken from Basilius' infatuation for Zelmane in the
Arcadia. Similarly Leucippus when enticed by the lecherous Queen
is modelled on Pyrocles and Musidorus when approached in the
same way by Andromana. Diaphantus, Pyrocles' loyal page, turns
out to be the disguised Zelmane, in love with Pyrocles but a daughter of his enemy, who dies in his arms as the similarly disguised
daughter of the *Cupid's Revenge* Queen dies with Leucippus. Beaumont and Fletcher reduce the range of characters and tighten the

[1] Savage, 'Beaumont and Fletcher's *Philaster* and Sidney's *Arcadia*',
op. cit.

plot by making her the Queen's daughter, so that the Queen can be punished by Cupid along with all the others through her death. The Queen's name, Bacha, is taken from a minor figure of lechery in the *Arcadia*, and those of the two other important characters, the loyal Ismenus and the self-seeking Timantus, are taken from similar minor figures with the required characteristics. In openly adopting Sidney's names the playwrights were explicitly acknow-ledging their debt.

In *Cupid's Revenge* two stories from Sidney and several of his characters are put together to make a tragedy for the stage. *Philaster* takes the seven chief character-types of *Cupid's Revenge* and fits them into the non-tragic Perez story. Leucippus the noble hero becomes Philaster, Hidaspes the chaste maiden becomes Arethusa, the disguised page becomes Bellario, the judicious courtier Ismenus is Dion, and the wicked trio—stupid King, lecherous and deceitful Queen, and self-seeking accomplice—are adjusted into Calabria's King and the league of Megra and Pharamond. The chief awkward-nesses of *Cupid's Revenge* are eliminated by the recombination. The play becomes a romance instead of an uncertain tragedy; instead of being stricken like Hidaspes by Cupid into falling for a dwarf, Arethusa is given an alliance equally unfortunate in her father's eyes but wholly virtuous in itself; similarly Philaster by loving her from the outset is saved from Leucippus' awkward character-switch from the lecherous young Prince with a mistress to the virtuous man resisting the seductions of the same woman once she has become his stepmother. The rôle of the disguised page in the play is changed so that she has a central function not only of exemplifying faithful love but also of disproving the allegations made against the heroine's virtue by the lecherous woman in the piece.

In redeploying the Arcadian characters and tightening up the plot Beaumont and Fletcher were not merely elaborating the *Diana*'s story. Sidney's fundamental design in the *Arcadia*, which Beaumont called 'an everlasting work',[1] was very different from the easy entertainment of Montemayor and Perez, and Beaumont and Fletcher took it over quite as thoroughly as they took his

[1] Dyce, XI, 509.

characters; it was in fact the Sidneian design which justified the
kind of characterization the collaborators employed. As J. F. Danby
has said,

> The ground-plan of Sidney's own heroical poem is ... the exem-
> plification of 'patience and magnanimity'. It is not, as Milton
> over-rashly asserted, merely 'vain and amatorious'. It is, on the
> contrary, as sage and serious as Spenser, or as anything Milton
> himself could have wished. The plan requires that the classical,
> romance and chivalric schemes should be brought within the or-
> bit of an instructed renaissance Christianity... The *Arcadia* is
> Sidney's Christian epic 'under the name of a romance'. As such
> it stands not with Montemayor, but with Tasso, Ariosto, Spenser,
> and (ultimately) Milton himself.[1]

Adversity in Sidney's design is the supreme testing of Christian
patience and Aristotelian magnanimity, nobility of mind, alike, and
the romance was constructed in order to display these qualities
under test, the stress being on the testing situation rather than on
the individuality of the characters tested. Beaumont and Fletcher
recognized this grand design in Sidney and attempted to follow it
in their plays. How they worked their imitation we shall see later.

The influence of *Hamlet* might understandably have been
brought to bear on the Sidneian version of Perez because it was a
drama not a prose romance. It was useful to Beaumont and Fletcher
because there were turns of situation where it became obviously
convenient to acknowledge a kinship with that most famous demonstration of indecision at work. Philaster's problem is close to
Hamlet's in that he is subject to the man who has usurped his title
and who plans to perpetuate his usurpation by marriage. Philaster
is held inactive because action against the usurper would be an
offence to the woman he loves, rather as Hamlet might be seen as
caught between the ghost's urgings to action and his concern for
his mother. The woman in one case is the usurper's daughter, in
the other his wife. The mental torment of Philaster is thus modelled
on Hamlet's, as later in the course of the play *Philaster*'s usurper
is tormented by his conscience in words like those of Claudius. It
is perhaps too much to say that *Philaster* was designed as a tidier

---

[1] J. F. Danby, *Poets on Fortune's Hill*, London, 1952, reissued as *Elizabethan and Jacobean Poets*, 1965, p. 71.

version of *Hamlet*,[1] but it was certainly felt to be desirable that audiences should be reminded of the play's already legendary predecessor and the similarity of the dilemma in which its hero is caught.

There is, of course, a good deal more to the sources behind *Philaster* than this drawing together of a plot-situation from Perez, character-types from Sidney, and an emotional situation from Shakespeare. With *Pericles* and *Cymbeline* it was the first successful work of its kind on the Jacobean stage, and its antecedents belong in theatre history as well as in literary prose traditions. Its relationships with Shakespeare's romances, with Beaumont and Fletcher's own previous plays, and its relevance to the political thought of its time are as important source materials for *Philaster* as its specific borrowings. Beaumont and Fletcher introduced something new to the stage, and the degree of its novelty is more than a question to be answered by source-hunting. To make clear sense of *Philaster* one must look beyond its immediate borrowings, even those which it was concerned more or less openly to acknowledge, to the theatre for which it was written, to the nature of the romantic drama in which it was a conscious innovation, to the contemporary political concerns which it was designed to illustrate, and finally to the achievement of the Sidneian design in the play itself.

4. THE BLACKFRIARS AND THE KING'S MEN

The acquisition of the 'private' Blackfriars theatre in addition to the public Globe by the King's Men is the reason usually given for Shakespeare writing *Cymbeline* and the other last plays as well as for Beaumont and Fletcher's success with *Philaster*. It does seem a limited and commercial explanation of such a striking change in theatrical fashion as those plays represent, and one which might bear a closer look. After all, had what the Burbages planned come about in 1596 the Globe, built as a second-best House when the plan fell through, might never even have existed. James Burbage bought the Blackfriars property in 1596 and spent £600 converting it for the use of his son's acting company; he died the following

---

[1] Clifford Leech, *The John Fletcher Plays*, 1962, p. 84.

year just as his plans were frustrated by a prohibition which prevented the company from using the building. Richard Burbage made what he could of the property in 1600 by leasing it to Henry Evans, an impresario for a new boy company, whose enterprise was presumably less objectionable to the residents of Blackfriars than the adult company's, and it was not until 1608 that Evans handed the possession back to Burbage for the adult company to use. Even then a prolonged outbreak of plague kept the theatre out of use till the beginning of 1610, fourteen years later than the Burbages had planned.

That Shakespeare and Beaumont and Fletcher did begin to write a new kind of play between 1608 and 1610 is of course unquestionable, and it is not likely to have been an entire coincidence that the company which employed them acquired a new venue at that time. But assessing its likely influence is a delicate task. One needs not only to ask how much influence the new theatre had in shaping the new plays of 1609 and after but also whether the changes were in the nature of the theatre itself and its traditions or in the audience. From 1610 to 1642 the King's Men used the Globe for the four summer months and the Blackfriars through the winter, a practice no other acting company could imitate. This, added to the fact that they were already the most favoured company at Court, gave them an extraordinary predominance over their competitors. Which came first, the venue, the audience, or the plays ?

The Blackfriars audiences who saw performances by the boys up to 1608 were used to a number of staging practices which differed from those of the adult actors at the Globe as Beckerman[1] has described them. The theatre itself was internally similar to the Globe in its fittings, though the disposition of its seating was different in some respects. It was an indoor theatre whereas the Globe was open to the sky, and its internal dimensions, including its stage, were smaller. But plays could be and were interchanged between the two theatres, and it had after all been designed by a man used to public theatres, builder of the original Theatre which formed the skeleton of the Globe in 1599. There were boxes at the Blackfriars

---

[1] Bernard Beckerman, *Shakespeare at the Globe, 1599–1609*, New York, 1962, pp. 63–108, 157–213.

adjacent to the stage for the wealthier patrons, and it was common for a dozen or so gallants to sit on stools on the stage itself, which must have restricted the acting area a little.[1] The boxes, too, seem to have been at the back or sides of the stage, and may have limited the upper stage or balcony area;[2] plays written for the Blackfriars have relatively little action taking place 'above'. Stage machinery was a little more elaborate, and was more heavily used. Periaktoi, for instance, great prisms with scenes painted on each of the three sides, which could be revolved to display one scene at a time, were in use at the early Blackfriars theatre in 1589,[3] and would have been familiar to the managers of the second Blackfriars children. Boys were flown in *The Widow's Tears* and *Cupid's Revenge* at Black-friars, but at the Globe Hymen in *As You Like It* and Diana in *Pericles* both entered on foot. The plays written after 1608 used flights. The emphasis in the boy company Blackfriars plays was on either fixed or simultaneous settings, so far as one can judge,[4] and the adult practice of unlocalized and variable settings was imported only after 1608.

The important Blackfriars feature not possessed by the Globe but adopted by the King's Men after 1608 was music. The famous Induction to *The Malcontent*, written in 1604 to smooth the adapta-

---

[1] The 1604 Induction to *The Malcontent*, played at the Globe, has the following passage:

'*Enter W. Sly, a Tyre-man following him with a stoole.*

TYRE. Sir, the Gentlemen will be angry if you sit heare.

SLY. Why? we may sit upon the stage at the private house.'

The Gull's Hornbook (1609) and *The Knight of the Burning Pestle* also make use of the practice.

[2] Herbert Berry, 'The Stage and Boxes at Blackfriars', *S.P.*, LXIII (1966), 163–86, and cf. I. A. Shapiro, 'Robert Fludd's Stage-Illustration', *Shakespeare Studies*, II (1966), 192–209. There is, of course, a great deal of uncertainty over how much inner or upper stage there was, if any, in all the Elizabethan playhouses. There was a 'tarras' or balcony at the Blackfriars, but it is doubtful if there was any considerable inner space.

[3] The early Blackfriars theatre was in a different part of the precinct from Burbage's property. William E. Miller ('*Periaktoi* in the Old Black-friars', *M.L.N.*, LXXIV, 1959, 1–3, and cf. *S.Q.*, xv (1964), 61–5) notes a reference in 1589 to a prism, otherwise not known to have been used before Inigo Jones's masques of 1605 and after.

[4] W. A. Armstrong, *The Elizabethan Private Theatres, Facts and Problems*, Society for Theatre Research Pamphlet Series No. 6, 1957–8, London, 1958.

tion of a private theatre play to the Globe, speaks of the 'not received custom of music in our Theatre'. The boy companies, of
course, had originated as choristers, but it was not in song that the
Blackfriars differed; one might regard the songs of the boys' Blackfriars plays, and those of *Cymbeline, The Winter's Tale*, and *The
Tempest* as less dramatically relevant than, for instance, those of
Ophelia or Desdemona, but they were by no means a new element
in the theatre. The chief difference between the boys' and the men's
performances before 1608 derived from the use of overture and
inter-act music. The Blackfriars in 1602 was noted by the visiting
Duke of Stettin-Pomerania as providing a whole hour's concert
before the play, the orchestra including lutes, mandolins, pandorins
(bandores, guitar-like instruments played as bass to a cittern),
violins, and flutes.[1] The musicians also provided mood music in
the course of the play; for instance, in Marston's *Wonder of Women*
'Infernal music plays softly while Erictho enters, and when she
speaks, ceaseth.'[2] *The Duchess of Malfi*, acted at Blackfriars in 1614,
has a song by madmen '*to a dismal kind of music*', and a dance of
'8 Madmen, *with music answerable thereunto*';[3] similar 'solemn
music' or something like it occurs in two places in *Cymbeline* (IV. ii
and v. iv), and in *The Tempest, Winter's Tale, Henry VIII, Two
Noble Kinsmen*, and many others.[4] Under the King's Men the
Blackfriars orchestra became highly regarded. Bulstrode White-
locke in 1633 noted that

> I composed an Aier myselfe, with the assistance of Mr. Ives, and
> called it *Whitelocke's Coranto*; which being cried up, was first
> played publiquely, by the Blackfryars Musicke, who were then
> esteemed the best of common musitians in London. Whenever I
> came to that house (as I did sometimes in those dayes,) though not
> often, to see a play, the musitians would presently play *White-
> locke's Coranto*, and it was so often called for, that they would have
> it played twice or thrice in an afternoon.[5]

---

[1] Chambers, *E.S.*, II, 47.

[2] *Sophonisba, or, The Wonder of Women*, IV. i. 126.1–2.

[3] *The Duchess of Malfi*, ed. J. R. Brown (Revels edn), IV. ii. 60.1 and
114.1.

[4] J. Isaacs, *Production and Stage Management at the Blackfriars Theatre*,
London, 1933.

[5] Charles Burney, *A General History of Music*, London, 1789, III, 377.

There were several important consequences of this musical accompaniment to the plays, notably that they had to be broken into five acts to permit pauses for the inter-act music (and so that the candles which lit the stage could be trimmed). The Globe plays have no overt acknowledgement even of an interval break, let alone regular pauses between the acts as the Blackfriars plays all have. *Wonder of Women* includes a requirement for inter-act music in its stage directions, and *The Knight of the Burning Pestle*, which in many respects is a play parodying the performance of a play, sitting on stage, inter-act gossiping and all, has not only music but in one of its inter-acts a boy dances while the pseudo-audience talks about the play, and makes various demands of the stage-keeper about how it should go; in another the spectator orders what the musicians should perform as their inter-act music.

The inter-act pause, of course, allowed a dramatist to begin an act with the characters who had left the stage at the end of the previous act, which the continuous staging of the Globe did not permit. This happens in three acts of *Philaster*, though in Shakespeare it happens only once, in *The Tempest*. What happened to plays written with the Blackfriars act-breaks when they transferred in summer to the Globe we don't know; possibly the Blackfriars musicians and therefore the inter-acts went with them, though the open theatres were less acoustically convenient for their kind of music. Act divisions did become more usual in all plays in the decade after 1610.

Masquing and dancing were another Blackfriars feature tied to the music and spectacle. There are thirteen masques in eleven boy company plays at the Blackfriars, ranging from simple processional masquerades to elaborate imitations of the Court masques. In that period, up to 1608, the King's Men had masques only in *The Revenger's Tragedy* and *Timon*, where they are integral to the story in a way few of the boys' masques are.[1] After 1608 even if we discount the vision of Jupiter in *Cymbeline* there are masques in *The Tempest*, *Henry VIII*, and eight Beaumont and Fletcher plays. It became a

---

[1] M. C. Bradbrook, *Pageantry in Timon of Athens*, Cambridge, 1966, suggests that *Timon* was written with the Blackfriars in mind. There is no evidence for where or even whether *Timon* was acted.

conspicuous feature of the King's Men's plays. Dances too were rare at the Globe but common in the boy company plays, and after 1608 we find one in *The Winter's Tale*, two in *The Tempest*, and one in *Two Noble Kinsmen*.

When the boy companies were revived in 1600 there is no doubt that they and their private playhouses had considerable snob appeal. Jonson made much of it in *Cynthia's Revels*, one of the first plays written for the new boy company at Blackfriars. The very name of 'private', obscure in its origin though widely current from 1600,[1] implied a social distinction from the public playhouses. The prices charged for admission reflected the distinction, too, ranging from sixpence to two shillings and sixpence, well above the Globe minimum of a penny. So far as the Globe/Blackfriars differences are concerned, though, this does not seem to have made their audiences as distinct as one might think. In the beginning there are references to the 'select' Blackfriars or Paul's audience, but by 1607/8 social mobility appeared. Jonson's prefatory verses to Fletcher's *Faithful Shepherdess*, put on by the boys of Blackfriars in 1608, speak of a 'many-headed bench' composed not only of 'gamester, captain, knight', but also the 'shop's foreman . . . That may judge for his sixpence'. The chief difference between the cheapest places at the two theatres was that the 'understanders' at the Globe paid a penny to stand in the open yard surrounding the stage, while the 'six-penny mechanicks' at the Blackfriars sat farthest from the stage, in the topmost gallery.

The evidence about the private playhouse audiences is in fact fairly variable before about 1615. There is a clear distinction between the repertories of the boy and the adult companies between 1600 and 1608, the boys producing mainly satirical comedy or rhetorical tragedy; the social and moral values too seem to have differed considerably from what the public theatre audiences of Shakespeare, Dekker, and Heywood liked.[2] Private theatre plays made fun of the citizenry and their values, and to some extent the

---

[1] The title-page of *Satiromastix*, 1602, says that it was presented 'publicly' by the Chamberlain's Men, and 'privately' by Paul's Boys.

[2] Alfred Harbage, *Shakespeare and the Rival Traditions*, New York, 1952, p. 85; cf. R. Ornstein, *The Moral Vision of Jacobean Tragedy*, Wisconsin, 1965, p. 12.

citizens' theatres, chiefly the Red Bull and the Fortune, seem to have retaliated with attacks on lords and lawyers.[1] The opening lines of Beaumont's private theatre play *The Knight of the Burning Pestle* actually polarize the difference as between the City (merchants and artisans) and the Court. At the beginning of the play, in which a citizen climbs on stage to stop a satire on the merchant class and is himself in the process doubly satirized, the boy Prologue enters to introduce his satire, saying:

> From all that's near the Court, from all that's great,
> Within the compass of the City walls
> We now have brought our Scene,[2]

implying, as the rest of the play goes on to demonstrate, that the middle-class pretension to greatness and courtly honour is misconceived. The point is made when the citizen orders the boys to act a play called 'the Grocer's Honour', an honour deriving from the improbabilities of the chivalric romances satirized by Cervantes, and immensely popular with the middle class. The whole play is based on the citizen's being out of his depth at the private theatre.

Beaumont's play suggests that there was a fundamental division between the two classes among theatrical audiences. If so, he was probably astray in seeing it at Blackfriars, because his own play had only the one unhappy performance there, the audience, as the publisher who rescued it from oblivion some years later tells us, missing the 'privy mark of irony about it', presumably displaying their middle-class tastes by accepting the citizen's concept of honour at face value. Just so a year later *The Faithful Shepherdess* was condemned by a similar audience for lacking the traditional trappings of country pastoral:

> It is a pastoral tragi-comedy, which the people seeing when it was played, having ever had a singular gift in defining, concluded to be a play of country hired shepherds in grey cloaks, with curtailed dogs in strings, sometimes laughing together, and sometimes killing one another; and missing Whitsun ales, cream, wassail and morris dances, began to be angry.

[1] Marco Mincoff, 'The Social Background of Beaumont and Fletcher', *English Miscellany* I (1950), 3, 13.
[2] *The Knight of the Burning Pestle*, Induction 1–3.

Dekker in his *Gull's Hornbook* used the Blackfriars audience for his satirical example of how a gallant should behave when seated on a playhouse stool, and his opinion of the audience's capacity is no higher than Fletcher's while free from the disappointed playwright's spleen.

In 1617 a law student called H. F[itzgeoffery] published a set of 'Satyres and Satyricall Epigrams', the third book of which was entitled *Notes from Blackfriars*, a set of verse characters of the kind of individuals you might expect to find in 'this *Microcosme*, Man's societie' attending a play. Fitzgeoffery itemizes a military captain standing in the 'middle region' (a gallery ?); a traveller, 'Sir Island Hunt', full of strange tales; 'A *Cheapside* Dame'; a gallant who is described as 'yon world of fashion'; then comes 'Monstrous! A Woman of the masculine gender'; a gigolo; and a prodigal, an expensively dressed pauper, who emerges from the tiring-house, presumably to sit on the stage.

Fitzgeoffery is useful as an indication of how supremely fashionable the Blackfriars was under the King's Men. Title-pages are another guide to its esteem: between 1616 and 1660 the Globe is mentioned as a venue on its own only five times (one of them the 1620 quarto of *Philaster*), plus ten in conjunction with the Blackfriars. The private playhouse, on the other hand, is mentioned by itself forty-nine times.[1] There is no question that the Blackfriars did come to stand as the supreme symbol of theatrical excellence, and that the Globe stood well in the background, even after its palatial rebuilding in 1614. The danger in this is of using hindsight to claim that the possibilities of the Blackfriars for the King's Men were recognized and consequently shaped the plays being written even before the King's Men finally took it over. It was not pre-eminent under the boys as it came to be under the King's Men. It never had under the boys the monopoly of the upper-class audience that it gained after 1610. Beaumont in his burlesque grammar lecture of *c*. 1602[2] speaks of lawyers seeing plays at the Bankside (meaning the Globe, which was the only public house regularly

---

[1] Irwin Smith, *Shakespeare's Blackfriars Playhouse*, New York, 1964, p. 211.

[2] Eccles, *op. cit.*, p. 404.

used there between 1600 and 1605), without any mention of a private playhouse. The King's Men were always preferred at Court, performing more plays there in the decade ending in 1610 than all the other companies, boy and adult, put together. They would have regarded it as an insult were it suggested that their pre-eminence after 1608 was owing to the theatre they acted in.

G. E. Bentley first formulated the theory that the King's Men in 1608, recognizing that they might imminently gain possession of the Blackfriars, wanted Shakespeare to write plays suitable for the new audience, the plays now generally known as the romances.[1] They also, he considers, commissioned Jonson and Beaumont and Fletcher, the former as a playwright experienced in writing both for the Blackfriars boys and for the King's Men, the latter as a socially more reputable pair of apprentice playwrights who had several plays already at the Blackfriars. He stresses the commercial risk for the King's Men's shareholders of facing a new audience of the aristocracy with a repertory of plays from the public theatre. Since the same public theatre repertory had made the company by far the most in demand at Court, this is an unlikely argument, and a closer inspection of the other points raises similar doubts about them.

In the first place Jonson was, as Bentley notes, celebrated in aristocratic circles for his brilliantly successful Court masques, and his name would have been a major attraction for the company's productions at the new playhouse. But the play he chose to write for them was *The Alchemist*, a play true to the traditional public theatre repertories, even though it was clearly designed to be played 'here, in the Friars', as Subtle says.[2] Secondly, Beaumont and Fletcher separately were only distinguished in the plays they had written for the Blackfriars boys by flops, which if anything proved that their tastes were *not* those of the Blackfriars audience. Their collaborated play, *Cupid's Revenge*, was presumably a moderate success, and was much closer to adult fare than its unhappy precursor *The Faithful*

---

[1] G. E. Bentley, 'Shakespeare and the Blackfriars Theatre', *Sh.S.*, I (1948), 38–50. Cf. D. L. Frost, *The School of Shakespeare*, Cambridge, 1968, p. 212.

[2] *The Alchemist* (Revels edn), I. i. 17.

Shepherdess. There is in fact no evidence for the success on the Blackfriars stage of any romances before the King's adults came to act in them. The only known success of the kind was *Pericles*, which was performed at the Globe before the Blackfriars was available. Furthermore, Simon Forman's 'Booke of Plaies'[1] lists four plays including *Cymbeline* and *The Winter's Tale* which he saw in 1611; three of them he notes as being seen at the Globe. Although *Cymbeline* is the one play of the four which he does not record as seeing there, it is unlikely that he saw it anywhere else; he saw the plays in quick succession, and *Cymbeline* was not the last of the four. Since we have no evidence that the King's Men switched houses in mid-season it seems that two of the four Shakespeare plays usually thought of as Blackfriars plays were in the Globe's season for 1611. The title-page of *Philaster*'s own first quarto tells us that it too was known as a Globe play. The implication is that the company did not vary its repertory to match any difference it may have thought existed in the tastes of its two playhouse audiences.

The Globe and the Blackfriars were used by the King's Men as seasonal playhouses. They did get a crop of new plays between 1608 and 1610; playing round the calendar as they now could they would have needed them. The romances which were written in the new crop did come with the Blackfriars to an eminence of favour amongst the upper classes in the Jacobean period, but they were performed at the Globe as well as the Blackfriars. One wonders whether the eventual eclipse of the Globe by its fellow was not partly a result of the open theatre's less favourable season, summer, when the aristocracy was in the country and the Inns of Court lawyers on vacation. The indoor playhouse always was more fashionable than the public, besides being more conveniently situated within the City walls, but these circumstances have little real connection with the changes in Shakespeare's plays and the success of *Philaster* in 1608–10.

---

[1] Simon Forman, *A Booke of Plaies*, quoted in Chambers, *W.S.*, II, 337–41.

5. *CYMBELINE* AND *PHILASTER*

Whatever the influence of the Blackfriars theatre, there is still the fact that Shakespeare's plays did change strikingly, and that Beaumont and Fletcher did find an extraordinarily successful and on the whole basically similar dramatic formula during the relatively short period of their collaboration, a formula by which Fletcher and his various partners produced all the most popular plays in the King's Men's repertory up to his death in 1625. The characteristics of this Fletcherian formula were shared by Shakespeare in more than just the 'polite tone' by which a recent critic has bound them together.[1] And the reason why they shared the formula, if it is anything more than the new playhouse, is as important as it is complicated.

The efforts of many critics to prove either that Shakespeare learnt from Beaumont and Fletcher's *Philaster* how to write *Cymbeline*, or that Beaumont and Fletcher learnt from Shakespeare, testify to the more than casual relationship of the two plays. The first view was elaborately expressed by A. H. Thorndike in 1901, the other most thoroughly by R. T. Thornberry in an unpublished dissertation of 1964.[2] Thornberry's conclusion is that Shakespeare's decision to write romantic tragicomedy grew out of the Globe tradition, and that *Cymbeline*, being a Globe play, must have preceded *Philaster*, which was written in 1609–10 after the Blackfriars had become available. Apart from the general relationship of tragicomic situations and characters, the only direct links between the plays are verbal recollections, and the resemblance of *Cymbeline*'s Belarius to *Philaster*'s Bellario. The resemblance is in name, not character, and could easily be a coincidence, as could one of the verbal echoes, the word-play on strange/stranger in *Cymbeline*, II. i. 31–9, and *Philaster*, I. i. 77–9. The other verbal recollection is

---

[1] Richard Proudfoot, 'Shakespeare and the New Dramatists of the King's Men, 1608–1613', *Later Shakespeare*, Stratford-upon-Avon Studies 8, pp. 234–61.

[2] A. H. Thorndike, *The Influence of Beaumont and Fletcher on Shakespeare*, Worcester (Mass.), 1901; R. T. Thornberry, 'Shakespeare and the Blackfriars Tradition', unpublished dissertation, Ohio State University, 1964, *D.A.*, XXVI (1965), 1029–30.

more precise, in situation as well as words. Iachimo in *Cymbeline*,
v. ii. 2–6, when defeated by Posthumus says:

> I have belied a lady,
> The Princess of this country; and the air on't
> Revengingly enfeebles me; or could this carl,
> A very drudge of nature's, have subdu'd me
> In my profession?

Philaster similarly when wounded by the Country Fellow after
attacking Arethusa says:

> The gods take part against me, could this boor
> Have held me thus else?   (IV. v. 103–4).

Each passage belongs quite properly in its place. The internal evidence of the plays, in other words, is indeterminate; we have to
look elsewhere for an explanation of why Shakespeare and the two
younger playwrights turned at about the same date to write the
same kind of play.[1]

It was not the theatre, if only because *Philaster* of all the Beaumont and Fletcher plays lacks any song, dance, or masque, the
most characteristic Blackfriars features, while *Cymbeline* has all of
them. All *Philaster* has of peculiarly private theatre features is its
act-breaks, which may very well be simply an inheritance from the
practices established in the five or so plays which the two dramatists had already written for the boy companies. Nor was it the
audiences of the Blackfriars, since Shakespeare had already given
Pericles and probably *Cymbeline* itself to the Globe.

A more plausible, if vaguer, answer might be found in the
changing taste of the time, a renewal of interest in the romantic
drama which had been quiescent a dozen years. The change may
have been speeded by an awareness of côterie audiences which
Beaumont for one shows he had in *The Knight of the Burning Pestle*.
For the younger dramatists, though, it was a change forced on by
a determination in the dramatists themselves to create the taste by
which they were to be appreciated. Fletcher's *Faithful Shepherdess*
is clearly a calculated attempt to introduce a new literary fashion

---

[1] The best account of the romantic tradition (a tradition rather than a
genre) is given in E. C. Pettet, *Shakespeare and the Romance Tradition*,
London, 1949.

into the Jacobean theatre. The preface he wrote for the published text about 1609 shows his awareness of what he had attempted to do. He began by saying 'If you be not reasonably assurde of your knowledge in this kinde of Poeme, lay downe the booke or read this, which I would wish had bene the prologue. It is a pastorall Tragic-comedie . . .' and he went on to describe how the audience at the first performance had misunderstood the genre.[1] In conclusion he defined his new genre for the reader's benefit:

> A tragie-comedie is not so called in respect of mirth and killing, but in respect it wants deaths, which is inough to make it no tragedie, yet brings some neere it, which is inough to make it no comedie: which must be a representation of familiar people with such kinde of trouble as no life be questiond, so that a God is lawfull in this as in a tragedie, and meane people as in a comedie. This much I hope will serve to justifie my Poeme, and make you understand it; to teach you more for nothing, I do not know that I am in conscience bound.

Fletcher was conscious of his innovation, and in both his definition and his title was explicitly acknowledging his literary debt to Guarini's *Il Pastor Fido*, which had appeared in a storm of contoversy in Italy some years before. Both Guarini's pastoral and Cinthio's romantic tragicomedy had been making headway in England as well as Italy. *Il Pastor Fido* had been translated in 1602; Cambridge had acted Guarini in Latin and in August 1605 Samuel Daniel had produced 'a Pastorall Trage-comedie', *The Queen's Arcadia*, for the Queen at Oxford; and now Fletcher was trying to introduce it to the commercial stage.[2]

It was not to Guarini, however, that he looked for the material of the new genre. Daniel's title shows where the English pastoral tradition saw its origin. Sidney's *Arcadia* had gone through five editions (counting an illegal Edinburgh edition) by this time, and a Latin version, Barclay's *Argenis*, was even more popular. It was, as Danby has put it, paraphrasing Greville, 'a book intended for

---

[1] Quoted above, p. xli.

[2] Studies in the development of tragicomedy include F. H. Ristine, *English Tragi-comedy*, New York, 1910; M. T. Herrick, *Tragicomedy*, Urbana, 1962; and J. J. Lievsay, 'Jacobean Stage Pastoralism', in *Essays on Shakespeare and Elizabethan Drama in Honor of Hardin Craig*, ed. R. Hosley, London, 1963.

the instruction in virtue and in the art of government of princes and gentlemen, in prosperity and adversity, limning out exact pictures of every posture of the mind'.[1] Its scene is 'the pastoral land, not exactly Edenic but exhibiting good and evil in pure and radical forms'.[2] It was eminently respectable literary material for an ambitious young dramatist to imitate.

The Faithful Shepherdess took Arcadian characters, exhibiting good and evil in pure and radical forms, and Arcadian situations, positions of stress especially as moral dilemmas, to exhibit the actions and reactions of such characters, presenting them in a drama shorn of almost all the conventional devices of stage realism, with pastoral song and dance in place of wassail and cream. The *Arcadia* was adapted into the drama by a drastic simplification of the story line and of the range of parallel characters. The play has four sets of lovers, whose relationships range 'from spiritual devotion to bestial sensuality',[3] the action of the play developing from the opposition of the lustful and the chaste lovers.

The important thing about *The Faithful Shepherdess* is that it presents in the pastoral setting the gamut of love-relationships which Fletcher retained in a courtly setting for the plays he wrote when Beaumont joined him, *Cupid's Revenge* and *Philaster*. Precisely the same sets of lovers, representing chaste and successful love, chaste and unsuccessful love, sensual infatuation, and a mutual sensuality, are constructed in *Cupid's Revenge* out of the *Arcadia*; and the same material is reworked in *Philaster* with the mutual love of Philaster and Arethusa, the chaste love of Bellario for Philaster, the indiscriminate lust of Pharamond, and its linking with Megra. The action in *Philaster* as in *The Faithful Shepherdess* proceeds initially from the difficulties in the way of Philaster's and Arethusa's love, and develops through the hostile devices of the lecherous Megra. What is important about this is the change in setting; the pastoral countryside of the first play becomes the hunting country of *Philaster*, and the concerns are not the loves of

---

[1] Danby, *op. cit.*, p. 47.

[2] W. R. Davis, *A Map of Arcadia*, Yale Studies in English No. 158, New Haven, 1965, p. 51.

[3] Waith, *op. cit.*, p. 6.

literary shepherds but the loves and related dynastic complications of princes and courts. *Philaster* even does without the descent of God Cupid and the attendant dance of youths and maidens that we find in *Cupid's Revenge*; its *deus ex machina* is not the descending God but a comic mob of City artisans. The patterning of love-characters is retained in a totally different, more theatrically realistic, environment.

Cupid's Revenge was written for the same boy company as *The Faithful Shepherdess*; *Philaster* was the first play in this kind that they wrote for the King's Men. The opening lines of *Philaster*, which probably are Fletcher's,[1] may signify his Global expectation: three gentlemen enter, and the first exclaims 'Here's nor lords, nor ladies', to which the second replies 'Credit me, gentlemen, I wonder at it. They received strict charge from the King to attend here'. Whether they do or not, the line of development from the failure of *The Faithful Shepherdess* to the triumph of *Philaster* does suggest that there was a gradual convergence between 1608 and 1610 of the taste of theatre audiences with what Beaumont and Fletcher provided for them.

The success with *Philaster*, whether at Globe or Blackfriars, was the result of two or three years of experimentation beginning well before the Blackfriars expansion of the King's Men. Shakespeare, writing throughout for the one company, up to a point seems to have followed a similar road, in *Pericles* and *Cymbeline*, over the same years within the limits 1607–10.

Not that the roads ever came really close together. H. S. Wilson has written:[2]

> *Philaster* is a lively series of incidents contrived with great ingenuity to provide constant excitement and surprise and to issue agreeably with the recognition and reward of virtue, the dismissal of the wicked in disgrace. And it is nothing more. *Cymbeline* is, by comparison, more old-fashioned in method, more complicated and altogether more ambitious. At least as ingeniously plotted, it employs an utterly different method in the conduct of the action: preparation of the audience to perceive the dramatic ironies of

[1] Cyrus Hoy, 'The Shares of Fletcher and his Collaborators in the Beaumont and Fletcher Canon (III)', *S.B.*, XI (1958), 91.

[2] H. S. Wilson, '*Philaster* and *Cymbeline*', *English Institute Essays* (1951), New York, 1952, pp. 162–3.

D

situation, the pathos of character, the joys and sorrows of reunion;
it aims at effecting the gratification of expectancy rather than the
shock of surprise. *Cymbeline* admits all kinds of ancient romance
conventions and stage devices in which Beaumont and Fletcher
were little interested—stately pageants, riddles, masques, the god
from the machine. The younger dramatists seem to have regarded
such effects as unnecessary. Their new technique in the dramatic
romance was actually a remarkable simplification of existing stage
conventions. In *Philaster*, apart from the ingenious plotting there
is scarcely any conspicuous stage device used save that of disguise
—and that in the single example of Bellario. But they carried their
economy much further, virtually eliminating character study and
stripping the play down to the bare essentials of swift emotional
dialogue and clever plot.

It is an overstatement to say that Beaumont and Fletcher were little
interested in the stage devices of masque and song which Shakespeare employed, since *Philaster* is almost unique in this respect,
coming between the god from the machine in *Cupid's Revenge* and
an elaborate masque and some beautiful songs in *The Maid's
Tragedy*. But Wilson's distinction between dramatic technique in
Philaster itself and *Cymbeline* holds true.

The two plays grew from a common soil in the popular romance
tradition, but beyond this ground their interests diverged markedly, because the playwrights saw different opportunities in their
material. Shakespeare's interests in the late plays are, of course, a
long distance from Beaumont and Fletcher's chief interests, which
show a withdrawal from broadly social considerations, the individual in the commonwealth, to an individualistic concern with
honour and personal gentlemanly conduct in love and politics, the
private and the public sides of the personal conduct of a prince. It
is in this divergence of interest that Beaumont and Fletcher show
their youth and Shakespeare his age. Beaumont and Fletcher pre-
figure the whole cavalier ethos of the later seventeenth century;[1]
as popularizers of the Arcadian ideals they disseminated Sidney's
concepts of courtly behaviour.

[1] Charles Barber, *The Idea of Honour in the English Drama, 1591–1700*,
Göteborg, 1957, p. 29; and Danby, *op. cit.*, p. 41: 'it was during this period
(particularly, if one might be definite, during the partnership of Beaumont
and Fletcher on the stage) that the cavalier mentality was shaped in all its
essentials.'

6. THE POLITICAL CONCERNS

We deduce from Fletcher's designs in *The Faithful Shepherdess* that his chief contribution to *Philaster* was probably the patterning of the love-relationships, and the plot structure as it grew from them. Beaumont's contribution was probably quite different. He has left no clear indication in his plays of the road that led him to *Philaster*, but the pervasive political concerns in the play relate so closely to his personal background and are in many ways so much at odds with what Fletcher came subsequently to write that it seems only possible to attribute them to him.

The opening situation in *Philaster* is a careful interlocking of a political and an amorous dilemma. Instead of Clorin in *The Faithful Shepherdess* or God Cupid in *Cupid's Revenge* the initiator of the action is a King, rightfully of Calabria, a sixteenth-century kingdom on the Italian mainland adjacent to Sicily, and wrongfully by conquest of Sicily itself, where the action is set. In the opening scene, set at the Sicilian Court, the King by his conquest has dispossessed the rightful heir Philaster, and now proposes to make his title sure by marrying his daughter to a Spanish prince in the hope that the might of Spain will subjugate Sicily as he cannot. The amorous concern is revealed in the second scene of the play when Arethusa, the King's daughter, declares her love to Philaster instead of to Pharamond, the Spanish prince. She sees her love as the 'secret justice of the gods' (I. ii. 103) because her marriage to Philaster will secure for him the throne which rightfully belongs to him, instead of the 'stranger' Pharamond.

The plot as it subsequently develops is largely Fletcherian, concerned with love more than politics in the exposure of Pharamond's and Megra's lechery and Megra's revenge, casting doubt on Arethusa's virtue, with the final happy resolution through the offices of Bellario, the selflessly devoted lover. The political situation is interwoven into this structure in Dion's reasons for urging Philaster to believe in Arethusa's unchastity, the reasons being the need to persuade him into active rebellion against the King, a course he was known to be reluctant to take because of his admiration for her, the King's daughter. The resolution is brought about initially by

Arethusa's constancy and ultimately, when the King threatens to disinherit her for her secret marriage to Philaster, by the mob which captures Pharamond and will be led only by Philaster.

Danby in his essay on *Philaster*[1] sees in the politics a set of what he calls 'clamorous absolutes' at work, the chief of which is kingship. They are absolutes because Beaumont 'lacks the supporting strength of an independent position from which to see with detachment what he is writing about'.[2] The detachment of Shakespeare's and Jonson's writing about kingship is lost to the younger playwright in Jacobean uncertainties, according to Danby, with the result that Beaumont is confused amidst his absolutes. I find this difficult to understand. Beaumont's attitudes to kingship in *Philaster*, particularly the question of usurpation, are very precisely Shakespearean; there is in fact a close parallel between *Philaster*'s handling of the kingship question and that of Shakespeare's Henry IV plays. The Calabrian King's guilt over his usurpation of Philaster's title bears an obvious resemblance to that of both Hamlet's uncle and Henry IV. What may be less immediately obvious is the further resemblance in the play to Shakespeare's version of the whole Henry V story. Arethusa's faith in the providential nature of her love for the true heir to the Sicilian throne is fully justified in the light of the traditional attitudes to usurpation and royal lineage, since by marrying the lawful heir she can restore to him the throne she will inherit from her father. As his daughter hers is the inherited title freed from the taint of usurpation, as was Henry V's. In political terms *Philaster* is an idyllically complete version of the elements in the Henry V legend: where Richard II and Henry IV each suffered as kings, the first by his human failure as God's justicer, the second because he was a usurper, Henry V triumphed both as a man (avoiding the traps set for him by Hotspur and Falstaff) and as a king, taking his title with 'better quiet, / Better opinion, better confirmation' (*2 Henry IV*, IV. v. 188–9) as lawful inheritor of his father's possession. *Philaster* adds to its parallel with this the further endorsement of the marriage alliance,

---

[1] 'Beaumont and Fletcher: Jacobean Absolutists', in Danby, *op. cit.*, pp. 152–83.
[2] *Ibid.*, p. 165.

as if Henry were securing his title not by testing it at Agincourt but by marrying a daughter of Richard II. The Shakespearean precedent is even there in the marriage's linking of the two kingdoms, Philaster's Sicily with Arethusa's Calabria, as Henry V clinched his possession of France by marrying Katherine. Beaumont in this respect is working from Shakespearean premises.

The reasons for ascribing this aspect of the play to Beaumont rather than Fletcher, or the collaborators together, are largely circumstantial, and may be in part due to *Philaster*'s being the first play they wrote for the adult acting company. But they are completely consistent with what we know of Beaumont. In the first place *Philaster*, like no other play in which Fletcher was concerned, but quite like *The Knight of the Burning Pestle* and *The Woman Hater*, involved itself with contemporary issues. The setting on the whole is generalized, even pastoral; all the characters' names are Arcadian, and Arethusa and Galatea, the two virtuous ladies of the Court, are named after famous places in the Sicily of Theocritus, the world of classical pastoral. Nonetheless, there are references such as the one to the 'new platform', which can have been a well-known talking-point only in 1609; and Philaster when approached by a group of courtiers protests 'I am no minion,' meaning he is not a royal favourite: James's love for young courtiers like Sir James Hay and Robert Carr had been notorious for some years. The history of James's characterization on the Jacobean stage has still to be written, but it is probable that Beaumont's *Woman Hater* contains a satirical portrait of James and his 'minion', and as such can be put alongside *Eastward Ho !*, *The Isle of Gulls*, Marston's *The Fawn*, and even *Catiline*.[1] Savage has also found glances at contemporary events with personal relevance to Beaumont in *Cupid's Revenge*.[2]

There are three matters in *Philaster* which may be more than incidental allusions to the contemporary situation. If they are, they

[1] Cf. A. W. Upton, 'Allusions to James I and his Court in Marston's *Fawn* and Beaumont's *Woman-Hater*', *P.M.L.A.*, XLIV (1929), 1048–65; and Geoffrey Hill, 'The World's Proportion: Jonson's dramatic poetry in *Sejanus* and *Catiline*', in *Jacobean Drama*, Stratford-upon-Avon Studies 1, London, 1961, pp. 113–31.

[2] Savage, 'The Date of Beaumont and Fletcher's *Cupid's Revenge*', *op. cit.*

were well disguised and unobtrusive enough for the official censor to allow them through.[1] The first of these is the coincidence between the stage King and James as rulers of two kingdoms. Union of Scotland and England had been a major parliamentary issue for years after James's accession to his second throne in 1603, and the minimal legal links which were all Parliament conceded James gave him little satisfaction. The play, however, does not really make use of its two kingdoms as a parallel to the Stuart position in 1609; it is perfectly justifiable in its own right as a means to avoid the tragic killing-the-king dénouement which would have been inevitable had the usurpation theme been tied to only one throne, as in *Hamlet*. And a happy resolution of the plot was necessary not only in the nature of the play as a romance but also because the heroine was daughter of the usurping King.

The second parallel to contemporary affairs comes a little closer to home in the King's proposal to marry Arethusa to the Spanish prince in order to secure his kingdom. James had initiated negotiations for two marriage alliances after the peace of 1604, one of his daughter to a Protestant prince, the other of his son Henry to a Catholic princess. The latter alliance, because the Spanish demanded Henry's conversion to Catholicism, proved a royal wild-goose chase, dragging on until 1612, when the Princess Elizabeth was successfully contracted to a German Protestant leader and her brother terminated his half of the negotiations by dying. A Spanish marriage in *Philaster* could, of course, be allowed in as a plausible happening in Sicilian politics, a traditional field of Spanish involvement.[2]

Neither of these parallels need be taken as significant in itself. The third allusion is an even more vague parallel, but altogether more significant in its implications. It justifies the use of the mob as god from the machine restoring Philaster to himself, and throws doubt not only on Coleridge's conviction that Beaumont and

---

[1] Savage, 'The "Gaping Wounds" in the Text of *Philaster*', *op. cit.*, has a theory that Q1 *Philaster* is a censored text. See below, p. lxxv.

[2] The events of *Philaster* cannot be precisely paralleled in Sicilian history, but the plot situation is constructed from the materials of a century in which such diplomatic and military affairs as the conflicts between Sicily and Calabria were familiar events. Cf. Waith, *op. cit.*, p. 15.

Fletcher were 'servile *jure divino* royalists'[1] but also on Danby's acceptance of their absolutism. The basic resemblance is between Lord Dion's standing up to the King in IV. iv and Sir Edward Coke's clash with King James on 13 November 1608. The incident occurred at one of a series of conferences summoned by James on the question of 'Prohibitions', an issue essentially concerned with the extent of the jurisdiction of common law judges. The reports of the incident itself are various,[2] but it appears that Coke, then Lord Chief Justice of Common Pleas and for several years the un-bowing champion of common law rights against the royal prerogative, infuriated James by asserting that the common law protected the King, and not the reverse. To quote Sir Julius Caesar's official report,

> The comon lawe protecteth the king, quoth the L. Cooke, which the King said was a traiterous speech: for the King protecteth the lawe and not the lawe the King. The King maketh Judges and Bishops. If the Judges interprete the lawes themselves and suffer none else to interprete, then they may easily make of the laws shipmen's hose.[3]

According to contemporary accounts, Coke was forced to fall 'flatt on all fower' before the royal wrath, and the Lord Treasurer had to intercede for him on his knees. Coke was unabashed, and added to his own subsequent story of the event a series of justifications for his attitude, specifically that the King was subject to the authority not only of God but of 'the artificiall reason and judgment of the law'.[4]

The clash between James and his Lord Chief Justice was no more in itself than an open display of the controversy implicit in James's constitutional position with regard to his subjects in general and particularly the House of Commons from 1607 till 1611, on the relations of government and the law. James's concept of his royal prerogative, by which he saw himself appointed by God and an-

---

[1] *Coleridge's Miscellaneous Criticism*, ed. T. M. Raysor, London, 1936, p. 69.

[2] Roland G. Usher, 'James I and Sir Edward Coke', *English Historical Review*, XVIII (1903), 664–75. Cf. also D. H. Willson, *King James VI and I*, London, 1956, pp. 257–9.

[3] Quoted by Usher, *op. cit.*, p. 669.   [4] Willson, *op. cit.*, p. 259.

swerable only to God,[1] was far too autocratic for the lawyers in the Commons, and their support for Coke's stand was strong enough in 1609–10 to make James adopt a markedly conciliatory attitude. He was forced, for instance, to condemn Cowell's *Interpreter* in a speech in Parliament on 21 March 1610 because of its extremely royalist views on prerogative. James was made reluctantly to deny the claim 'that I would have wished the Civill Law to have bene put in place of the Common Law for government of this people'.[2] James suffered until February 1611 when he angrily dismissed Parliament, to rule through his favourites for the rest of the decade.

It was a lawyer's quarrel rather than a revolutionary movement. As C. H. McIlwain has said, 'the debates in the Commons in 1610 leave little doubt that Parliament's attack on the royalist doctrines was made as much in the interests of the common law as of the liberty of the subject.'[3] It is inconceivable that Beaumont could not have been concerned with the issue; his father was a Common Law judge, and he himself was a member of Coke's own Inn of Court, the Inner Temple. The version of the Coke incident he heard would have been Coke's rather than James's.

There may, in other words, have been more than just the hint of satire in the comic confrontation of *Philaster*'s King making impossible demands of his subjects and being confined by Dion to 'things possible and honest'. The King's reaction is to call Dion a traitor (IV. iv. 36–8), which is what James called Coke. His frenzied self-pity is cast into legal terms; as Dion says (ll. 62–3), 'He articles with the gods; would somebody would draw bonds for the performance of covenants betwixt them.' (James in his *Trew Law* of

---

[1] In *The Trew Law of Free Monarchies* (1603), James wrote: 'out of the lawe of God, the duetie, and alleageance of the people to their lawfull king, their obedience, I say, ought to be to him, as to Gods Lieutenant in earth, obeying his commands in all thing, except directly against God, as the commands of Gods Minister, acknowledging him a Judge set by GOD over them, having power to judge them, but to be judged onely by GOD, whom to onely hee must give count of his judgement; fearing him as their Judge, loving him as their father; praying for him as their protectour; for his continuance, if he be good; for his amendment, if he be wicked; following and obeying his lawfull commands, eschewing and flying his fury in his unlawfull, without resistance, but by sobbes and teares to God' (*Political Works*, ed. C. H. McIlwain, Cambridge (Mass.), 1916, p. 61).

[2] *Ibid.*, p. 307.   [3] *Ibid.*, p. lxxxviii.

1603 denied the validity of any covenant between King and people.)[1]
Dion's rôle throughout the play is that of a leader of the common
opinion; he is genially contemptuous of the City folk, 'the multitude (that seldom know anything but their own opinions)', but has
no hesitation in applauding their action in rising to rescue their
Prince Philaster in order to see justice done. He even goes so far as
to say that Pharamond was born a slave 'but that people / Please
to let him be a Prince' (III. i. 12–13). He is presented as well versed
in the Law; when Arethusa asks for the custody of the captured
Philaster and Bellario so that she can arrange their deaths, Dion's
reaction is 'Death? Soft; our law will not reach that for this fault'
(IV. vi. 151). He performs something of the function of the Lord
Chief Justice in Shakespeare's *2 Henry IV*. Certainly Beaumont's
King behaves in a manner far removed from Henry V's model
attitude to his Common Law representative.

There are further, more general, parallels in the attitudes and
beliefs of Beaumont's King and James noted in articles by Mary
G. M. Adkins and Peter H. Davison,[2] which suggest that Beaumont recognized the power of the people and the fallibility of
monarchs. Miss Adkins also sees Philaster's respectful treatment
of the mob in Act v as a model of the sovereign's attitude to his
subjects, 'an impressive ending for the citizens, demonstrating
their power and, as well, the desirable relationship between a ruler
and his people'.[3] There is an assumption, as in *The Knight of the
Burning Pestle*, of fundamental goodwill in the citizenry.

One must be careful not to take this reading of Beaumont's interests in the play too far, however. Fletcher certainly would not on
the evidence of his later plays have agreed with his partner's ques-
tioning of kingship,[4] and the political concerns of the play presumably gave few qualms either to the official censor or to the King's
Men, who wasted little time before they performed it at Court.

[1] *Ibid.*, p. 61.

[2] M. G. M. Adkins, 'The Citizens in *Philaster*: their Function and Significance', *S.P.*, XLIII (1946), 203–12; and Peter H. Davison, 'The Serious
Concerns of *Philaster*', *ELH*, XXX (1963), 1–15.

[3] Adkins, *op. cit.*, p. 208.

[4] *Ibid.*, p. 209. Cf. also M. Mincoff, 'Fletcher's Early Tragedies', *Renais-
sance Drama*, VII (1964), 75.

The central issue is largely by-passed on stage by the two kingdoms device, which makes the King at the same time a true king, not to be dislodged from his kingship, and a usurper on the throne which the play is concerned with. It is still a strictly hypothetical situation in the best Arcadian fashion, surpassed in its theoretical neatness only by *The Maid's Tragedy*'s presentation of a dilemma in which the would-be revengers of a wronged woman, husband and brother, find the object of their vengeance to be their king. The resolution in the later play, leaving one revenger dead through the torment of his inability to solve the dilemma and the other revenging and tormented by penitence, by its very neatness takes that play further from any direct application to local and specific concerns such as are in *Philaster*. Still, other such essentially theoretical situations were felt to be fully meaningful in relation to contemporary politics. Fulke Greville saw Sidney posthumously criticizing James's rule of favourites:

> doe not his Arcadian Romanties live after him, admired by our soure-eyed Criticks? who, howsoever their common end upon common arts be to affect reputation by depraving censure; yet where nature placeth excellencie above envy, there (it seemeth) she subjecteth these carping eyes to wonder, and shewes the judicious reader, how he may be nourished in the delicacy of his own judgement.
>
> For instance; may not the most refined spirits, in the scope of these dead images (even as they are now) finde, that when Soveraign Princes, to play with their own visions, will put off publique action, which is the splendor of Majestie, and unactively charge the managing of their greatest affaires upon the second-hand faith, and diligence of Deputies, may they not (I say) understand, that even then they bury themselves, and their Estates in a cloud of contempt, and under it both encourage, and shaddow the conspiracies of ambitious subalternes to their false endes, I meane the ruine of States and Princes?[1]

Greville characterizes James as a lover of masques in relating him to Sidney's King. Beaumont depicted his love of hunting in the Calabrian King. While far from being a satire, Beaumont's *Philaster* held the mirror up to princes as Greville saw the *Arcadia* doing.

[1] Fulke Greville, *The Life of Sir Philip Sidney* (1652), ed. by Nowell Smith, Oxford, 1907, pp. 11–12.

7. THE PLAY

Philaster has lain for most of its life in a critical backwater moved
only occasionally by eddies from Shakespeare's romances. Seeing
no grounds for the presumption of high artistry automatically conceded even to *Cymbeline*, the most opaque of that complicated group
of plays, critics have in the past given not much more than a dis-
missive acknowledgement of the place in literary history of a work
popular enough in its own time, and in some way related to Shakespeare. Most of the attention paid to the play in the earlier years of
this century has come from the historians of tragicomedy,[1] and it
is only fairly recently that the basic tasks, the prerequisites for any
sort of comprehension of the design in the Beaumont and Fletcher
plays, have been tackled with success. Waith accomplished the first
step in explaining the careful design of *The Faithful Shepherdess*
and how the succeeding plays followed from it. Danby's essays on
the social background of *Philaster* and the structural virtues of *The
Maid's Tragedy*, relating the plays as he does to the *Arcadia*, show
what could be gained from a fresh approach and a close examination, and more recently Clifford Leech has extended this closeness
of scrutiny more widely through the canon with admirable effect.
The view common to them all suggests that all the romances, like
Shakespeare's last plays, require a delicate approach, a shedding of
the preconceptions and habits of reading acquired from Shakespeare's tragedies and early comedies, setting aside the chronic over-
familiarity with subtle characterization in the sensitive rehand-
ling of uncomplicated old stories which still tempts us to read Elizabethan plays as if they were embryonic nineteenth-century novels.

The basis of a better understanding of *Philaster* as a romantic
tragicomedy is to be found in the literature rather than the drama
of its time. It is best seen as a dramatization of the designs which
Sidney and Spenser embodied in genres more solemn and respectable than stage fare. At least that is how its authors and their contemporaries saw it. Beaumont in his elegy on Sidney's daughter
expressed the wish that the *Arcadia* might beget successors. Sidney,
he wrote,

---

[1] For instance, Ristine, Herrick, and Lievsay, *op. cit.*

> left two children, who for virtue, wit,
> Beauty, were lov'd of all—thee and his writ:
> Two was too few; yet death hath from us took
> Thee, a more faultless issue than his book,
> Which, now the only living thing we have
> From him, we'll see, shall never find a grave
> As thou hast done. Alas, would it might be
> That books their sexes had, as well as we,
> That we might see this married to thy worth,
> And many poems like itself bring forth![1]

The *Arcadia* was not an entertainment but an education, according to Greville.[2] Shirley's epistle *To The Reader* in the 1647 Beaumont and Fletcher Folio gives their plays the same praise:

> *this being the Authentick witt that made Blackfriers an Academy, where the three howers spectacle while* Beaumont *and* Fletcher *were presented, were usually of more advantage to the hopefull young Heire, then a costly, dangerous, forraigne Travell, with the assistance of a governing Mounsieur, or Signior to boot; And it cannot be denied but that the young spirits of the Time, whose Birth & Quality made them impatient of the sowrer wayes of education, have from the attentive hearing these pieces, got ground in point of wit and carriage of the most severely employed Students, while these Recreations were digested into Rules, and the very Pleasure did edifie.*

Of course, these were the orthodox terms for commending serious literature, and even plays, when the opposition had shut the theatres for licentiousness; they are the terms of Sidney's own *Defence of Poesy*. The best of the romantic dramas did imitate the serious literature of Sidney and Spenser, and were written to this morally educational formula, one quite explicitly distinct from the pattern which Sidney and Spenser themselves exploited, the chivalric romances burlesqued by Cervantes and *The Knight of the Burning Pestle*. Beaumont's burlesque attacked the middle-class genre; his later plays offered the other face of the coin, the true 'heroick' vein which the Restoration imitated. In a sense the collaborators, and Shakespeare with them, were writing 'literary' drama for the first time. Their plays are distinct from earlier romantic stories such as *Two Gentlemen of Verona*, which like *Philaster* was based on an episode in the *Diana*. The difference lies in the shift of priorities

[1] Dyce, XI, 509.   [2] Greville, *op. cit.*, pp. 15–16.

from the designs either of comedy or of character-centred tragedy
to the Sidneian scheme of moral paradigms or patterns of situation.

Spenser's design in *The Faerie Queene*, minutely exhibiting the
twelve virtues which made in their total Magnificence,[1] was the
same as Sidney's, the aristocratic ideal of works displaying magnanimity or magnificence, nobility of mind or nobility of conduct.
Spenser's plan of twelve books for the private virtues and twelve
more for the politic in his total picture of the ideal prince differed
from Sidney's only in its exclusive concern with the portrait of
perfection. Sidney and after him Beaumont and Fletcher were more
various and less ambitious, leaving out Prince Arthur in favour of
a wide range of lesser characters with more immediate human relevance, mingling heroic and amatorious, external and internal
worlds in interlocking situations which put both sets of virtues on
trial together.

The Maid's Tragedy, the most self-evidently great play of the
collaboration, shows more obviously than *Philaster* the thorough-
ness with which the basic Sidneian design was adapted into dramatic form. The genesis of its testing situation can be found in Fuller's
anecdote of the man who overheard Fletcher in a tavern plotting
to kill the King.[2] The same patterning of 'amatorious' contrasts as
in the *Arcadia* and the earlier Beaumont and Fletcher plays, the
lecherous and chaste women, the virtuous subject and profligate
King, with the lecherous and virtuous loves in conflict, is set in a
hypothetical 'heroical' situation where two types of honourable
subject, lover and soldier, find their personal honour destroyed by
their adulterous King, and are tested by the problem of what course

---

[1] In the letter to Raleigh explaining the plan of his book Spenser wrote:
'The generall end ... of all the booke is to fashion a gentleman or noble
person in vertuous and gentle discipline... I labour to pourtraict in
Arthure, before he was king, the image of a brave knight, perfected in the
twelve private morall vertues, as Aristotle hath devised, the which is the
purpose of these first twelve bookes: which if I finde to be well accepted,
I may be perhaps encoraged, to frame the other part of polliticke vertues
in his person, after that hee came to be king... So in the person of Prince
Arthure I sette forth magnificence in particular, which vertue for that
(according to Aristotle and the rest) it is the perfection of all the rest, and
conteineth in it them all' (*Works*, ed. F. M. Padelford, etc., I, 167–8).

[2] T. Fuller, *The Worthies of England*, London, 1662, Sig. Ooo1ᵛ.

honour then dictates. The collision of personal and public honour, the dilemma of choice between the honourable man's twin duties of virtue in love and allegiance to the King, is the problem set out in the play. The initiating action is that of Amintor, the younger hero of the play, the lover, in following the command of his King to marry the royal nominee instead of Aspatia, the maid to whom Amintor was contracted. The forlorn Aspatia wanders through the play as a not entirely mute reproach to Amintor for his putting public duty before love, for taking the masque of ceremonious love as in the wedding celebration of Act I to be reality, and the play has its title from her. When Amintor finds that his sense of duty has led him into marriage with the King's mistress, the train of tragic consequences is laid. The subsequent complications involving the older hero Melantius, whose honour is similarly destroyed because the King's mistress is his sister, are mainly refinements on the questions of honourable conduct in its various aspects, private and politic, chastity and reputation, love and duty, suffering and revenge. There is a perfectly Sidneian balancing of parallels and contrasts.

Recognition of the same design in *Philaster* is complicated by its mood as a tragicomedy. Beaumont and Fletcher have frequently been condemned for writing plays in which the choice of happy or unhappy ending is merely fortuitous. It is a difficult contention to uphold. Nothing at any stage in the development of *The Maid's Tragedy*'s situation gives any hope of escape from the problems honour poses; the only relief from the sombre mood is in the minor figure of Calianax. Conversely, everything in *Philaster* unwaveringly points to its happy conclusion. Its evil characters (with the only partial exception of Megra) like those of *Cymbeline* are merely comic, and every unhappy turn of events is followed by a switch to a lighter mood; the final confrontation of Philaster with Arethusa, for instance, in IV. v, is broken into by the Country Fellow, and the pathos of the sacrificial wedding scene is swallowed in Dion's exuberance over the citizen mutiny. Above all, the gods behind the play are benign; their 'secret justice' provides an amatorious resolution of the heroical dilemma in the second scene of Act I. The beneficent powers of virtuous love display themselves from the beginning, openly in Arethusa and covertly in Bellario. Arethusa's prayer before her declaration of love to Philaster looks to a happy ending in its hint of innocent double-think, submissive to the will of the gods whose interest it is to see her love consummated:

> You gods that would not have your dooms withstood,
> Whose holy wisdoms at this time it is
> To make the passions of a feeble maid
> The way unto your justice, I obey.   (I. ii. 31-4)

There is no proleptic irony in this, no foreboding. The tragicomic atmosphere differs from the purely tragic in its lightness of touch, and especially in this suggestion of an indulgent mockery of the little weaknesses of the central characters. Comedy distances the viewers from the protagonists, and we see Arethusa here as Shakespeare means us to see Imogen, human as well as virtuous. The same note as Arethusa's is struck in Philaster's first impulse to praise the gods when Bellario's sex is finally revealed, in a moment of superbly serio-comic relief:

> *Dion.* . . . . It is a woman; let her speak the rest.
> *Phi.* How ? That again.
> *Dion.*   It is a woman.
> *Phi.* Blessed be you powers that favour innocence!
> *King.* Lay hold upon that lady. [*Megra is seized.*]
> *Phi.* It is a woman, sir! Hark, gentlemen,
>   It is a woman! Arethusa, take
>   My soul into thy breast that would be gone
>   With joy. It is a woman!   (V. v. 133-40)

In both these instances we are aware of the benignity of fortune not only through the words of the principals but most thoroughly by what Danby has described as dramatic situations performing the work of metaphysical conceits, 'moral puns' in which turns of situation express and illuminate the moral problem. Danby has subtly analysed the conceits of situation in the tragedy, but his essay on *Philaster* fails to catch the pervasive and brilliantly successful tragicomic mood of its situational puns. The sympathy in the audience for the protagonist which tragedies are traditionally expected to evoke is irrelevant in a tragicomedy as it is in a comedy.

Viewing Philaster as if he were Amintor or Hamlet is to take him
more at his own valuation than his authors'. His joyful hysteria, at
the discovery that his page who has been accused of fornication
with his chaste mistress is a girl, is a delicate blend of comic and
pathetic incongruities. Its immediate impact lightens the tension
before the implications of the discovery are set out. The whole
point of this penultimate twist in the story lies not in the confirmation of a happy ending—we have never been given any reason to
doubt Arethusa's virtue or the course of justice—nor in the comic
ridicule it throws on Megra's accusation, but in the ironies first of
Dion's having been led into falsely testifying to Philaster against
his own daughter, which in its own way is a lesson in means which
are not justified by their ends, and secondly in the realization that
had Bellario not been so faithful a 'servant' of Philaster the events
following from Megra's accusation need never have happened. As
she admits,

> understanding well
> That when I made discovery of my sex
> I could not stay with you, I made a vow,
> By all the most religious things a maid
> Could call together, never to be known
> Whilst there was hope to hide me from men's eyes
> For other than I seemed, that I might ever
> Abide with you.   (v. v. 183–90)

It is the slightest of final twists when Arethusa then shows that
Bellario had no such reason to fear discovery. The whole conclusion of the play in this respect is an intensely dramatic presentation
through the situation of the familiar verbal pun on the 'service' of
love and loyalty. The improbability of the father failing to recognize
his disguised daughter is a small price to pay for it, if the standard
Elizabethan disguise convention is not enough wrapping.

'Service' and 'servant', in fact, are key words in the play. Their
primary sense of duty to lord or king occurs with regard to Philaster's relationship to the King and the King's daughter, and Bellario's and Dion's to Philaster. The related sense of a lover's service
to his mistress appears in I. i when Pharamond describes himself
as Arethusa's servant; Philaster and Arethusa come to address each
other as 'dearest mistress' and 'dearest servant' (III. ii). The sexual

ambiguity in the word is brought out in the King's accusation to
Arethusa that Bellario has

> done you that good service
> Shames me to speak of   (III. ii. 27–8)

and is suggested earlier when Pharamond's visit 'to do his service'
to Arethusa turns out to be for the purpose of inviting her not to
wait for the wedding ceremonies but to 'prevent our joys to come'
(I. ii. 201). In the conclusion of the play Bellario is revealed as a
metaphor of true service, uniting the two respectable meanings of
the word in her actions and denying its third implication by the
fact of her sex. The neat reversal of expectation in the discovery
of her sex, when she is found to be not the false servant of Philaster
and the lustful 'servant' of the Princess but the platonically loving
and loyal servant to both, makes her the exemplification of the twin
ideals of service in love and government, honest love and duty
without lust or self-interest.

The amatorious and heroic senses of service fused in the 'conceit'
of Bellario show clearly enough the Sidneian design of *Philaster*,
but the theme is established by more than the service metaphor.
With true service goes being oneself; Arethusa, who at the beginning is described as having

> knowledge
> Only of what herself is to herself,   (I. i. 94–5)

triumphs by her constancy. Under the King's threat of disinherit-
ance for her marriage to Philaster she declares:

> There's nothing that can stir me from myself.
> (v. iii. 68)

Her selfhood is her virtue. Philaster's selfhood is his rightful title
and position; he reassures the citizens in v. iv by saying:

> I am myself,
> Free as my thoughts are; by the gods I am
> (ll. 88–9)

and elaborates a little later with:

> I am what I was born to be, your Prince.   (l. 98)

The concept of selfhood was orthodox, of course, in the Eliza-

E

bethan scheme of things. The Chamberlain's comment on Wolsey in *Henry VIII*—

> My heart weeps to see him
> So little of his great self   (III. ii. 335–6)

—reads the office in the man while expressing the standard psychology of any man who is out of his 'character' being not himself. Self is inward character in the new King Henry's declaration 'I have turn'd away my former self' (*2 Henry IV*, v. v. 59) and in Spenser's *Amoretti*, xlv:

> And in my selfe, my inward selfe I meane,
> Most lively like behold your semblant trew.

It is because Philaster is not himself again till he can be King that he suffers the Hamlet-like distraction of the first acts.

The same terminology is used over the destruction of Pharamond's brave front. Dion's analysis of Pharamond in the first scene, following directly on the disagreement between the ladies over his character ('O, 'tis a Prince of wax. / A dog it is.') is a prediction that his 'bravery' will eventually be seen as a bold face rather than his true self, unlike Philaster whose quality is 'the bravery of his mind' (I. i. 21–2). At this stage in the play the point is a simple one:

> Every man in this age has not a soul of crystal, for all
> men to read their actions through; men's hearts and
> faces are so far asunder that they hold no intelligence.
> Do but view yon stranger well, and you shall see a
> fever through all his bravery, and feel him shake like a
> true tenant ... (ll. 247–52)

When the citizens do make him shake like the mere tenant of the throne he hopes to occupy, the Captain's comment is:

> the man begins to fear and know himself.
>   (v. iv. 44)

The orthodoxy of selfhood also indicates how the double theme of love and politics derives from the ethos which underlies the situational conceits. Philaster ultimately attains his honour and becomes himself through his love, specifically through Arethusa's constancy and Bellario's selfless devotion: a thematic principle close to Sidney's in the marriage of Arethusa's patience to Philaster's magnanimity (the 'bravery' of his mind). 'Perfection will be a co-operative rather than an individual achievement.'[1] Love, in all the possible meanings of 'service', was one half of the ethos; the other was honour with its even more complex set of meanings. The central question in *The Maid's Tragedy* is one of honourable conduct, and the word 'honour' itself (with its middle-class equivalent 'honesty') is used more than forty times in a range of contexts to exemplify the many niceties of its meanings. There is no such minute examination in *Philaster*, but it lies as a presupposition behind all the shifts in the hero's situation, and works with love as the arbiter of good conduct through the play. It was this minute demonstration of the testing of honourable conduct which led to Beaumont and Fletcher's elevation as the formative educational forces behind the Cavalier ethos in Jacobean England.

One cannot stress too much that Beaumont and Fletcher were literary gentry, that they wrote to a bookish rather than a theatrical specification, and that they expected their audiences to understand their work as they understood Sidney and Spenser, at large and not only in mighty lines. They wrote for the Fulke Grevilles of their day. However many more concessions *Philaster* made to theatrical realism than its predecessors *The Faithful Shepherdess* and *Cupid's Revenge* had done, in keeping the gods and their machinery off-stage, it still belongs more in the magic, allegorizing world of the court masque than the theatre world of Shakespearean tragedy. The appeal which Ben Jonson made on behalf of his masques demands the same kind of attention to the significances which lie behind the spectacle as the authors of *Philaster* expected:

> This it is hath made the most royall *Princes*, and greatest *persons* (who are commonly the *personaters* of these *actions*) not onely studious of riches, and magnificence in the outward celebration, or shew; (which rightly becomes them) but curious after the most high, and heartie *inuentions*, to furnish the inward parts: (and those grounded vpon *antiquitie*, and solide *learnings*) which, though their *voyce* be taught to sound to present occasions, their *sense*, or doth, or should alwayes lay hold on more remou'd *mysteries*.[2]

[1] Danby, *op. cit.*, p. 51.
[2] Jonson, VII, 209. Frost, *op. cit.*, pp. 217–24, has a full account of the Elizabethan allegorizing mentality.

The tribe of Ben were agreed in regarding understanding of 're-moved mysteries' as the test of a good audience.

Every Elizabethan or Jacobean writer with literary pretensions who took up the popular middle-class prose romance for his medium was going to follow the *Defence*'s dictum about poets figuring a golden world and allegorize his romance world essentially into a golden one. The world of *Philaster* is as much a golden one as in the masques, where evil is an intrusion, to be isolated and in the end banished from the scene. It is a precise opposite of the worlds of Middleton's and Webster's tragedies, where earthly cor-ruption is the only datum. The witches in the antimasque of Jon-son's *Masque of Queenes* (1609) are exhorted by their leader to do evil because 'Ill lives not, but in us', and '*Vertue*, else, will deeme / Our powers decreas't, . . . and, bold / Upon our sloth, retrive her *Age of Gold*.'[1] Evil in the antimasque is no more than a foil to the gold of the masque proper. Realism here as in *Philaster* presupposes an ideal reality; the concern is not with the inevitably corrupt sub-lunary world of the majority of Jacobean plays. When Pharamond deplores the return of the golden age of virtuous wives (II. ii. 59), his evil is comic and his rôle is only that of a foil to true virtue. Where in Middleton his words would be cynical, in *Philaster* they are comically foolish. Dion is the only courtier to produce a cynical witticism of the same kind (II. iv. 128–9), and it is precisely his sexual cynicism which makes him credulous towards Megra's story of Arethusa's and Bellario's lechery, and so to foster the temporary success of evil in the play. Even he figures the golden world when he is punished for his would-be cynicism.

The same 'literary' devotion to the underlying ideal is the reason why there are few mighty lines or purple passages in the verse. A drama of sublunary corruption permits epigrams and sententious proverbs at appropriate points throughout (since in such a world everything is to be summed up as corruption and therefore subject for comment at any point); the literature of the golden world, on the other hand, makes its main summing-up in its conclusion. *Philaster* is noticeably short of aphorisms. The only two proverbs (IV. i. 7 and 33–4) are insignificant, and sententious sayings such

[1] Jonson, VII, 288.

as Philaster's attack on womankind (III. ii. 127–40) have no place
outside their context. The verse, as Philip Edwards has pointed
out,[1] is organized by scenes strictly according to the requirements
of the dramatic situation. Verbal exuberance and extensively pun-
ning word-play are confined to the scenes of excited prose (v. iii.
128–70 and v. iv), and to the bawdy joking in the sequences involving Megra and Pharamond. Pope's maxim that expression is the
dress of thought is a fair description of the status of the verse in
Philaster, governed as it is by an almost Augustan sense of the
decorum of fitting speeches to mood and situation in each scene.
It is perhaps this as much as anything else which has caused critics
of Fletcherian verse to disagree over whether it is 'natural' or 'rhetorical'.[2] The syntax and vocabulary are 'natural', by which of
course one means simple, with few involved subordinate clauses
and relatively few inversions, the 'conversation of gentlemen', as
Dryden took it to be.[3] In v. iii, the scene of greatest dramatic in-
tensity before the play's dénouement, there are three set speeches
which might be considered as appropriately rhetorical in their contexts: Dion's lengthy aside (ll. 6–19), threatening violence; Bellario's 'glad story' (25–44), a speech of calculated prettiness; and
finally Philaster's speech of persuasion to the King (74–103), in
fulfilment of his promise to

> deliver words will mollify
> The hearts of beasts.   (v. ii. 11–12)

The only obtrusive rhetorical device in any of these speeches is the
extended simile in Dion's aside. The only one of the three which is
a speech of persuasion has sentences as short and syntax as simple
as the others, and seems forceful more in its bluntness than its
ingenuity:

> If you aim
> At the dear life of this sweet innocent,
> Y' are a tyrant and a savage monster
> That feeds upon the blood you gave a life to ...
> (v. iii. 76–9)

---

[1] P. Edwards, in *Jacobean Theatre*, p. 161.
[2] Moody E. Prior, *The Language of Tragedy*, New York, 1947, and
Leech, *op. cit.*, among others consider Fletcherian verse to be natural;
Waith, *op. cit.*, considers it rhetorical.   [3] Dryden, *op. cit.*, I, 61.

Perhaps most significantly the speech is barely concluded when it
is overtaken by events and the need to persuade the King of anything disappears. Eloquence is only a frill on the dress of events.
The rhetoric is more a matter of decorum than an occasion for
poetry.

Decorum in the speeches shows in the 'low' style passages as
well as the high. Pharamond woos Megra in 'pretty begging blanks',
but as soon as they turn to the real business of their lust they switch
to prose. Pharamond has already done the same with the Princess;
in I. ii. 159–201 he addresses her in stately verse, but his comment,
once she has rejected his improper suggestion and left him, follows
in flat prose. The King similarly stands on his dignified verse
throughout the play, except for v. iii. 151–60, when he enters in
confusion after being routed by the citizens. The asides of the
gentlemen, particularly in the opening scene, are conspicuously set
in prose to contrast them with the verse being spoken centre-stage;
at I. i. 173 Dion's brief prose aside is even interjected between two
half-lines of verse shared by the King and Philaster:

> King.   As a subject,
>   We give you freedom.
> Dion. [Aside]   Now it heats.
> Phi.   Then thus I turn
>   My language to you, Prince, you foreign man . . .
>   (I. i. 172–4)

Prose performs an important rôle by signalling contrasts of tone
and shifts of mood. The prose comments of the courtiers in the
first scene show the falsity of the King's formal verse declarations,
as Pharamond's prose exposes the emptiness of his verse façade.
Appearances are kept up in verse, and reality cuts through in prose.
The mood of the scene is altered similarly when the Country
Fellow's simplicity in prose lowers the tension of the moment when
Philaster wounds Arethusa. It is the tragicomic deflation of the
tragic.

In some sense recent criticism of Beaumont and Fletcher seems
only to have been dotting the i's of Lamb's summary judgment
that 'after all, Beaumont and Fletcher were but an inferior sort of

Shakespeares and Sidneys'.[1] Translating Sidney's ingenious design, of capturing a popular genre for serious ends, into the other popular genre, drama, meant adapting snippets of Shakespearean theatre, and translators and borrowers in their function as imitators are evidently less than their sources. But judgment cannot afford to be so summary. Beyond any dramatist of their time the collaborators were adept at the theatre of situation; the extraordinary ingenuity of plotting which gave them the accomplishment of metaphysical conceits of situation on stage was a splendidly right vehicle for their design of translating the educative functions of Sidneian literature into the different medium.

8. STAGE HISTORY

The publisher of the third quarto of *Philaster* in 1628 prefaced his edition with a note 'To the Understanding Gentrie', beginning 'This Play, so affectionately taken, and approved by the Seeing Auditors, or Hearing Spectators, (of which sort, I take, or conceive you to bee the greatest part) hath received (as appeares by the copious vent of two Editions,) no lesse acceptance with improovement of you likewise the Readers'. On the evidence of the number of seventeenth-century editions, a rather indiscriminate gauge of popularity, *Philaster* would rank with *The Maid's Tragedy* as the most successful Beaumont and Fletcher play, going into nine quartos in addition to the Second Folio of 1679. With this number it ranks only a little way behind Shakespeare's *Hamlet*, *Richard III*, and *1 Henry IV*, which in their turn follow the immense though perhaps different successes of *Mucedorus*, *The Spanish Tragedy*, *Dr Faustus*, and Heywood's *If You Know Not Me, You Know Nobody*. A better gauge for the kind of popularity *Philaster* had is in the record of what was probably an exceptional double performance at Court in the 1612–13 season. In the list of payments made to the King's Company for fourteen performances in the season, the fourteen were noted as thirteen plays, including *The Maid's Tragedy* and *A King and No King*, with *Philaster* listed twice, at

[1] Charles Lamb, note on *The Maid's Tragedy* in *Specimens of the English Dramatick Poets*, London, [1907], p. 285.

the beginning and end of the list, the second time under its sub-title.[1] The double entry may have been a clerical error, of course, but Chambers accepts that it was performed twice against once for the other plays.

It seems to have appeared at Court again in 1619–20, when the first quarto was published, and it was certainly at Court in 1630 and 1637.[2] During the Commonwealth the Citizen scene (v. iv) was acted as a Droll called 'The Club Men'.[3] When the theatres were closed after 1642 there was no prohibition on reading plays, and it was through this time, notably about 1647 with the production of the First Folio, that Beaumont and Fletcher's reputations reached their greatest heights.[4] Understandably, therefore, in 1660 the theatres reopened with a staple diet of Beaumont and Fletcher, *Philaster* figuring prominently in the repertory till 1662; it was re-vived five years later, and was played for Charles II, probably with Nell Gwyn as Bellario. Pepys in 1661 went 'To the Theatre to see "Philaster", which I never saw before, but I found it far short of my expectations.' He returned in 1668 more happily:

> To the King's playhouse, and there was 'Philaster', where it is pretty to see how I could remember almost all along, ever since I was a boy, Arethusa, the part which I was to have acted at Sir Robert Cook's; and it was very pleasant to me, but more to think what a ridiculous thing it would have been for me to have acted a beautiful woman.[5]

It played again in 1672 (once possibly with an entirely female cast), 1674, and 1676, disappearing then until 1683 when an adaptation called *The Restoration* was performed,[6] with prologue and epilogue by the Duke of Buckingham, who may have written the whole adaptation. The object of the adapter seems largely to have been to comment on the contemporary political scene. Another adapted

---

[1] Chambers, *E.S.*, IV, 180.   [2] Bentley, I, 95–8.

[3] Printed in Francis Kirkman's *The Wits, or Sport upon Sport*, ed. J. J. Elson, New York, 1926, pp. 146–50.

[4] Cf. A. C. Sprague, *Beaumont and Fletcher on the Restoration Stage*, Cambridge (Mass.), 1936, p. 26.

[5] W. B. Van Lennep, *The London Stage 1660–1800*, Part I, 1660–1700, Carbondale (Ill.), 1965, pp. 42, 137.

[6] *Ibid.*, pp. 194, 223, 244, 319.

version by Elkanah Settle, a more royalist text which made Philaster an exiled Prince of Aragon and changed the wounding scene to make Arethusa wound herself, was performed and published in 1695, the last appearance for fifteen years. Waller in 1687 followed Dryden in coupling it with *The Maid's Tragedy* as the most popular play of the two collaborators, but by the end of the century their popularity was more in the study than on the stage.[1]

It had to fade in any case with the fading of the Restoration theatre world in the eighteenth century. The original version was successfully revived in 1711–12, and again in 1714–16 and 1722, but after that it was not seen until 1763–4, when a version by George Colman the Elder had an exceptionally popular eighteen performances. Colman's sole object was 'to remove the objections to the performance of this excellent play on the modern stage',[2] which he did by eliminating the scenes of Dion's confrontation with the King, the citizens' taunting of Pharamond, the wooing scene between Megra and Pharamond, and Philaster's wounding of Arethusa and Bellario. To make the last two cuts possible he made Megra a Spanish lady, already Pharamond's mistress, sent by the Spanish Queen to serve Arethusa; and in the wounding scene he made the Country Fellow arrive in the nick of time to save Arethusa, then had Bellario wounded in trying to separate the Country Fellow and Philaster. Colman also, after some hesitation, omitted III. i, where Dion reveals Megra's story to Philaster, because of Dion's falsification of the facts and because 'Philaster's emotions appeared impossible to be exhibited with any conformity to truth and nature'.[3] The discovery is left to happen off-stage.

Colman's version reappeared in 1765, 1767–8, and 1773–4, but a further revival in 1780 was not a success and the play went down for the last time on the professional London stage in 1796.[4] A revival at the Theatre Royal, Bath, on 12 December 1817, suggests that it survived a little longer in the provinces. There are no records

---

[1] Sprague, *op. cit.*, p. 42.

[2] *The Dramatick Works of George Colman*, 4 vols., London, 1777, III, Sig. B3^r.

[3] *Ibid.*, Sig. B4^r.

[4] Donald J. Rulfs, 'Beaumont and Fletcher on the London Stage, 1776–1833', *P.M.L.A.*, LXIII (1948), 1245–64.

of performance in America, and in modern records there is only a production in June 1947, in the gardens of Worcester College, Oxford, and in November 1953, at the Guildhall School of Music and Drama in London.

9. THE TEXT

The provenance of *Philaster*'s text is complicated by the question of the relationship between the first two quartos. The play was entered on the Stationers' Register on 10 January 1620, and first printed in the same year by Nicholas Okes for Thomas Walkley.[1] The title-page reads:

PHYLASTER. / Or, Loue lyes a Bleeding. / *Acted at the Globe by his Maiesties Seruants.* / Written by $\left\{\begin{array}{c} \textit{Francis Baymont} \\ \text{and} \\ \textit{Iohn Fletcher} \end{array}\right\}$ Gent. / Printed at *London* for *Thomas Walkley*, and are to be sold at his / shop at the *Eagle and Child* in Brittaines Burse. / 1620.

The second edition appeared from the same printer and publisher in 1622, with a new title-page, reading

PHILASTER. / OR, / Loue lies a Bleeding. / *As it hath beene diuerse times Acted,* / at the Globe, and Black-Friers, by / his *Maiesties* Seruants. / Written by $\left\{\begin{array}{c} \textit{Francis Beaumont.} \\ \text{and} \\ \textit{Iohn Fletcher.} \end{array}\right\}$ Gent. / The second Impression, corrected, and / amended. / *LONDON,* / Printed for THOMAS WALKLEY, and are to / be solde at his shoppe, at the signe of the / Eagle and Childe, in *Brittaines Bursse.* / 1622.

The claim that the second quarto was 'corrected, and amended' was amplified by Walkley in a prefatory note to the reader which spoke of 'dangerous and gaping wounds' suffered by the text in Walkley's first impression, and hastened to deny responsibility for them. The third quarto of 1628 was published by Richard Hawkins, who bought the copy from Walkley in that year, and who printed

---

[1] W. W. Greg, *A Bibliography of the English Printed Drama to the Restoration*, London, II, 1951, 510.

from Q2 with a number of minor emendations to the text.[1] Subsequent quartos, in 1634, 1639 (two issues), 1652, and two probably dating from early in the Restoration (*c.* 1661), before the play was collected into the second Folio of 1679, were all reprints of the early quartos.[2] The 'corrected and amended' second quarto has been taken as the copy text by all editors of the play.

Q1 (1620) undoubtedly does present a text inferior in almost all respects to that of Q2 (1622). The two texts differ in numerous words and phrases throughout. Q1 is shorter by 200 lines; in particular its first and last few hundred lines are widely divergent from Q2, evidently written by a different hand from those of the authors, with only broad resemblances of plot in the first section and occasional verbal echoes in the last. Various explanations have been given for these differences and for the inferiority of Q1. Thorndike in his edition held that Q1 was in some way a piracy and that Q2 was the authorial text, a theory later supported by Leo Kirschbaum and others.[3] The only substantial alternative view has been J. E. Savage's suggestion that Q1 is an authorized version of Q2 written at the demand of the censor.[4]

The possibility of Q1's being a censored text needs to be looked at if only because there are in Q2 sufficient parallels to the contemporary political situation to have conceivably justified such a happening.[5] Savage pointed out that Q1 shows some evidence of performance, whereas Q2 has all the signs of a text which never reached the actors. He notes that Q1 has no reference to Calabria, the second kingdom of the play, and that in all but two instances the plural

---

[1] *Philaster*, ed. Robert K. Turner, in *The Dramatic Works in the Beaumont and Fletcher Canon*, I, 371. This critical textual edition is by far the best yet to appear, and all subsequent editors must be in its debt. Its discussion of the textual problems and its textual apparatus are more elaborate than is possible or desirable in this edition. Before Turner's, the only editions showing substantial editorial care were those of P. A. Daniel in the uncompleted *Variorum*, Ashley Thorndike's edition, and the Brooke and Paradise edition of 1933. The last good complete edition of Beaumont and Fletcher's works was that of Dyce in 1843–6.

[2] *Ibid.*, p. 370.

[3] L. Kirschbaum, 'An Hypothesis concerning the Origin of the Bad Quartos', *P.M.L.A.*, LX (1945), 707.

[4] Savage, 'The "Gaping Wounds" in the Text of *Philaster*', *op. cit.*

[5] See above, pp. liii–lvii.

'kingdoms' is made singular. Similarly in the opening and closing scenes references to royalty and the court are minimized. Savage also sees the conclusion of Q1, where Bellario and Galatea are married off to Cleremont and Thrasiline, as an attempt to reduce any parallelism with the case of Arabella Stuart, who had a distant claim to the throne and was refused permission to marry by both Elizabeth and James until December 1609: 'This seemingly happy marriage of Bellario might well have been a device by which the dramatists, at the instigation of the censor, made Bellario look less like the Lady Arabella.'[1] Against Savage's theory, we should first note that Pharamond remains a Spanish prince and that the clash between the King and Dion in IV. iv is also unchanged; the references to 'kingdoms' which stay unaltered are two out of only four, while three references to 'both' kingdoms and three more to 'them' in the scene where Arethusa declares her love to Philaster (I. ii) remain. Nor is it easy to see how the ending which marries off the womenfolk so summarily can be authorial. It is written more clumsily than the original and contains words like 'golls', 'porcupines', and 'dowcets' which suggest that the writer remembered some of the more unusual words from the original but not their context. Again, whereas the divergence of the first section ends abruptly at I. i. 106, the divergence at the end is curiously gradual.[2] In neither the beginning nor the ending is there any obvious reason in the matter of the play why the divergences should occur where they do. The differences are much more likely to be the result of the conditions under which the Q1 copy was transcribed than of an expedient set of alterations made under direction from the censor.

Q1 is a botched text throughout, with nonce-constructions and variants which are evident misreadings of the Q2 text's readings on an average of one line in four. In addition to literals and misspellings Q1 has misreadings such as 'Lyon' or 'Leon' for 'Dion' throughout, 'gentle heauens' for Q2's 'Gentlemen, by heauen' (I. i. 206), 'or no, derectly' for 'no directlier' (I. ii. 163), 'sighes' for 'fights' (II. i. 54), 'fayre leaps' for 'layes, leaps' (II. iv. 156), 'sufficient' for 'suffice it' (III. i. 55), 'make talke' for 'wak'd, talk'd' (III.

---

[1] 'The "Gaping Wounds" in the Text of *Philaster*', *op. cit.*, p. 451.
[2] See Appendix A.

ii. 3), 'know him well' for 'know he will' (IV. vi. 137), and 'iniurious' for 'Murriens' (V. iii. 140). More revealing as to the nature of the Q1 copy are mishearings such as 'vnseene to sound enough' for Q2's 'one sinnew sound enough' (I. i. 163), 'way the danger' for 'weigh the danger' (I. i. 330), 'at the high Altar' for 'I at the Altar' (I. ii. 187), 'time' for 'theame' (II. ii. 73), 'the presents' for 'the presence' (II. iii. 25), and 'ore againe' for 'ouer of a game' (III. i. 267). These errors are not likely to have been entirely or even largely compositorial. Even if we hesitate to accept Walkley's assurance that it was neither he nor the printer who hurt Q1, R. K. Turner has shown that in other texts Okes's compositors were competent enough.[1] The errors in Q1 must mainly have originated with the copy that came into Walkley's hands.

The characteristics of the copy for Q1 besides the misreadings and mishearings include mislineation so persistent that the manuscript most probably was written in prose throughout, a mark of hurried if not of surreptitious transcription, and probably a mark of copying from dictation, which would explain the mishearings as well as the mislineations. The scribe was distracted to the extent that after 'sea' in III. ii. 107 he wrote 'sterne' as 'deepe' and 'flung it by' as 'flowing it by'. He was also evidently familiar with the play in performance, and used his memory to assist his eyes in places. Bellario's exhortation 'Fly, fly' to Philaster in IV. vi. 36 becomes in Q1 'Hide, hide', which is what Philaster eventually does. The stage directions are elaborate and explanatory, and entries are consistently placed two or three lines earlier than in Q2, where they appear only immediately before the entrant speaks.

On the evidence it seems that Q1 was printed from a clumsy, dictated transcript of the central part of authorial foul papers, by a scribe familiar with the play in performance. It may very likely have been surreptitious, since it was clearly not a transcript of the kind often made for presentation to a patron, the only sort of person besides the players likely to receive an authorized transcript.[2] The

---

[1] R. K. Turner, jr, 'The Printing of *Philaster* Q1 and Q2', *Library*, 5th series, XV (1960), 28.

[2] See above, p. xxiii. There is some possibility that the difficulties which the King's Men suffered in 1619, the death of Burbage and an attempt at restraining their activities at Blackfriars, may be linked with the publish-

beginning and end were missing from the transcript originally, possibly from the same cause as led the Pied Bull *King Lear*'s first and last scenes to be transcribed largely from memory.[1] *Philaster*'s beginning and ending were replaced by a hack, possibly the scribe, who had a perfunctory acquaintance with the story and was commissioned to make the incomplete text good.

A comparison of Q1 and Q2 suggests also that they derive from different states of the authors' copy. Turner has noted as evidence for Q1's being the earlier draft some apparent uncertainty over names.[2] Arethusa and Bellario are named only as 'Princesse' and 'Boy' until Act III, and Cleremont and Thrasiline, not mentioned in the text by name at all, appear only as names in stage directions as late as Act IV. Their designation with Dion simply as 'three Gentlemen' in the stage directions may represent the authors' initial uncertainty over names, and would explain why fifty of their speeches are differently assigned in Q1 and Q2.

Such differences as these indicate only a degree of tidying up in the Q2 copy. Other differences, however, suggest a rather more positive revision. Q1's 'Countrey gallant', as Turner notes, is demoted into the mere 'Country Fellow' of Q2 with some consistency (the 'man' of Q1 becomes a 'mean man' and 'a good fellow' in Q2, at IV. v. 80 and 88). What seems to be a late insertion in Q2 (IV. iii. 26–31)[3] is similarly designed to emphasize the distance between country and court.

If these changes do signify different states of copy behind Q1 and Q2, then several indifferent variants may represent authorial second thoughts. Q2's 'nobler' where Q1 has 'worthier' at I. ii. 102, Q2's 'Mercers' for Q1's 'silke-mans' (II. ii. 26), 'spirits' for 'anymales' (II. ii. 42), 'coldly' for 'milder' (III. i. 105), 'guiltily' for 'vile' (III. ii. 149), and 'hurt her?' for 'done it?' (IV. v. 124) are

---

ing of several of their more popular plays between 1619 and 1622; three of them, *Philaster*, *The Maid's Tragedy*, and *Othello*, first appeared in versions which had subsequently to be revised.

[1] Cf. Alice Walker, *Textual Problems of the First Folio*, Cambridge, 1953, p. 40, and *King Lear*, ed. G. I. Duthie, Cambridge, 1960, p. 133.

[2] *Philaster*, ed. Turner, *op. cit.*, p. 395.

[3] See Commentary note, and below, p. lxxxi.

some instances; they may in some cases be Beaumont's rewriting of Fletcher's text.[1]

The crucial difficulty of the text is whether or to what extent Q1, with all its imperfections, may have been used to print Q2. There are several common errors between the two texts which almost certainly indicate contamination: the transposed lines at I. i. 178–9, transposed words at II. iii. 28, a punctuation error in II. iii. 30, and a number of possible mislineations.[2] Other errors which occur in both texts may have been produced by Q1's contamination of Q2 or may equally well have originated with the authorial transcriber whose hand lies behind the copy for both quartos. These are the textual cruxes at I. i. 241 and 299, punctuation at II. iv. 53, the pronouns in V. ii. 39, and 'deliuer' in V. iii. 31. The common errors would seem to imply that a copy of Q1, extensively corrected by reference to an authorial manuscript, formed the printer's copy for Q2. Against this conclusion one must note that there is little sign of the copying of accidentals usual when a corrected copy of one printed text is used in the setting of another, except for some odd italicization and some rather idiosyncratic punctuation. The differences are much more striking than the resemblances. If Q1 did serve as the basis for Q2's copy then the corrector of the Q1 text must have been extraordinarily conscientious in making his annotations and the compositors exceptionally strong-minded in following them and ignoring the Q1 accidentals. The first compositor of Q2, who set sheets B–H (up to IV. vi. 35), had probably also set Q1 two years before, yet he altered his former layout by setting to a different measure and indenting the speechprefixes, even though (to judge by the common errors) his original layout must have been to hand. One cannot question the evidence of the transpositions: they are clearly compositorial errors made in setting up Q1, not authorial errors made in the Q1 copy, and equally clearly they occur in Q2 as a result of the Q2 compositor's following Q1. On the other hand fresh errors in Q2 such as 'understanding'

---

[1] Beaumont transcribed the final copy of all the plays in which he had a hand, to judge by the absence in them of Fletcher's orthographic characteristics. Cf. Hoy, III (1958), 86.

[2] Cf. *Philaster*, ed. Turner, *op. cit.*, pp. 378–9.

(II. iv. 63), 'stagge' (II. iv. 128), 'metled' (II. iv. 188), 'women' (v. ii. 33), and 'Chast' (v. iii. 63) appear to derive from misreadings of a manuscript where Q1 if consulted could have given the correct reading.

Quantitatively the largest number of Q1 errors which appear to carry over into Q2 involve lineation, and here the evidence is ambiguous. In the first scene of the play the Q2 compositor evidently did consult Q1 as soon as it began to agree with his copy. Q1 sets the first scene very largely in prose, with occasional attempts, usually in the shorter speeches, to set lines of verse, and still more occasional capitalization of the first letter in the verse lines. Several of the interjections by the gentlemen are set as lines of verse length but lacking capitals, and four such pairs of lines (117–18, 121–2, 169–70, and 194–5) were taken over as verse by the Q2 compositor and supplied with capitals. Q1 seems also to have been responsible for some anomalies of capitalization in Q2 through the compositor ignoring Q1's lineation but following its capitalization at III. ii. 174 and v. iv. 20.[1]

Some copying of Q1's lineation, then, is apparent in Q2. Far less certain is the general presumption of editors that Q2's verse was quite frequently mislined as a result of the Q1 contamination. *Philaster*'s text has suffered more than most plays from the attentions of Procrustean editors. Mason noted as early as 1798 that

> the most striking, and most unfortunate error in Seward's [i.e., Theobald's] edition is, a preposterous affectation of reducing to metre, many passages which the author intended for prose. This plan was ill conceived, and miserably executed; it has led the editors into many difficulties, and, instead of adding honour to the poets they wished to illustrate, has tended to degrade them, for there is a degree of harmony in good prose, which bad verse can never arrive at.[2]

Fleay's belief that Fletcher in general wrote no prose but only a loose verse with a preference for feminine endings is in the Theobald tradition. Even Turner in his otherwise splendid old-spelling edition has emended the lineation of more than sixty passages, in many cases 'reducing to metre' lines which should be prose. The

---

[1] See Collation.   [2] *Op. cit.*, p. vii.

presumption of the need to adjust almost every line on a Procrustean bed of ten syllables can only too successfully conceal the balance which exists in *Philaster* between verse and prose, the balance between dignity and everyday reality and between differing tragicomic moods which has been examined above.

One particularly difficult aspect of the lineation question has been created by the modern practice of setting split lines of verse across the page as if one speaker is completing the incomplete verse line of the former speaker. The difficulty in this is first the invariable practice of Elizabethan and Jacobean compositors of setting all speakers' first lines to the left margin, making no distinction between short lines of prose and half-lines of verse. The problem of distinguishing between them lies with the modern editor, whose task is complicated by the common practice of most authors, including those who wrote *Philaster*, of using half-lines either to begin or to end verse speeches without bothering to see the lines completed by another speaker. One suspects that Jonson was alone among his contemporaries in trying to complete all his half-lines. In *Philaster*'s case it is doubtful whether Beaumont and Fletcher conceived of their half-lines as split-line verse at all. Short lines are used to begin speeches when the preceding line is complete at I. i. 229, 237, and 255, III. ii. 99, and at least forty other places; and half-lines at the end of speeches which are followed by a full line occur at I. ii. 162, II. ii. 76, III. i. 57 and 246, III. ii. 118, and at many other places. The insertion at IV. iii. 26–31 does not fit the metre of its context, leaving two unmatched half-lines at the end of each of its three-line speeches. Twice in IV. vi, at 61–2 and 69–71, three short lines of dialogue divided between different speakers make a total of one and a half metrical lines, and the irregularity is still more marked in longer interchanges of dialogue such as those at I. ii. 170–9, II. iii. 1–24, III. ii. 11–33, IV. v. 109–40, and IV. vi. 135–44. To spread such dialogue across the page in simulation of metrical regularity makes the page layout visually awkward and the speeches metrically absurd. It would take an abnormally mathematical ear, for instance, to detect V. ii. 40–51 as six and a half lines of regular decasyllabics, and it is to be doubted whether it was written with that intention.

F

Turner, like slashing Theobald, justifies much of his relineation on the ground that Q2 is following Q1's almost wholly mistranscribed lineation. He lists three speeches in prose and twenty-one verse passages, in which Q2 is thought to follow Q1's erroneous lineation, as a not insubstantial part of the evidence for Q2 being printed from a corrected copy of Q1.[1] The three prose passages, however, are each a matter of a line and a half, and since each complete line is set to the full measure, and the words are substantially the same in each quarto, it is a not impossible coincidence. The measures used to set Q1 and Q2 are not so different as to affect the number of words in the measure to any extent. Of the twenty-one verse passages, two (I. i. 117–18 and v. iii. 122–6) are Dion's prose; the first is one of the four short passages which Q2 lines as verse in the opening scene, following Q1, but the second is prose in both quartos and does not need altering to verse. Seventeen of the remaining nineteen examples are split lines,[2] so placed as a result of the practice of starting all speeches at the left margin; it is difficult to see how else they could have been set in either text. The eighteenth example is Pharamond's rather prosaic instructions, IV. v. 141–3, at the end of a series of quick exchanges. It is set as prose in both quartos, probably again correctly, though all editors, following Theobald, have relined it as verse. The last example, II. i. 6–10, is verse which is certainly slightly irregular, but hardly enough so to justify emendation except on the presumption that Q1 has worked its corruption.

One is in the circumstances led to adopt conservatism as the alternative to anarchy. If Q2's lineation is really in doubt through the whole text as a result of its dependence on Q1, then such passages as the four lines at IV. vi. 141–4, the first and last of which are half-lines, should be adjusted to make a total of three complete lines; and the whole passage in the vicinity of Q2's sole mid-speech half-line (III. ii. 124) should similarly be smoothed out of sight. Similar drastic treatment would be necessary for the captain's first speeches in v. iv, which have so far resisted every such attempt

---

[1] *Op. cit.*, p. 379.

[2] i.e., II. ii. 69–70; III. i. 36–7, 102, 127–9, 262–3; ii. 9–10, 24, 27–8, 73–84; IV. i. 18; iv. 20–3, 41; v. 127–8; vi. 68, 136–40; V. ii. 34–6, 40–51.

(Q2 sets it all as impossible verse, leaving the citizens' speeches in prose). There is some possibility that parts of it should be verse, notably the section following l. 48, which is a mock proclamation of Pharamond as king. Q2's version of the lines addressed to Philaster makes quite good verse, and the verse-arrangement has been retained as verse in this edition. But a more radical attitude to the text than it requires, an acceptance of its general instability, would be necessary to justify large-scale emendation.

Contamination of Q2 by Q1 must be acknowledged to exist, though I would not go so far as Turner in concluding that the whole central portion of Q2 was set from a heavily annotated copy of Q1.[1] It is evident that the compositors of Q2 did have a copy of Q1 close enough beside them to lead them into error, particularly where the two texts begin to correspond; it would have been useful for consultation, of course, in checking difficult readings in the Q2 manuscript and for guidance in casting-off copy. The differences in layout, accidentals, and spelling, and the sheer bulk of the annotation which would have been necessary argue strongly against much more than that.

Q2, then, must serve as copy-text for editions of *Philaster*, with the moving shadows of Q1 looming over it. Reference to Q1 is useful in correcting Q2's cruxes, either to find the possible source of the corruption or as a back-door way of ascertaining when the Q2 compositor may have nodded. The text was set in formes, with little press correction except for the inner forme of sheet I, the second forme to be set by the second compositor, and probably the only one corrected by reference to copy. The number of corrections in this forme and the lack in others suggests that as many as one compositorial error in twenty lines may have passed uncorrected into the Q2 text.[2]

[1] There is also some anomalous page-numbering in the outer forme of sheet K in Q2, which reproduces the equivalent Q1 numbering and might again suggest a Q2 compositor led astray by Q1. Turner, however (*op. cit.*, p. 377), suggests that it may have been an accidental equivalence resulting from the machining of sheet K (outer) after L (outer), and a subsequent miscalculation of the compositor in deducting twice as much as he should have to get the page-numbers of the earlier forme. There is no correspondence with Q1's numbers on the inner forme of sheet H, where there is a similarly miscalculated pagination.   [2] Turner, *op. cit.*, p. 379.

For this edition the copies of Q2 in the British Museum (two copies), the Bodleian Library, and the Dyce Collection have been collated and checked against the readings of the three American copies noted in Turner.[1] The copy-text is that in British Museum C.34.c.4. Copies of Q1 in the same libraries have also been checked against Turner. Only the Q1 variants which have some significant bearing on the differences between Q1 and Q2 have been recorded in the Collation of this edition. Where a Q1 stage direction has been adopted it is noted in the Collation. Where Q1 is given as authority and Q2 not named, substantial identity between them is implied. All departures from the Q2 lineation, and Theobaldian emendations to lineation, are listed separately in Appendix B. The punctuation of Q2, which is uniformly heavy and probably compositorial, since it does not always follow the sense adequately, has been silently regularized. Spelling has been modernized, contracted forms regularized in accordance with current Revels practice, and proper names regularized throughout. The capitalization of titles (e.g., 'lord' and 'lady') has been dropped except where it clearly refers to an individual (as in 'my Lord Dion', I. i. 318, etc., and 'my Lord', referring to Philaster, at II. i. 51, etc.), in accordance with modern practice. Line-numbering has given this editor some problems. Where a half-line of verse by one speaker seems to match a subsequent half-line by a second, the two half-lines have been counted as a single line of verse. Elsewhere, each line or part-line has a number to itself.

In the Collation Q1 = quarto of 1620; Q2 = quarto of 1622; $Q2^c$ = quarto of 1622 (corrected); $Q2^u$ = quarto of 1622 (uncorrected); Q3 = quarto of 1628; Q4 = quarto of 1634; Q5 = quarto of 1639; Q6 = quarto of 1652; Q7 = quarto of c. 1661 (published by Kirkman); F2 = folio of 1679; Q9 = quarto of 1687; other editions are as cited in the list of Abbreviations.

---

[1] *Ibid.*, pp. 492–3.

PHILASTER

PHILASTER.

OR,

Loue lies a Bleeding.

As it hath beene diuerse times Acted,
at the Globe, and Blacke-Friers, by
his *Maiesties Seruants.*

Written by {
Francis Beaumont.
and
Iohn Fletcher.
} *Gent.*

The second Impression, corrected, and
amended.

LONDON,

Printed for THOMAS WALKLEY, and are to
be solde at his shoppe, at the signe of the
Eagle and Childe, in *Brittaines Bursse.*
1622.

To the Reader

Courteous reader, Philaster and Arethusa his love have lain so
long a-bleeding, by reason of some dangerous and gaping
wounds which they received in the first impression, that it is
wondered how they could go abroad so long or travel so far as
they have done. Although they were hurt neither by me nor   5
the printer, yet I, knowing and finding by experience how
many well-wishers they have abroad, have adventured to bind
up their wounds, and to enable them to visit upon better terms
such friends of theirs as were pleased to take knowledge of
them, so maimed and deformed as they at the first were; and   10
if they were then gracious in your sight, assuredly they will
now find double favour, being reformed and set forth suitable
to their birth and breeding,

> By your serviceable friend,
> Thomas Walkley.   15

To the Reader . . . Walkley] *Q2; not in Q1.*

2–3. *dangerous . . . wounds*] See Introduction, p. lxxv.

[*CHARACTERS in the order of their appearance*[1]

DION,
CLEREMONT, } *gentlemen of Sicily.*
THRASILINE,

GALATEA,
MEGRA, } *Ladies in Waiting.*
Lady,

KING, *of Calabria and Sicily.*

ARETHUSA, *his daughter, the Princess.*

PHARAMOND, *a Spanish Prince, betrothed to Arethusa.*

PHILASTER, *heir to the throne of Sicily.*

Lady, *attending the Princess.*

BELLARIO, *page to Philaster.*

Guard, *to the King.*

Two Woodmen.

Country Fellow.

Captain.

Six Citizens.]

---

[1] Q2 contains no list of characters. Q1's unauthorized list is printed in Appendix A.

4

Philaster,

or, Love Lies a-Bleeding

Act I

[I. i]

Enter DION, CLEREMONT, *and* THRASILINE.

Cle. Here's nor lords, nor ladies.

Dion. Credit me, gentlemen, I wonder at it. They received
strict charge from the King to attend here; besides, it was
boldly published, that no officer should forbid any gentlemen that desired to attend and hear.   5

Cle. Can you guess the cause?

Dion. Sir, it is plain about the Spanish Prince that's come to
marry our kingdom's heir and be our sovereign.

Thra. Many that will seem to know much say she looks not on
him like a maid in love.   10

Dion. Faith, sir, the multitude (that seldom know anything
but their own opinions) speak that they would have. But
the Prince, before his own approach, received so many
confident messages from the state that I think she's resolved to be ruled.   15

I. i.] *Actus* I. *Scæna* I. *Q2.*

---

1. i. 0.1. *Dion*] named after a Syracusan aristocrat who lived in Sicily in
the 4th century B.C., one of the subjects of Plutarch's *Parallel Lives*. A
friend of Plato, he led a successful revolt against the Syracusan tyrant
Dionysius the Younger.

1.] See Introduction, p. xlix.

2. *Credit me*] take my word.

4. *boldly published*] loudly proclaimed.

forbid] prevent.

12. *that they would have*] what they wish were true.

5

Cle. Sir, it is thought, with her he shall enjoy both these kingdoms of Sicily and Calabria.

Dion. Sir, it is, without controversy, so meant. But 'twill be a
troublesome labour for him to enjoy both these kingdoms
with safety, the right heir to one of them living, and living   20
so virtuously; especially, the people admiring the bravery
of his mind and lamenting his injuries.

Cle. Who, Philaster?

Dion. Yes; whose father, we all know, was by our late King of
Calabria unrighteously deposed from his fruitful Sicily.   25
Myself drew some blood in those wars, which I would
give my hand to be washed from.

Cle. Sir, my ignorance in state policy will not let me know
why, Philaster being heir to one of these kingdoms, the
King should suffer him to walk abroad with such free   30
liberty.

Dion. Sir, it seems your nature is more constant than to
enquire after state news. But the King (of late) made a
hazard of both the kingdoms, of Sicily and his own, with
offering but to imprison Philaster. At which the City was   35
in arms, not to be charmed down by any state order or
proclamation, till they saw Philaster ride through the
streets pleased and without a guard; at which they threw
their hats and their arms from them; some to make bon-
fires, some to drink, all for his deliverance. Which (wise   40

---

16. *enjoy*] possess, have the use of (*O.E.D.* s.v.3, 4a).

17. *Sicily and Calabria*] The play is set in the kingdom of Sicily. Calabria
was the kingdom nearest to it, in the toe of the Italian mainland.

21. *bravery*] (1) valour or fortitude; (2) splendour. Cf. Holinshed,
Scottish Chronicle, I, 29: 'Their apparel was not made for bravery and
pomp'.

22. *injuries*] injustices practised on him.

28. *state policy*] diplomacy, politics; with an adverse implication of subtle
courses of action (*O.E.D.* 'policy', s.v.1.i.3).

32–3. *your nature ... state news*] implying that Cleremont is too un-
varying in his mind to be interested in the changeable business of politics.

33–4. *made a hazard of*] gambled with, ran the risk of losing.

40. *for*] because of.

men say) is the cause the King labours to bring in the
power of a foreign nation, to awe his own with.

Enter GALATEA, *a* Lady, *and* MEGRA.

Thra. See, the ladies; what's the first?

Dion. A wise and modest gentlewoman that attends the
Princess.   45

Cle. The second?

Dion. She is one that may stand still discreetly enough, and
ill-favouredly dance her measure; simper when she is
courted by her friend, and slight her husband.

Cle. The last?   50

Dion. Faith, I think she is one whom the state keeps for the
agents of our confederate princes; she'll cog and lie with
a whole army, before the league shall break; her name is
common through the kingdom, and the trophies of her
dishonour advanced beyond Hercules' Pillars. She loves 55
to try the several constitutions of men's bodies; and in-

42.1. *a* Lady, *and Megra*] *Theobald;* Megra *and a Lady Q2.*

42.1.] Theobald altered the order of entry to suit the order in which
Dion describes those entering. The order in Q2 was determined by the
convention of listing named characters before unnamed. The reversal of
speech-prefixes for Megra and the Lady in ll. 60–79 was a further conse-
quence of the muddle caused by the convention.

Galatea] a name taken from the Sicily of Theocritus' pastorals, where
her story is elaborated from its origin in Homer. She was a sea-nymph in
love with Acis, a son of Pan, who offended the Cyclops Polyphemus. The
giant crushed him with a rock and as he did so Galatea turned Acis into
the river at the foot of Etna which bears his name. Virgil's *Eclogues* and
Ovid's *Metamorphoses* also have versions of the story.

Megra] The name of the villainess of the piece may have been intended
to suggest Megaera, one of the Erinyes, a Fury or goddess of vengeance.
In II. iv. 161 she describes herself as 'a fury'.

48. *measure*] a dance, often with a sexual quibble.

52. *cog*] cheat at dice or cards, specifically to manipulate the dice in the
dice box. *O.E.D.* allows it to be less of a technical term than it really was;
here the suggestion is that Megra was capable of outdoing men at their
own tricks even in gambling.

53. *league*] i.e., the confederation.

55. *Hercules' Pillars*] the rocks on either side of the Straits of Gibraltar.

56. *several constitutions*] varying physiques, with a play on legal or gov-

deed has destroyed the worth of her own body by making
experiment upon it, for the good of the commonwealth.

Cle. She's a profitable member.

Meg. Peace, if you love me; you shall see these gentlemen   60
stand their ground and not court us.

Gal. What if they should?

La. What if they should!

Meg. Nay, let her alone. What if they should? Why, if they
should, I say they were never abroad; what foreigner   65
would do so? It writes them directly untravelled.

Gal. Why, what if they be?

La. What if they be!

Meg. Good madam, let her go on. What if they be? Why, if
they be, I will justify they cannot maintain discourse with   70
a judicious lady, nor make a leg, nor say excuse me.

Gal. Ha, ha, ha!

Meg. Do you laugh, madam?

Dion. Your desires upon you, ladies.

Meg. Then you must sit beside us.   75

Dion. I shall sit near you then, lady.

Meg. Near me, perhaps; but there's a lady endures no stranger; and to me you appear a very strange fellow.

La. Methinks he's not so strange; he would quickly to be
acquainted.   80

Thra. Peace, the King.

60–79. *Meg. . . . La.*] *Theobald; speech-headings reversed in Q2.*

ernmental constitutions. The whole speech is an elaborate quibble on
sexual and political unions.

59.] (1) She adds to the common good; (2) her sexual member is profitable. The same quibble is evident in *Love's Labour's Lost*, IV. i. 41: 'Here
comes a member of the commonwealth', and in *The Coxcomb*, I. v. 63:
'You'le keep no whores, Rogue, no good members?'

71. *make a leg*] bow, make an obeisance.

74. *Your desires upon you*] an elliptical version of an elaborately courteous
greeting: 'May you have your desires.'

76. *near you*] (1) close to you; (2) intimate with you (*O.E.D.* s.v.2.III.
1 and 2).

77–8. *stranger*] a foreigner. The word-play on 'strange' and 'stranger'
may be related to *Cymbeline*, II. i. 31–9. See Introduction, p. xlv.

Enter KING, PHARAMOND, ARETHUSA, *and* Train.

King. To give a stronger testimony of love
  Than sickly promises (which commonly
  In princes find both birth and burial
  In one breath), we have drawn you, worthy sir, 85
  To make your fair endearments to our daughter,
  And worthy services, known to our subjects,
  Now loved and wondered at. Next, our intent
  To plant you deeply our immediate heir
  Both to our blood and kingdoms. For this lady 90
  (The best part of your life, as you confirm me,
  And I believe), though her few years and sex
  Yet teach her nothing but her fears and blushes,
  Desires without desire, discourse and knowledge
  Only of what herself is to herself, 95
  Make her feel moderate health; and when she sleeps,
  In making no ill day, knows no ill dreams.
  Think not, dear sir, these undivided parts,
  That must mould up a virgin, are put on
  To show her so, as borrowed ornaments, 100
  To talk of her perfect love to you, or add

84–5. burial / . . . breath),] *F2;* buriall.) / . . . breath, *Q2.* 101. talk of]
Q2; speake *Q3.*

81.1. *Pharamond*] The authors presumably took the name from Fauchet's
Lez Antiquitez et Histoires Gauloises et Françoises, which gave Fletcher the
plot of *Thierry and Theodoret* (1613–17). It was the name of the legendary
first king of the Franks; nothing more than the name is relevant to the
play.
 Arethusa] The heroine's name, like Galatea's, comes from Theocritus.
Arethusa was a Nereid, guardian of a fountain in Sicily, whose waters were
so pure they gave longevity to the men and cattle drinking them. A spring
known as Arethusa's well still exists close to the port of Syracuse.
 91. *confirm*] assure.
 94. *discourse*] understanding.
 97. *making no ill day*] 'performing no evil in the daytime'; dreams were
believed to reflect conduct while awake.
 98. *undivided parts*] inseparable qualities; the sense is that all these 'parts'
are intrinsic to the truly virginal nature.
 101. *To talk of*] to give the impression of.

An artificial shadow to her nature.
No, sir; I boldly dare proclaim her yet
No woman. But woo her still, and think her modesty
A sweeter mistress than the offered language   105
Of any dame, were she a Queen, whose eye
Speaks common loves and comforts to her servants.
Last, noble son (for so I now must call you),
What I have done thus public, is not only
To add a comfort in particular   110
To you or me, but all; and to confirm
The nobles and the gentry of these kingdoms
By oath to your succession, which shall be
Within this month at most.

Thra. This will be hardly done.   115

Cle. It must be ill done, if it be done.

Dion. When 'tis at best, 'twill be but half done, whilst so
brave a gentleman is wronged and flung off.

Thra. I fear.

Cle. Who does not?   120

---

110. a] *Q1; not in Q2.*

102. *artificial shadow*] A 'shadow' was a parasol or sunscreen, or sometimes a form of head-dress; the King is claiming that her virginal appearance is not a disguise for a more sophisticated temperament. Cf. *O.E.D.*
s.v. 'shadow', III.3.a, b.

105.] Q1 and Q2 begin to correspond at this line, the last of B2ʳ in Q1
and the eleventh of B2ᵛ in Q2.

111–13. *to confirm ... your succession*] i.e., to make the leading subjects
of both kingdoms swear personal loyalty to Pharamond as heir-apparent.

115–22.] The three gentlemen make comments throughout the play from
the periphery of the action. Apart from the few moments when they are
alone together on stage, only in IV. iv and V. v when Dion is addressed by
the King, and on the two occasions when the three approach Philaster, do
they move to the centre of the stage and speak in verse. Q2 at no point
marks their speeches as asides, and this edition does so only when it is not
immediately apparent that they are. They are not in any case strictly asides
in the sense that they are spoken to the audience; they are rather a separate
dialogue conducted out of the hearing of the central characters. The ladies
have a similar side-dialogue, probably at a distance from the gentlemen,
since they do not speak except to their own sex.

115. *hardly*] (1) with difficulty; (2) with harshness.

118. *flung off*] dispossessed, disinherited.

Dion. I fear not for myself, and yet I fear too; well, we shall
  see, we shall see. No more.

Pha. Kissing your white hand, mistress, I take leave
  To thank your royal father; and thus far
  To be my own free trumpet. Understand,   125
  Great King, and these your subjects, mine that must be
  (For so deserving you have spoke me, sir,
  And so deserving I dare speak myself),
  To what a person, of what eminence,
  Ripe expectation, of what faculties,   130
  Manners and virtues, you would wed your kingdoms,
  You in me have your wishes. O, this country,
  By more than all the gods, I hold it happy;
  Happy in their dear memories that have been
  Kings great and good; happy in yours that is; 135
  And from you (as a chronicle to keep
  Your noble name from eating age) do I
  Opine myself most happy. Gentlemen,
  Believe me in a word, a Prince's word,
  There shall be nothing to make up a kingdom 140
  Mighty and flourishing, defencèd, feared,
  Equal to be commanded and obeyed,
  But through the travails of my life I'll find it,

---

131. kingdoms,] *This ed.;* kingdomes; *Q2.* 132. your] *Q1;* you *Q2.*
138. Opine] *F2;* Open *Q2.* 143. travails] *Q2* (trauells).

---

125. *trumpet*] herald, proclaimer of his titles.

129. *what a*] whatever. 'Understand that whatever eminence you would
desire in the person you would marry your daughter to is embodied in me.'

136. *chronicle*] written record, here used metaphorically.

137. *eating*] devouring, destroying.

138. *Opine*] Spencer, followed by Turner, accepts Q2's 'Open' in the
sense of 'declare' or 'disclose'. The preposition in l. 136, however, suggests
that F2's is the correct spelling, and that the sense is 'I hold this country
fortunate in its memories of its great and good kings, fortunate too in the
memory of you who are great and good, and from your account (a story to
keep your name memorable) I gain the opinion that I am the most fortunate.'

143. *travails*] labours, with a suggestion of the 'travels' appropriate to
the 'strange' Prince.

And tie it to this country. By all the gods
My reign shall be so easy to the subject   145
That every man shall be his Prince himself,
And his own law; yet I his Prince and law.
And, dearest lady, to your dearest self
(Dear in the choice of him whose name and lustre
Must make you more and mightier) let me say,   150
You are the blessèd'st living; for, sweet Princess,
You shall enjoy a man of men to be
Your servant; you shall make him yours, for whom
Great Queens must die.

Thra. Miraculous.   155

Cle. This speech calls him Spaniard, being nothing but a
large inventory of his own commendations.

Dion. I wonder what's his price? For certainly he'll sell himself, he has so praised his shape.

Enter PHILASTER.

But here comes one more worthy those large speeches   160
than the large speaker of them. Let me be swallowed
quick, if I can find in all the anatomy of yon man's virtues one sinew sound enough to promise for him he shall
be constable. By this sun, he'll ne'er make King, unless
it be of trifles, in my poor judgment.   165

Phi. [*Kneeling*] Right noble sir, as low as my obedience,
And with a heart as loyal as my knee,
I beg your favour.

King.   Rise, you have it, sir.   [*Philaster rises.*]

159.1.] *so Q1; at end of l. 157 Q2.*

149. *Dear*] i.e., made precious.
153. *Your servant*] See Introduction, p. lxiv.
159. *shape*] appearance (as distinct from inner qualities).
162. *quick*] alive.
164. *constable*] either Lord High Constable, traditionally commander of
the army, or village bailiff. In England the former office had been merged
in the Crown by the time of Henry VIII. 'Controller' in I. ii. 194 is a
similarly ambiguous office. The implication in both cases points to the
lesser rôle.

Dion. Mark but the King, how pale he looks, he fears. O,
    this same whoreson conscience, how it jades us!   170
King. Speak your intents, sir.
Phi.   Shall I speak 'em freely?
    Be still my royal sovereign.
King.   As a subject,
    We give you freedom.
Dion. [*Aside*]   Now it heats.
Phi.   Then thus I turn
    My language to you, Prince, you foreign man:
    Ne'er stare nor put on wonder, for you must   175
    Endure me, and you shall. This earth you tread upon,
    A dowry, as you hope, with this fair Princess,
    By my dead father (O, I had a father,
    Whose memory I bow to) was not left
    To your inheritance, and I up and living,   180
    Having my self about me, and my sword,
    The souls of all my name and memories,
    These arms and some few friends beside the gods,
    To part so calmly with it, and sit still
    And say I might have been. I tell thee, Pharamond,   185
    When thou art King, look I be dead and rotten,
    And my name ashes, as I; for hear me, Pharamond,

171. intents] *Q1;* intent *Q2.*   177–9.] *Theobald;* (A dowry . . . Princesse,/
Whose . . . left / By . . . father) *Q1.*

---

170. *jades*] galls.

173. *heats*] works towards a climax. Dion's aside appears to be a prose
interjection between two half-lines of verse.

175. *put on wonder*] an internal stage direction: Pharamond expresses
mute amazement that a subject should address him so unceremoniously.

181.] Q2's punctuation (here retained) of this line is ambiguous; the
passage may either mean 'having the souls of my distinguished ancestors
to support myself and my sword, together with my own strength, a few
friends and the gods on my side', which could be the reading if the comma
after 'me' were shifted to follow 'my self'; or else and more probably it
means 'having my selfhood with me, together with my sword, the souls
of my distinguished ancestors, etc.' All these stand in the way of Philaster's
calmly parting with his inheritance.

185. *I might have been*] i.e., what my inheritance should make me, my
'self'. See Introduction, pp. lxv–lxvii.

G

This very ground thou goest on, this fat earth
My father's friends made fertile with their faiths,
Before that day of shame shall gape and swallow   190
Thee and thy nation, like a hungry grave,
Into her hidden bowels; Prince, it shall;
By the just gods it shall.

Pha.   He's mad, beyond cure, mad.

Dion. Here's a fellow has some fire in 's veins; the outlandish
Prince looks like a tooth-drawer.   195

Phi. Sir Prince of popinjays, I'll make it well
Appear to you I am not mad.

King.   You displease us,
You are too bold.

Phi.   No, sir, I am too tame,
Too much a turtle, a thing born without passion,
A faint shadow, that every drunken cloud   200
Sails over, and makes nothing.

King.   I do not fancy this.
Call our physicians! Sure he's somewhat tainted.

Thra. I do not think 'twill prove so.

Dion. Has given him a general purge already for all the right
he has, and now he means to let him blood. Be constant,   205
gentlemen; by heaven, I'll run his hazard, although I
run my name out of the kingdom.

194.] *outlandish*] foreign, with a hint of 'uncouth' (*O.E.D.* s.v.2).

195. *a tooth-drawer*] J. Ray, *Proverbs* (1742), p. 65, quotes this phrase
(without specifically referring to the play), and defines it as meaning 'very
thin and meagre'. But Pharamond is described at I. i. 161 as 'large' and at
II. ii. 36 as fat, which suggests that the comparison is meant to describe
him as deflated, or simply an ignoble type of person.

196. *popinjays*] parrots, commonly taken as a type for vanity or noise and
emptiness.

199. *turtle*] turtle-dove.

201. *fancy*] like.

202. *tainted*] diseased, insane.

204–5. *general purge . . . blood*] a comment on the King's calling for
physicians; purgation and blood-letting were the two most common treat-
ments for mental as well as physical disorders. 'Philaster has already been
purged of his inheritance, and now the King threatens his life.'

206. *run his hazard*] share his risk.

Cle. Peace, we are all one soul.

Pha. What you have seen in me to stir offence
    I cannot find, unless it be this lady,   210
    Offered into my arms with the succession;
    Which I must keep, though it hath pleased your fury
    To mutiny within you, without disputing
    Your genealogies, or taking knowledge
    Whose branch you are. The King will leave it me,   215
    And I dare make it mine. You have your answer.

Phi. If thou wert sole inheritor to him
    That made the world his, and couldst see no sun
    Shine upon any thing but thine; were Pharamond
    As truly valiant as I feel him cold,   220
    And ringed amongst the choicest of his friends,
    Such as would blush to talk such serious follies
    Or back such bellied commendations,
    And from this presence; spite of all these bugs,
    You should hear further from me.

King.   Sir, you wrong the Prince;
    I gave you not this freedom to brave our best friends;   226
    You deserve our frown. Go to; be better tempered.

Phi. It must be, sir, when I am nobler used.

Gal. Ladies,
    This would have been a pattern of succession,   230

---

209. me] *Q1;* me; *Q2.*   211–12. succession; / . . . keep,] *Theobald;* succession, / . . . keepe: *Q2.*   223. bellied] *Q3;* belied *Q2.*   224. spite . . . bugs] *Q3;* Spight of these bugs *Q2;* Spit all those bragges *Q1.*

---

208. *one soul*] of one mind.

213–14. *disputing | Your genealogies*] 'arguing about your ancestry and right of inheritance'.

217–18. *him | That . . . his*] Alexander the Great.

223. *bellied*] extravagant, inflated. Q2's 'belied' is possible, though Q3 fits the metre more easily, and accords with the picture of 'fat' Pharamond. A homonymic pun is not unlikely.

224. *from this presence*] out of the royal presence (*O.E.D.* 'presence', s.v. 2.b), which gives him protection.

    bugs] terrors, intimidations.

226. *to brave*] to confront, defy.

230. *pattern of succession*] model heir to the throne.

Had he ne'er met this mischief. By my life,
He is the worthiest the true name of man
This day, within my knowledge.

Meg. I cannot tell what you may call your knowledge,
But th' other is the man set in my eye.   235
O, 'tis a prince of wax.

Gal.   A dog it is.

King. Philaster, tell me
The injuries you aim at in your riddles.

Phi. If you had my eyes, sir, and sufferance,
My griefs upon you and my broken fortunes,   240
My wants great, and now-nothing hopes and fears,
My wrongs would make ill riddles to be laughed at.
Dare you be still my King, and right me ?

King. Give me your wrongs in private.

Phi.   Take them,
And ease me of a load would bow strong Atlas. *They whisper.*

Cle. He dares not stand the shock.   246

241.] *Turner;* My want's great, and now nothing ... feares *Q2;* ... wants
... *Q1;* ... nought but hopes ... *Q4;* ... nothing-hopes ... *Boas.*
243. right me ?] *Q2;* right me not ? *Q3.*   244–5. *Phi.* ... Atlas.] *Q2;*
not in Q1.   245. *They whisper*] *so Boas; after* 'private' (*l. 244*) *Q2.*

---

231. *mischief*] misfortune.

236. *a prince ... A dog*] In *Romeo and Juliet,* I. iii. 77, 'a man of wax' is
used by the Nurse of Paris as a term of praise. In *Sir John Oldcastle* (Malone
Society Reprints, London, 1908, ll. 754–5), 'a dog of wax, a horse of cheese,
a prick and a pudding' is a list of futilities. How either Megra's or Galatea's
expressions arose is not known.

238. *aim at*] i.e., refer to; not the injuries Philaster intends to inflict but
the harms he claims to have suffered.

239. *sufferance*] sufferings, the necessity of suffering.

241. *now-nothing*] reduced now to nothing.

243. *and right me ?*] Philaster is posing a paradox: dare the King be kingly
in seeing justice done, and at the same time fill his judicial function by
returning Philaster his right, the throne ?

244–5. *Phi. ... Atlas*] probably an accidental omission in Q1 rather than
a late insertion in the manuscript which lies behind Q2. Cleremont's comment in l. 246 is on Philaster's acceptance of the King's demand to speak
his wrongs privately, instead of delivering the public speech for which the
riddle posed in l. 243 was a prologue.

Dion. I cannot blame him, there's danger in 't. Every man
　　in this age has not a soul of crystal, for all men to read
　　their actions through; men's hearts and faces are so far
　　asunder that they hold no intelligence. Do but view yon　250
　　stranger well, and you shall see a fever through all his
　　bravery, and feel him shake like a true tenant; if he give
　　not back his crown again upon the report of an elder-
　　gun, I have no augury.

King. Go to;　　　　　　　　　　　　　　　　　　255
　　Be more yourself, as you respect our favour;
　　You'll stir us else. Sir, I must have you know
　　That y' are and shall be at our pleasure, what
　　Fashion we will put upon you. Smooth your brow,
　　Or by the gods—　　　　　　　　　　　　　260

Phi. I am dead, sir; y' are my Fate. It was not I
　　Said I was wronged; I carry all about me
　　My weak stars lead me to, all my weak fortunes.
　　Who dares in all this presence (speak, that is
　　But man of flesh, and may be mortal) tell me　265
　　I do not most entirely love this Prince,
　　And honour his full virtues?

King.　　　　　　　　　　　Sure, he's possessed.
Phi. Yes, with my father's spirit. It's here, O King,

252. tenant] *Q2;* truant *Q1;* recreant *Theobald conj.;* tyrant *Brooke conj.*
262–3. me / . . . to,] *Theobald;* me, / . . . too; *Q2.*　　264. (speak, that] *Q2;*
speake, (that *Q1.*　　265. man] *Q1;* men *Q2.*　　me] *Q1;* me? *Q2.*

---

252. *tenant*] Many editors accept Q1's 'truant', but Q2 makes good sense:
'yon stranger' Pharamond, who will gain the crown by marrying Arethusa,
is truly only a tenant, not the owner of his property, which of course truly
belongs to Philaster. Dion shifts from speaking of Philaster by way of his
dispossession to the foreigner who will perpetuate the dispossession, and
who like any tenant lacking lawful possession will give up what he holds
with little dispute.
253–4. *elder-gun*] a pop-gun, so called because it was usually made from
elder wood.
254. *no augury*] no ability to read omens, to prophesy.
256. *our favour*] (1) the royal patronage; (2) the King's face.
257. *stir us*] move us to anger.
267. *possessed*] i.e., by spirits.

A dangerous spirit; now he tells me, King,
I was a King's heir, bids me be a King,   270
And whispers to me, these are all my subjects.
'Tis strange, he will not let me sleep, but dives
Into my fancy, and there gives me shapes
That kneel and do me service, cry me King.
But I'll suppress him, he's a factious spirit,   275
And will undo me. Noble sir, your hand,
I am your servant.
King.   Away, I do not like this.
I'll make you tamer, or I'll dispossess you
Both of life and spirit; for this time
I pardon your wild speech, without so much   280
As your imprisonment.

       Exeunt KING, PHARAMOND, ARETHUSA [*and* Attendants].

Dion. I thank you, sir. You dare not for the people.
Gal. Ladies, what think you now of this brave fellow?
Meg. A pretty-talking fellow, hot at hand; but eye yon stranger, is he not a fine complete gentleman? O, these   285
strangers, I do affect them strangely; they do the rarest
home things, and please the fullest; as I live, I could love
all the nation over and over for his sake.
Gal. Gods comfort your poor head-piece, lady, 'tis a weak
one, and had need of a night-cap.   *Exeunt* Ladies. 290

---

273. *shapes*] apparitions.
276.] Turner suggests that Philaster here turns to speak to Pharamond,
which is plausible. But a request to kiss the King's hand as a formal gesture
of homage, however ironically made, is a rather more appropriate conclusion to Philaster's speech. The King's response, 'Away', may signify the re-
fusal of his hand. His next lines certainly relate to Philaster's, not only in the
play on 'spirit' but in the acceptance of their rôles as master and 'servant'.
282. *for the people*] because of how the people might react.
284. *hot at hand*] hot-blooded.
286. *affect*] have an affection for.
286–7. *rarest home things*] (1) things not often done at home, in one's
own country; (2) things that strike home most remarkably. There is also
probably a sexual innuendo.
290. *night-cap*] i.e., marriage. Cf. *The Taming of a Shrew*, IV. ii. 8–9: 'For
forward wedlock, as the proverb says, / Hath brought him to his night-cap
long ago', where there is also a bawdy pun in the word. Lightheadedness

Dion. See how his fancy labours; has he not spoke
  Home, and bravely ? What a dangerous train
  Did he give fire to! How he shook the King,
  Made his soul melt within him, and his blood
  Run into whey! It stood upon his brow   295
  Like a cold winter dew.
Phi.   Gentlemen,
  You have no suit to me ? I am no minion.
  You stand, methinks, like men that would be courtiers,
  If I could well be flattered at a price
  Not to undo your children. Y' are all honest.   300
  Go get you home again, and make your country
  A virtuous court, to which your great ones may
  In their diseasèd age retire and live recluse.
Cle. How do you, worthy sir ?
Phi.   Well, very well;
  And so well that if the King please I find   305
  I may live many years.
Dion.   The King must please,
  Whilst we know what you are and who you are,
  Your wrongs and injuries. Shrink not, worthy sir,

297. me ?] *Q2;* me, *Q1.*   299. I] *Mason;* you *Q2.*

---

and lechery went together, and marriage was a cure for both, in Galatea's
expression.
    294. *Made . . . him*] The heat of passion was thought to melt solid flesh
and cause sweating.
    297. *minion*] a court favourite; Marlowe in *Edward II* (ed. H. B.
Charlton and R. D. Waller, London, 1933), I. iv. 30 and II. ii. 4, uses the
term of Gaveston. King James first elevated Sir James Hay into the royal
favour and probably the royal bed in 1605. The most successful of all the
favourites, Robert Carr, obtained his ascendancy in 1606 when he fell from
his horse in front of the King. He remained in favour until 1615. Horatio
Busino in 1618 described Carr's successor, the Duke of Buckingham, as
'his Majesty's most favoured minion' (Bentley, IV, 671).
    299. *If I*] A court favourite was inevitably to be solicited for his powers
of intercession with the King. Q2's reading is possible, as Turner points
out: 'You are dancing attendance on me like courtiers, as if you could be
flattered (pleased) for a price not to undo your own children'; but it is
more strained than Mason's emendation, and takes insufficient account of
the strength of the 'minion'.

But add your father to you; in whose name
We'll waken all the gods, and conjure up   310
The rods of vengeance, the abusèd people,
Who like to raging torrents shall swell high,
And so begirt the dens of these male-dragons
That through the strongest safety they shall beg
For mercy at your sword's point.

Phi.   Friends, no more;   315
Our ears may be corrupted; 'tis an age
We dare not trust our wills to. Do you love me?

Thra. Do we love heaven, and honour?

Phi.   My Lord Dion, you had
A virtuous gentlewoman called you father;
Is she yet alive?

Dion.   Most honoured sir, she is;   320
And for the penance but of an idle dream,
Has undertook a tedious pilgrimage.

Enter a Lady.

Phi. Is it to me, or any of these gentlemen, you come?

Lady. To you, brave lord: the Princess would entreat
Your present company.   325

Phi. The Princess send for me? Y' are mistaken.

Lady. If you be called Philaster, 'tis to you.

Phi. Kiss her fair hand, and say I will attend her.   [*Exit* Lady.]

Dion. Do you know what you do?

Phi.   Yes; go to see a woman.

Cle. But do you weigh the danger you are in?   330

Phi. Danger in a sweet face?

---

312. *like . . . torrents*] The same image is used in v. iii. 9–19 and 185.
313. *begirt*] surround.
male-dragons] an obscure term, presumably a parallel form to 'she-dragons'. The image seems to imply floods quenching the fires of the dragons.
314. *through . . . safety*] however strongly entrenched.
316. *Our . . . corrupted*] i.e., someone amongst us may be an informer.
325. *present company*] immediate attendance.

By Jupiter, I must not fear a woman.

Thra. But are you sure it was the Princess sent?
    It may be some foul train to catch your life.

Phi. I do not think it, gentlemen; she's noble.   335
    Her eye may shoot me dead, or those true red
    And white friends in her face may steal my soul out;
    There's all the danger in 't; but, be what may,
    Her single name hath armed me.   *Exit.*

Dion.   Go on,
    And be as truly happy as th' art fearless.   340
    Come, gentlemen, let's make our friends acquainted,
    Lest the King prove false.   *Exeunt.*

[I. ii]

Enter ARETHUSA *and a* Lady.

Are. Comes he not?

Lady.   Madam?

Are.   Will Philaster come?

Lady. Dear madam, you were wont to credit me
    At first.

Are.   But didst thou tell me so?
    I am forgetful, and my woman's strength
    Is so o'ercharged with dangers like to grow   5
    About my marriage, that these under things
    Dare not abide in such a troubled sea.
    How looked he when he told thee he would come?

Lady. Why, well.

Are.   And not a little fearful?

---

334. *train*] treachery; literally, a lure for catching birds.

339. *Her single name*] (1) her name for honesty, absence of duplicity; (2) her name in itself. Philaster is concealing his love from the courtiers.

I. ii. 3. *At first*] the first time I say a thing.

4–7.] It is a characteristic paradox of tragicomedy that the first speech of the heroine should be an obvious evasion of the truth.

6. *under things*] matters of small importance.

Lady. Fear, madam? Sure, he knows not what it is.   10
Are. You all are of his faction; the whole Court
          Is bold in praise of him, whilst I
          May live neglected, and do noble things,
          As fools in strife throw gold into the sea,
          Drowned in the doing. But I know he fears!   15
Lady. Fear? Madam, methought his looks hid more
          Of love than fear.
Are.   Of love? To whom? To you?
          Did you deliver those plain words I sent,
          With such a winning gesture and quick look
          That you have caught him?
Lady.   Madam, I mean to you.   20
Are. Of love to me? Alas, thy ignorance
          Lets thee not see the crosses of our births.
          Nature, that loves not to be questionèd
          Why she did this or that, but has her ends,
          And knows she does well, never gave the world   25
          Two things so opposite, so contrary,
          As he and I am; if a bowl of blood
          Drawn from this arm of mine would poison thee,
          A draught of his would cure thee. Of love to me?
Lady. Madam, I think I hear him.
Are.   Bring him in. [*Exit* Lady.]   30
          You gods that would not have your dooms withstood,

26. contrary] *Q2* (contraty)*; bound to put *Q1*.

14-15. *As fools ... doing*] an obscure allusion. Turner (p. 487) suggests
that the peculiar positioning of 'and do noble things' (l. 13) in Q1, where a
space is left both before and after the phrase, denotes the omission of a
line or more elaborating the simile, which the annotator making up the
copy for Q2 failed to supply.

22. *crosses*] (1) contrarieties, opposite tendencies; (2) afflictions. Philaster's birth as rightful heir is an affliction to him in that he has lost his
heritage, and Arethusa's being daughter of the usurper is an affliction in
that it puts her in opposition to Philaster, 'crossed' against his cross.

29. *A draught of his*] Every poison was thought to have as its antidote a
medicine with the opposite qualities.

31. *dooms*] edicts, the destinies of man as laid down by the gods.

Whose holy wisdoms at this time it is
To make the passions of a feeble maid
The way unto your justice, I obey.

Enter [Lady *with*] PHILASTER.

Lady. Here is my Lord Philaster.
Are.   O, it is well.   35
Withdraw yourself.   [*Exit* Lady.]
Phi.   Madam, your messenger
Made me believe you wished to speak with me.
Are. 'Tis true, Philaster; but the words are such
I have to say, and do so ill beseem
The mouth of woman, that I wish them said,   40
And yet am loath to speak them. Have you known
That I have aught detracted from your worth?
Have I in person wronged you? Or have set
My baser instruments to throw disgrace
Upon your virtues?
Phi.   Never, madam, you.   45
Are. Why then should you in such a public place
Injure a Princess, and a scandal lay
Upon my fortunes, famed to be so great,
Calling a great part of my dowry in question?
Phi. Madam, this truth which I shall speak will be   50
Foolish: but for your fair and virtuous self
I could afford myself to have no right
To anything you wished.
Are.   Philaster, know
I must enjoy these kingdoms.

---

48. famed] *Q2;* found *Q1.*

---

44. *My baser instruments*] my less honest servants.
49. *Calling . . . question*] by laying claim to the Kingdom of Sicily which she will inherit from her father along with Calabria.
51–3.] a paradox: it is because he loves her that he cannot afford to give up his right to her inheritance. He could more easily leave it to her if she were less than her 'fair and virtuous self', because then, not loving her, he would have less cause to seek his own selfhood.

Phi.   Madam, both?

Are. Both, or I die: by heaven I die, Philaster,   55
    If I not calmly may enjoy them both.

Phi. I would do much to save that noble life;
    Yet would be loath to have posterity
    Find in our stories that Philaster gave
    His right unto a sceptre and a crown   60
    To save a lady's longing.

Are.   Nay then hear:
    I must and will have them, and more.

Phi.   What more?

Are. Or lose that little life the gods prepared
    To trouble this poor piece of earth withal.

Phi. Madam, what more?

Are.   Turn then away thy face.   65

Phi. No.

Are. Do.

Phi. I can endure it; turn away my face?
    I never yet saw enemy that looked
    So dreadfully, but that I thought myself   70
    As great a basilisk as he; or spake
    So horrible but that I thought my tongue
    Bore thunder underneath as much as his;
    Nor beast that I could turn from; shall I then
    Begin to fear sweet sounds? A lady's voice,   75
    Whom I do love? Say you would have my life,
    Why, I will give it you; for it is of me
    A thing so loathed, and unto you that ask
    Of so poor use, that I shall make no price.
    If you entreat, I will unmovedly hear.   80

Are. Yet for my sake a little bend thy looks.

---

75. lady's voice] *Q2;* womans tongue *Q1.*

---

71. *basilisk*] the mythical cockatrice, the breath and look of which were
said to be fatal.

79. *make no price*] put no valuation on it.

81. *bend thy looks*] do not look straight, look away.

Phi. I do.

Are.   Then know I must have them, and thee.

Phi. And me ?

Are.   Thy love; without which, all the land
      Discovered yet will serve me for no use
      But to be buried in.

Phi.   Is 't possible ?   85

Are. With it, it were too little to bestow
      On thee. Now, though thy breath do strike me dead
      (Which know it may) I have unripped my breast.

Phi. Madam, you are too full of noble thoughts
      To lay a train for this contemnèd life,   90
      Which you may have for asking; to suspect
      Were base, where I deserve no ill; love you!
      By all my hopes, I do, above my life;
      But how this passion should proceed from you,
      So violently, would amaze a man   95
      That would be jealous.

Are. Another soul into my body shot
      Could not have filled me with more strength and spirit
      Than this thy breath; but spend not hasty time
      In seeking how I came thus: 'tis the gods,   100
      The gods, that make me so; and sure our love
      Will be the nobler and the better blessed
      In that the secret justice of the gods
      Is mingled with it. Let us leave and kiss,
      Lest some unwelcome guest should fall betwixt us,   105
      And we should part without it.

86–7. *to bestow | On thee*] Arethusa envisages herself marrying Philaster
and so bestowing Sicily on him, fulfilling the 'secret justice of the gods'
(l. 103). It is characteristic of the tragicomic hero that he should react only
to the revelation of love and not to the further implications.

87. *breath*] words. Cf. l. 99.

88. *unripped my breast*] (1) revealed what is in my heart; (2) laid my
breast bare for your blow.

96. *jealous*] suspicious, distrustful.

99. *hasty time*] time which hurries by.

106. *without it*] i.e., a kiss.

Phi.   'Twill be ill
        I should abide here long.
Are.   'Tis true; and worse
        You should come often. How shall we devise
        To hold intelligence, that our true loves
        On any new occasion may agree   110
        What path is best to tread ?
Phi.   I have a boy,
        Sent by the gods, I hope, to this intent,
        Not yet seen in the Court. Hunting the buck,
        I found him sitting by a fountain's side,
        Of which he borrowed some to quench his thirst,   115
        And paid the nymph again as much in tears;
        A garland lay him by, made by himself
        Of many several flowers breded in the bay,
        Stuck in that mystic order that the rareness
        Delighted me; but ever when he turned   120
        His tender eyes upon 'em, he would weep,
        As if he meant to make 'em grow again.
        Seeing such pretty helpless innocence
        Dwell in his face, I asked him all his story;
        He told me that his parents gentle died,   125

---

110. agree] *Colman;* agree; *Q2.*   118. breded in the bay] *This ed.;*
bred... bay *Q2;* bred ... vayle *Q1.*

---

109. *hold intelligence*] exchange messages.
110. *new occasion*] change of circumstances (*O.E.D.* s.v.III.1).
116. *nymph*] the resident spirit of the fountain.
118. *breded in the bay*] entwined (braided) in the garland (laurel). Mason
suggested that Q2's 'bred' was a past participle of the verb 'to braid', in
apposition with 'Stuck', but could offer no parallel instances, and Weber,
the first editor to use Mason's commentary, did not adopt this suggestion.
All editors have taken the word to mean 'grown', although no usage in
connection with flowers is known, and have been forced to gloss 'bay' consequently as a small dell or glen, or to adopt Q1's 'vayle'. It is possible that
the past participle, being unmetrical, was written in an elided form in the
manuscript. A precedent for the full form is in *The Faerie Queene*, III. iii.
50: 'Taking thrise three heares from off her head, / Them trebly breaded
in a threefold lace'.
119. *mystic*] symbolical. Cf. ll. 130–3.

Leaving him to the mercy of the fields
Which gave him roots; and of the crystal springs,
Which did not stop their courses; and the sun,
Which still, he thanked him, yielded him his light.
Then took he up his garland, and did show   130
What every flower, as country people hold,
Did signify, and how all, ordered thus,
Expressed his grief; and, to my thoughts, did read
The prettiest lecture of his country art
That could be wished, so that methought I could   135
Have studied it. I gladly entertained him,
Who was glad to follow; and have got
The trustiest, loving'st, and the gentlest boy
That ever master kept. Him will I send
To wait on you, and bear our hidden love.   140

Enter Lady.

Are. 'Tis well; no more.
Lady. Madam, the Prince is come to do his service.
Are. What will you do, Philaster, with yourself?
Phi. Why, that which all the gods have appointed out for me.
Are. Dear, hide thyself;   145
    [*To Lady*] Bring in the Prince.   [*Exit* Lady.]
Phi.   Hide me from Pharamond?
    When thunder speaks, which is the voice of God,
    Though I do reverence, yet I hide me not;
    And shall a stranger Prince have leave to brag
    Unto a foreign nation, that he made   150
    Philaster hide himself?
Are.   He cannot know it.
Phi. Though it should sleep for ever to the world,

140.1.] *so Q3; at end of l. 141 Q2.*   144. appointed] *Q2; pointed Weber conj.*

---

136. *studied it*] committed it to memory (*O.E.D.* s.v.II.3.b).
entertained him] took him into employment (*O.E.D.* s.v.4).
140. *bear*] carry the messages of.
142. *to do his service*] See Introduction, p. lxiv.

It is a simple sin to hide myself,
Which will for ever on my conscience lie.

Are. Then, good Philaster, give him scope and way   155
In what he says; for he is apt to speak
What you are loath to hear; for my sake do.

Phi. I will.

Enter PHARAMOND.

Pha. My Princely mistress, as true lovers ought,
I come to kiss these fair hands, and to show   160
In outward ceremonies the dear love
Writ in my heart.

Phi. If I shall have an answer no directlier,
I am gone.

Pha.   To what would he have answer?

Are. To his claim unto the kingdom.   165

Pha. Sirrah, I forbare you before the King—

Phi. Good sir, do so still, I would not talk with you.

Pha. But now the time is fitter; do but offer
To make mention of right to any kingdom,
Though it lie scarce habitable—   170

Phi. Good sir, let me go.

Pha. And by the gods—

Phi. Peace, Pharamond; if thou—

Are. Leave us, Philaster.

Phi. [*Going*] I have done.   175

Pha. You are gone; by heaven I'll fetch you back.

Phi. [*Returning*] You shall not need.

Pha. What now?

Phi. Know, Pharamond,

---

162. Writ in] *Q3;* Writ it *Q2;* within *Q1.*   164. To what] *Q2;* To what?
what *Q1.*   166. King—] *Theobald;* King. *Q2.*   170. habitable—] *Theobald;* habitable. *Q2.*   172. gods—] *Boas;* gods. *Q2.*

---

153. *a simple sin*] undeniably a sin.
163–4.] an ethical nicety: Philaster will not hide to save himself but he
will dissemble to save the Princess.
166. *forbare*] tolerated, showed indulgence to.

I loathe to brawl with such a blast as thou,   180
Who art nought but a valiant voice; but if
Thou shalt provoke me further, men shall say,
Thou wert, and not lament it.
Pha.   Do you slight
My greatness so, and in the chamber of the Princess?
Phi. It is a place to which I must confess   185
I owe a reverence; but were 't the church,
Ay, at the altar, there's no place so safe
Where thou darest injure me, but I dare kill thee;
And for your greatness, know, sir, I can grasp
You and your greatness thus, thus, into nothing.   190
Give not a word, not a word back. Farewell.   *Exit.*
Pha. 'Tis an odd fellow, madam; we must stop his mouth
with some office when we are married.
Are. You were best make him your controller.
Pha. I think he would discharge it well. But, madam,   195
I hope our hearts are knit; and yet so slow
The ceremonies of state are that 'twill be long
Before our hands be so: if then you please,
Being agreed in heart, let us not wait
For dreaming form, but take a little stolen   200
Delights, and so prevent our joys to come.
Are. If you dare speak such thoughts, I must withdraw in
honour.   *Exit.*
Pha. The constitution of my body will never hold out till the
wedding; I must seek elsewhere.   *Exit.* 205

195. *Pha.* I ...] *Q1; Phi.* I ... *Q2.*   200. stolen] *Weber*; stolne *Q2.*

---

180. *blast*] (1) a loud wind; (2) a curse or blight.
194. *controller*] (1) treasurer or bursar; (2) master. Cf. note to I. i. 164.
200. *dreaming form*] unpurposeful ceremony.
201. *prevent*] anticipate.

H

Act II

Enter PHILASTER *and* BELLARIO.

Phi. And thou shalt find her honourable, boy;
Full of regard unto thy tender youth,
For thine own modesty; and for my sake
Apter to give than thou wilt be to ask,
Ay, or deserve.   5

Bel. Sir, you did take me up when I was nothing,
And only yet am something by being yours;
You trusted me unknown, and that which you were apt
To conster a simple innocence in me
Perhaps might have been craft, the cunning of a boy   10
Hardened in lies and theft; yet ventured you
To part my miseries and me; for which
I never can expect to serve a lady
That bears more honour in her breast than you.

Phi. But, boy, it will prefer thee; thou art young,   15
And bearest a childish overflowing love
To them that clap thy cheeks and speak thee fair yet;
But when thy judgment comes to rule those passions

II. i.] *Actus 2. Scœna 1. Q2.*

II. i. 0.1. *Bellario*] There is a Bellaria in Greene's *Pandosto* (1588), who became the Hermione of *The Winter's Tale*; *Cymbeline* has Belarius. It was evidently felt to be a suitable pastoral-romance name for a virtuous character. There is probably no link between the Italian 'bell' aria' (sweet song) and a misunderstanding of the alternative name, Euphrasia. The correct meaning of Euphrasia ('mind-gladdening') is pertinent when it is revealed at the end of the play.

9. *conster*] a common variant of 'construe', to interpret; it was pronounced to rhyme with 'monster', with the stress on the first syllable.

15. *prefer*] give advancement to, obtain a promotion for.

17. *clap*] pat fondly.

      Thou wilt remember best those careful friends
      That placed thee in the noblest way of life;   20
      She is a Princess I prefer thee to.

Bel. In that small time that I have seen the world,
      I never knew a man hasty to part
      With a servant he thought trusty; I remember
      My father would prefer the boys he kept   25
      To greater men than he, but did it not
      Till they were grown too saucy for himself.

Phi. Why, gentle boy, I find no fault at all
      In thy behaviour.

Bel.   Sir, if I have made
      A fault of ignorance, instruct my youth.   30
      I shall be willing if not apt to learn;
      Age and experience will adorn my mind
      With larger knowledge; and if I have done
      A wilful fault, think me not past all hope
      For once. What master holds so strict a hand   35
      Over his boy that he will part with him
      Without one warning? Let me be corrected
      To break my stubbornness if it be so,
      Rather than turn me off; and I shall mend.

Phi. Thy love doth plead so prettily to stay   40
      That, trust me, I could weep to part with thee.
      Alas, I do not turn thee off; thou knowest
      It is my business that doth call thee hence,
      And when thou art with her, thou dwellest with me.
      Think so, and 'tis so; and when time is full,   45
      That thou hast well discharged this heavy trust,
      Laid on so weak a one, I will again
      With joy receive thee; as I live, I will;
      Nay, weep not, gentle boy. 'Tis more than time
      Thou didst attend the Princess.

Bel.   I am gone.   50

---

35. *For once*] i.e., for one fault.
45. *when time is full*] when our plans have come to fruition.

But since I am to part with you, my Lord,
And none knows whether I shall live to do
More service for you, take this little prayer:
Heaven bless your loves, your fights, all your designs;
May sick men, if they have your wish, be well;   55
And heaven hate those you curse, though I be one.   *Exit.*

Phi. The love of boys unto their lords is strange;
I have read wonders of it, yet this boy
For my sake (if a man may judge by looks
And speech) would outdo story. I may see   60
A day to pay him for his loyalty.   *Exit.*

[II. ii]

Enter PHARAMOND.

Pha. Why should these ladies stay so long? They must come
this way. I know the Queen employs 'em not, for the
reverend mother sent me word they would all be for the
garden. If they should all prove honest now, I were in a
fair taking; I was never so long without sport in my life,   5
and in my conscience, 'tis not my fault. O, for our country
ladies!

Enter GALATEA.

Here's one bolted; I'll hound at her. Madam.
Gal. Your Grace.

II. ii. 7.I.] *so Q1; at end of l. 8 Q2.*   8. Madam.] *Q1; not in Q2.*

---

60. *outdo story*] i.e., do more than the legends of loyal boys.

II. ii. 2–3. *the reverend mother*] the chief lady-in-waiting, in charge of the
Maids of Honour. Her connivance with Pharamond perhaps is meant to
imply a willingness to act as pander for him.
4. *honest*] chaste.
4–5. *a fair taking*] a desperate condition.
6–7. *our country ladies*] the ladies of Pharamond's own country, with a
sexual quibble in 'country'.
8.] a hunting image. 'Here's one that has broken from cover. I'll be after
her like a hound.'
Madam] Turner notes that Q1 has 'Madam' here and omits it at l. 116,

Pha. Shall I not be a trouble?   10

Gal. Not to me, sir.

Pha. Nay, nay, you are too quick. [*Offers to take her hand.*]
By this sweet hand—

Gal. You'll be forsworn, sir, 'tis but an old glove. If you will
talk at distance, I am for you; but, good Prince, be not   15
bawdy, nor do not brag; these two I bar; and then I think
I shall have sense enough to answer all the weighty apoph-
thegms your royal blood shall manage.

Pha. Dear lady, can you love?

Gal. Dear Prince, how dear? I ne'er cost you a coach yet, nor   20
put you to the dear repentance of a play and a banquet;
here's no scarlet, sir, to blush the sin out it was given for;
this wire mine own hair covers; and this face has been so
far from being dear to any that it ne'er cost penny paint-
ing; and for the rest of my poor wardrobe, such as you see,   25
it leaves no hand behind it to make the jealous mercer's
wife curse our good doings.

Pha. You mistake me, lady.

Gal. Lord, I do so; would you or I could help it.

20. coach] *Q2;* Couch *Q1.*   21. a play and] *Q1; not in Q2.*

---

while Q2 reverses the positions. He conjectures (p. 487) that the Q2 compositor in correcting his proofs placed the word in the right position but
on the wrong leaf.

20. *I ne'er . . . yet*] elaborating her own quibble on 'dear', in its sense of
'costly', as well as its obvious sense.

21. *a play and*] The reference is to the old joke of whores exacting a 'dear'
repentance. This elaboration may equally well be authorial or an inter-
polation of the players which stuck in the memory of the Q1 scribe. Cf.
notes to ll. 30–2 and v. iii. 29.

22. *scarlet . . . given for*] Scarlet was the colour of the finest cloth; by
implication those who wore the colour were seen as women whose favours
could be bought.

23. *this wire*] the frame on which the cloth of her head-dress was fixed.
Cf. *Michaelmas Term* (ed. R. Levin, London, 1967), III. i. 15–16: 'a narrow-
eared wire sets out a cheek so fat and so full'.

26. *no hand*] no note of hand, signifying an unpaid debt.

29. *I do so*] playing on the senses of 'mistake' as (1) misunderstand,
Pharamond's meaning, and (2) find you offensive (*O.E.D.* s.v.2), the sense
which Galatea chooses to adopt.

Pha. Y' are very dangerous bitter, like a potion.   30

Gal. No, sir, I do not mean to purge you, though I mean to
purge a little time on you.

Pha. Do ladies of this country use to give no more respect to
men of my full being?

Gal. Full being? I understand you not, unless your Grace   35
means growing to fatness, and then your only remedy
(upon my knowledge, Prince) is in a morning a cup of neat
white wine brewed with carduus, then fast till supper;
about eight you may eat; use exercise, and keep a sparrowhawk; you can shoot in a tiller; but of all your Grace must   40
fly phlebotomy, fresh pork, conger, and clarified whey;
they are all dullers of the vital spirits.

Pha. Lady, you talk of nothing all this while.

Gal. 'Tis very true, sir, I talk of you.

Pha. [*Aside*] This is a crafty wench, I like her wit well; 'twill   45
be rare to stir up a leaden appetite: she's a Danaë, and
must be courted in a shower of gold. Madam, look here,
all these and more than—

Gal. What have you there, my Lord? Gold? Now as I live, 'tis

30–2.] *Q1; not in Q2.*

30–2.] a rather weak joke, which appears to have been added late. Since
it is in Q1, behind which lies an earlier text than Q2's, it may be non-
authorial, possibly an actor's insertion.

34. *full being*] (1) virile manhood; (2) stoutness.

37. *neat*] pure.

38. *carduus*] *Carduus benedictus*, a herbal medicine for settling the
stomach.

40. *tiller*] a crossbow. Tillers were the standard weapon used in hunting
by those who chose to shoot instead of following the chase.

41. *fly phlebotomy*] avoid blood-letting. Cf. note to l. 104.

conger] usually taken to mean jellied eels. 'Conger', however, was a
common term for 'cucumber' in the Midlands, where Beaumont may have
known it; cucumber was more distinctly noted as a chilling or unsexing
food than eels. Cf. *O.E.D.* 'conger', 3.

clarified] purified, separated.

42. *vital spirits*] semen. Galatea returns at the end of her recipe to the
innuendo of Pharamond's 'full being' (l. 34).

46. *Danaë*] daughter of the King of Argos. Locked in a tower, she was
impregnated by Zeus appearing in the form of a shower of gold.

fair gold; you would have silver for it to play with the 50
pages; you could not have taken me in a worse time, but if
you have present use, my Lord, I'll send my man with
silver and keep your gold for you.   [*Takes gold.*]

Pha. Lady, lady—

Gal. She's coming, sir, behind, will take white money.   55
[*Aside*] Yet for all this I'll match ye. *Exit behind the hangings.*

Pha. If there be but two such more in this kingdom, and near
the Court, we may even hang up our harps; ten such
camphor constitutions as this would call the golden age
again in question, and teach the old way for every ill-   60
faced husband to get his own children; and what a mischief that will breed let all consider.

Enter MEGRA.

Here's another. If she be of the same last, the devil shall
pluck her on. [*To her*] Many fair mornings, lady.

Meg. As many mornings bring as many days,   65
Fair, sweet, and hopeful to your Grace.

Pha. [*Aside*] She gives good words yet; sure this wench is free.
[*To her*] If your more serious business do not call you,
Let me hold quarter with you; we'll talk an hour
Out quickly.

69. talk] *Q2ᶜ;* take *Q2ᵘ.*

50–1. *silver . . . pages*] small change for gambling with the boys.

51–2. *if . . . use*] if you want it immediately.

55. *white money*] silver coins. Galatea's implication is that Megra's favours can be bought at a lower price than gold.

56. *hangings*] the curtain, probably fronting the discovery-space or entry doors.

58. *harps*] the equipment of the courtly lover.

59. *camphor constitutions*] Camphor was used as a medicament for its coldness. 'Ten women as frigid as Galatea would probably bring back the golden age of marital fidelity.'

63. *last*] a shape for forming objects on, a cobbler's last.

64. *pluck her on*] pull her on, i.e., wear her (as a boot), with a sexual innuendo.

67. *free*] loose, unbound by moral considerations.

69. *hold quarter*] have good relations: *O.E.D.* s.v.III.6.a.

Meg.   What would your Grace talk of?   70
Pha. Of some such pretty subject as yourself.
     I'll go no further than your eye, or lip;
     There's theme enough for one man for an age.
Meg. Sir, they stand right, and my lips are yet even,
     Smooth, young enough, ripe enough, and red enough,   75
     Or my glass wrongs me.
Pha. O, they are two twinned cherries dyed in blushes
     Which those fair suns above with their bright beams
     Reflect upon and ripen; sweetest beauty,
     Bow down those branches, that the longing taste   80
     Of the faint looker-on may meet those blessings,
     And taste, and live.   *They kiss.*
Meg. [*Aside*]   O delicate sweet Prince!
     She that hath snow enough about her heart
     To take the wanton spring of ten such lines off,
     May be a nun without probation.   85
     [*To him*] Sir, you have in such neat poetry gathered a kiss
     That if I had but five lines of that number,
     Such pretty begging blanks, I should commend
     Your forehead or your cheeks, and kiss you too.
Pha. Do it in prose; you cannot miss it, madam.   90
Meg. I shall, I shall.
Pha. By my life you shall not; I'll prompt you first. [*Kisses
     her*] Can you do it now?
Meg. Methinks 'tis easy, now I ha done 't before; but yet I
     should stick at it.   95

82. *They kiss*] *Q1; not in Q2.*   94. I ha done 't before] *Q2;* you ha dont
before me *Q1.*

---

74. *they stand right*] i.e., she is not cross-eyed.
78. *those fair suns*] i.e., her eyes.
83–5.] 'Any woman with enough winter weather in her heart to destroy
the springtime fecundity of ten such lines is chaste enough to enter a
nunnery without spending any time as a probationer.'
87. *number*] metre.
88. *blanks*] blank verse.
95. *stick at it*] (1) have scruples over it; (2) remain steadfast in pursuing
it (the sense which Pharamond takes up).

Pha. Stick till tomorrow; I'll ne'er part you, sweetest. But
  we lose time; can you love me?

Meg. Love you, my Lord? How would you have me love you?

Pha. I'll teach you in a short sentence, 'cause I will not load
  your memory; this is all: love me, and lie with me.   100

Meg. Was it lie with you that you said? 'Tis impossible.

Pha. Not to a willing mind that will endeavour; if I do not
  teach you to do it as easily in one night as you'll go to bed,
  I'll lose my royal blood for 't.

Meg. Why, Prince, you have a lady of your own that yet   105
  wants teaching.

Pha. I'll sooner teach a mare the old measures than teach her
  anything belonging to the function; she's afraid to lie
  with herself, if she have but any masculine imaginations
  about her; I know when we are married I must ravish   110
  her.

Meg. By mine honour, that's a foul fault indeed, but time and
  your good help will wear it out, sir.

Pha. And for any other I see, excepting your dear self, dearest lady, I had rather be Sir Tim the schoolmaster, and   115
  leap a dairy maid.

Meg. Has your Grace seen the court star, Galatea?

---

116. maid.] *Q1;* maid. Madam *Q2.*

---

 96. *part*] (1) leave; (2) separate (playing on 'stick', l. 95).

 99. *sentence*] an apophthegm, maxim.

 104.] a bawdy joke. In Elizabethan physiology semen was believed to be
a distillation or essence of the blood (cf. Lawrence Babb, 'The Physio-
logical Conception of Love in Elizabethan and Early Stuart Drama',
P.M.L.A., LVI (1941), 1020–35); hence the traditional description of lineage in terms of blood. In Pharamond's case it also foreshadows the events
to follow in the play. Cf. N. Highmore, *The History of Generation* (1651),
C3ᵛ: 'The purest part of this blood being extracted like a quintessence out
of the whole Mass, is reserved in convenient receptacles till there be use
of it; which is the seed, of which a new Animal is made.'

 107. *teach a ... measures*] possibly proverbial, though it does not appear
to be recorded elsewhere. There is probably a sexual innuendo in 'the old
measures'. Cf. note to I. i. 48.

 115. *Sir Tim*] Surly in *The Alchemist* (Revels edn), IV. vii. 46, is contemptuously called a 'tim'.

 116. *leap*] copulate with.

Pha. Out upon her; she's as cold of her favour as an apoplex;
    she sailed by but now.

Meg. And how do you hold her wit, sir ?   120

Pha. I hold her wit ? The strength of all the Guard cannot
    hold it; if they were tied to it, she would blow 'em out of
    the kingdom. They talk of Jupiter; he's but a squib-
    cracker to her; look well about you, and you may find a
    tongue-bolt. But speak, sweet lady, shall I be freely   125
    welcome ?

Meg. Whither ?

Pha. To your bed; if you mistrust my faith, you do me the
    unnoblest wrong.

Meg. I dare not, Prince, I dare not.   130

Pha. Make your own conditions, my purse shall seal 'em;
    and what you dare imagine you can want, I'll furnish you
    withal. Give two hours to your thoughts every morning
    about it. Come, I know you are bashful; speak in my ear,
    will you be mine ? Keep this, [*gives her money*] and with   135
    it me; soon I will visit you.

Meg. My Lord, my chamber's most unsafe, but when 'tis
    night I'll find some means to slip into your lodging; till
    when—

Pha. Till when, this and my heart go with thee.   140
                             [*Kisses her.*] *Exeunt.*

Enter GALATEA *from behind the hangings.*

Gal. O, thou pernicious petticoat Prince, are these your
    virtues ? Well, if I do not lay a train to blow your sport

---

   118. *apoplex*] paralysis, a stroke; (as here) someone suffering from paralysis.

   119. *sailed by*] i.e., through the sky, like a star.

   125. *tongue-bolt*] an arrow fired from her tongue.

   135. gives her money] Weber, Dyce, and Daniel suggest he gives her a
ring, the usual token of loyalty in love contracts. Thorndike, more plaus-
ibly, suggests money, which would follow from Galatea's claim that Megra
would take 'white money' (l. 55), and Pharamond's promise in l. 131. It is
possible that he gives her a kiss, however, as at l. 140.

   142. *train*] a gunpowder fuse.

up, I am no woman; and, Lady Towsabel, I'll fit you
for 't.   *Exit.*

[II. iii]
                    Enter ARETHUSA *and a* Lady.

Are. Where's the boy?
Lady. Within, madam.
Are. Gave you him gold to buy him clothes?
Lady. I did.
Are. And has he done 't?   5
Lady. Yes, madam.
Are. 'Tis a pretty sad-talking boy, is it not?
        Asked you his name?
Lady. No, madam.
                        Enter GALATEA.

Are. O, you are welcome. What good news?   10
Gal. As good as anyone can tell your Grace
        That says she has done that you would have wished.
Are. Hast thou discovered?
Gal. I have strained a point of modesty for you.
Are. I prithee, how?   15
Gal. In listening after bawdry. I see, let a lady live never so
        modestly, she shall be sure to find a lawful time to hearken
        after bawdry. Your Prince, brave Pharamond, was so hot
        on 't.
Are. With whom?   20

---

143. *Towsabel*] a tousled dowsabel or dulcibella, a sweetheart; cf. Turner,
p. 488.
    fit you] (1) provide what you need; (2) punish you appropriately. Cf.
The Spanish Tragedy (Revels edn), IV. i. 70, note.

II. iii. 7. *sad-talking*] serious in his speech.
    13.] It would seem from this query that Arethusa is being portrayed as
a woman of action, furthering the desires of the gods as she sees them
by trying to break the contract with Pharamond. Her announced intention
to do so (ll. 27–30) is in direct contrast to Philaster's paralysis.
    14.] Galatea quibbles on the two senses of 'discovered': (1) made a dis-
covery; (2) uncovered herself.

Gal. Why, with the lady I suspected; I can tell the time and
place.

Are. O, when, and where?

Gal. Tonight, his lodging.

Are. Run thyself into the presence; mingle there again   25
With other ladies; leave the rest to me.   [*Exit* GALATEA.]
If Destiny (to whom we dare not say,
Why didst thou this) have not decreed it so,
In lasting leaves (whose smallest character
Was never altered yet), this match shall break.   30
Where's the boy?

Lady. Here, madam.

Enter BELLARIO.

Are. Sir,
You are sad to change your service, is 't not so?

Bel. Madam, I have not changed; I wait on you,   35
To do him service.

Are.   Thou disclaim'st in me;
Tell me thy name.

Bel. Bellario.

Are. Thou canst sing and play?

Bel. If grief will give me leave, madam, I can.   40

Are. Alas, what kind of grief can thy years know?
Hadst thou a curst master when thou went'st to school?
Thou art not capable of other grief;
Thy brows and cheeks are smooth as waters be
When no breath troubles them; believe me, boy,   45
Care seeks out wrinkled brows and hollow eyes,
And builds himself caves to abide in them.

---

28. didst thou] *Langbaine;* thou didst *Q1.*   29. character] *This ed.;*
Carracters *Q2.*   30. Was] *Q2;* Were *F2.*   altered yet),] *Dyce;* atlterd:)
yet, *Q2;* altred, yet *Q1.*   32.1.] *so Q6; at l.31.1 Q2.*

---

29. *leaves*] pages.
character] letter.
30. *break*] be broken off.
36. *Thou . . . in me*] 'You deny that you are serving me.'
42. *curst*] malignant, cantankerous (*O.E.D.* s.v.4).

Come, sir, tell me truly, doth your lord love me?

Bel. Love, madam? I know not what it is.

Are. Canst thou know grief, and never yet knewest love?   50
  Thou art deceived, boy; does he speak of me
  As if he wished me well?

Bel.   If it be love
  To forget all respect to his own friends
  With thinking of your face; if it be love
  To sit cross-armed and think away the day,   55
  Mingled with starts, crying your name as loud
  And hastily as men i' the streets do 'fire';
  If it be love to weep himself away
  When he but hears of any lady dead
  Or killed, because it might have been your chance;   60
  If when he goes to rest (which will not be)
  'Twixt every prayer he says, to name you once
  As others drop a bead, be to be in love,
  Then, madam, I dare swear he loves you.

Are. O, y' are a cunning boy, and taught to lie   65
  For your lord's credit; but thou knowest a lie
  That bears this sound is welcomer to me
  Than any truth that says he loves me not.
  Lead the way, boy. [*To Lady*] Do you attend me too.
  [*To Bellario*] 'Tis thy lord's business hastes me thus. Away.

                                                        Exeunt.

60. chance;] *Theobald;* chance. *Q2.*

---

53. *respect to*] consideration for.

55. *cross-armed*] a lover's posture. The anonymous author of *The Cyprian Conqueror* (1633) specifies 'closed eies, hanging downe lookes, & crossed armes' (quoted by A. Harbage, *P.M.L.A.*, LIV (1939), 691).

60. *your chance*] an accident which happened to you.

63. *drop a bead*] i.e., in a rosary.

70. *thy lord's*] i.e., Philaster's; possibly a biblical echo.

[II. iv]

Enter DION, CLEREMONT, THRASILINE,
MEGRA, GALATEA.

Dion. Come, ladies, shall we talk a round ? As men
  Do walk a mile, women should talk an hour
  After supper; 'tis their exercise.
Gal. 'Tis late.
Meg. 'Tis all   5
  My eyes will do to lead me to my bed.
Gal. I fear they are so heavy you'll scarce find
  The way to your own lodging with 'em to-night.

Enter PHARAMOND.

Thra. The Prince.
Pha. Not abed, ladies ? Y' are good sitters-up;   10
  What think you of a pleasant dream to last
  Till morning ?
Meg. I should choose, my Lord, a pleasing wake before it.

Enter ARETHUSA *and* BELLARIO.

Are. 'Tis well, my Lord, y' are courting of these ladies.
  Is 't not late, gentlemen ?   15
Cle. Yes, madam.
Are. [*To Bellario*] Wait you there.   *Exit.*
Meg. She's jealous, as I live.
  [*To Pharamond*]   Look you, my lord,
  The Princess has a Hylas, an Adonis.
Pha. His form is angel-like.   20
Meg. Why, this is he must, when you are wed,
  Sit by your pillow like young Apollo, with

II. iv. 7. you'll] *Q1;* theile *Q2.*   13.1.] *Q1 adds: 'and a woman'.*
14. Lord,] *F2;* Lord: *Q2.*

II. iv. 1. *round*] session, with the implication of a circuitous course.
13. *a pleasing ... it*] something pleasant to happen while we are still
awake.
19. *Hylas*] the boy loved by Hercules. Adonis was loved by Venus.

His hand and voice binding your thoughts in sleep;
The Princess does provide him for you and for herself.
Pha. I find no music in these boys.
Meg.   Nor I.   25
They can do little, and that small they do
They have not wit to hide.
Dion.   Serves he the Princess?
Thra.   Yes.
Dion. 'Tis a sweet boy; how brave she keeps him!
Pha. Ladies all, good rest; I mean to kill a buck
Tomorrow morning ere y' have done your dreams.   30
Meg. All happiness attend your Grace.

                              [*Exit* PHARAMOND.]

Gentlemen, good rest. Come, shall we to bed?
Gal. Yes. All, good night.
Dion. May your dreams be true to you.

                         Exeunt GALATEA *and* MEGRA.

What shall we do, gallants? 'Tis late. The King   35
Is up still. See, he comes; a Guard along
With him.

            Enter KING, ARETHUSA *and* Guard.

King.   Look your intelligence be true.
Are. Upon my life it is; and I do hope
Your Highness will not tie me to a man
That in the heat of wooing throws me off,   40
And takes another.
Dion. [*Aside*] What should this mean?
King.   If it be true,
That lady had been better have embraced

34.1.] *after* 'good night' (*l. 33*) *Q2.*

_____

25.] (1) 'I do not enjoy the music these boys play'; (2) 'I get no pleasure
from boys', with a sexual implication elaborated by Megra in the next
lines.
28. *brave*] richly dressed.
37. *intelligence*] information.
43. *had been better*] would have done better to.

Cureless diseases; get you to your rest,
You shall be righted.   *Exeunt* ARETHUSA, BELLARIO.
                              Gentlemen, draw near;   45
We shall employ you. Is young Pharamond
Come to his lodging?
Dion.   I saw him enter there.
King. Haste some of you, and cunningly discover
If Megra be in her lodging.   *Exit* DION.
Cle.   Sir,
She parted hence but now with other ladies.   50
King. If she be there, we shall not need to make
A vain discovery of our suspicion.
[*Aside*] You gods, I see that who unrighteously
Holds wealth or state from others shall be cursed
In that which meaner men are blessed withal: 55
Ages to come shall know no male of him
Left to inherit, and his name shall be
Blotted from earth; if he have any child,
It shall be crossly matched; the gods themselves
Shall sow wild strife betwixt her lord and her.   60
Yet, if it be your wills, forgive the sin
I have committed; let it not fall
Upon this undeserving child of mine;
She has not broke your laws. But how can I
Look to be heard of gods that must be just,   65

---

49. *Exit Dion*] *Q1; not in Q2.*   53. You gods, I see] *Langbaine;* You
gods I see, *Q1.*   63. undeserving] *Q1;* vnderstanding *Q2.*

---

44. *Cureless*] incurable.
52. *vain discovery*] unnecessary revelation.
59. *crossly matched*] married to an incompatible partner. Cf. note to I. ii.
22.
63. *undeserving*] i.e., guiltless. Turner accepts Q2's 'understanding' on
the principle of adopting the harder reading, glossing it as 'standing under',
i.e., the generation following the King's. This sense was rarely used except
punningly, however, as in the Prologue's description of the *Burning Pestle*'s
Citizen as 'an understanding man', i.e., one who stood around the public
stage, a groundling (Induction, 42), and it is hard to see the word's appro-
priateness here.

Praying upon the ground I hold by wrong?

Enter DION.

Dion. Sir, I have asked, and her women swear she is within;
   but they I think are bawds. I told 'em I must speak with
   her; they laughed, and said their lady lay speechless. I
   said my business was important; they said their lady was   70
   about it. I grew hot, and cried my business was a matter
   that concerned life and death; they answered so was
   sleeping, at which their lady was; I urged again she had
   scarce time to be so since last I saw her; they smiled again,
   and seemed to instruct me that sleeping was nothing but   75
   lying down and winking. Answers more direct I could not
   get. In short, sir, I think she is not there.

King. 'Tis then no time to dally: you o' the Guard,
   Wait at the back door of the Prince's lodging,
   And see that none pass thence, upon your lives.   80

                                           Exeunt Guard.

   Knock, gentlemen; knock loud; louder yet.

                    [*Dion and Cleremont knock at the door.*]

   What, has their pleasure taken off their hearing?
   I'll break your meditations; knock again;
   Not yet? I do not think he sleeps, having his
   'Larum by him; once more, Pharamond! Prince!   85

Enter PHARAMOND *above.*

Pha. What saucy groom knocks at this dead of night?
   Where be our waiters? By my vexèd soul,
   He meets his death that meets me for this boldness.

80.1. *Exeunt* Guard.] *Q1; not in Q2.*   83. your] *Q2;* their *Turner conj.*
85.1. Enter] *Q1; not in Q2.*

---

66. *Praying*] (1) offering prayers; (2) preying.
71. *about it*] i.e., about important business.
76. *winking*] closing the eyes.
84–5. *his | 'Larum*] i.e., Megra.
85.1. Enter *Pharamond* above] i.e., on the upper stage or 'tarras'.
87. *waiters*] lookouts, watchmen (*O.E.D.* s.v.1.1).

I

King. Prince, you wrong your thoughts; we are your friends.
　　Come down.
Pha.　　　　　　The King ?
King.　　　　　　　　　The same, sir. Come down,　　90
　　We have cause of present counsel with you.

　　　　　PHARAMOND [*appears*] *below.*

Pha. If your Grace please to use me, I'll attend you
　　To your chamber.
King. No, 'tis too late, Prince, I'll make bold with yours.
Pha. I have some private reasons to myself　　　　95
　　Makes me unmannerly, and say you cannot.
　　Nay, press not forward, gentlemen; he must come
　　Through my life that comes here.
King. Sir, be resolved, I must and will come. Enter.
Pha. I will not be dishonoured!　　　　　　　100
　　He that enters, enters upon his death.
　　Sir, 'tis a sign you make no stranger of me,
　　To bring these renegados to my chamber
　　At these unseasoned hours.
King.　　　　　　　Why do you
　　Chafe yourself so ? You are not wronged nor shall be;　105
　　Only I'll search your lodging, for some cause
　　To ourself known. Enter, I say.
Pha. I say, no.

　　　　　[*Enter*] MEGRA *above.*

Meg.　　　Let 'em enter, Prince, let 'em enter;

97–8.] *Q1 adds in margin: 'They prease to come in.'*　103. renegados] *Q2;*
runagates *Q1.*

---

　　89. *you wrong . . . thoughts*] you degrade your mind by thinking unworthy
thoughts.
　　99. *be resolved*] be sure, accept.
　　102.] It is a sign that you treat me familiarly, not as a guest.
　　103. *renegados*] Q2's Spanish word was commonly used in the seventeenth century with the sense of apostate or turncoat. Its origin seems
more appropriate here than its precise meaning. Q1 substitutes the more
conventional word for ruffians.
　　104. *unseasoned*] inappropriate, unnatural.

I am up and ready; I know their business:
'Tis the poor breaking of a lady's honour   110
They hunt so hotly after; let 'em enjoy it.
You have your business, gentlemen: I lay here.
O, my Lord the King, this is not noble in you,
To make public the weakness of a woman.

King. Come down.   115

Meg. I dare, my Lord; your hootings and your clamours,
Your private whispers and your broad fleerings,
Can no more vex my soul than this base carriage;
But I have vengeance yet in store for some
Shall, in the most contempt you can have of me,   120
Be joy and nourishment.

King.   Will you come down ?

Meg. Yes, to laugh at your worst; but I shall wring you,
If my skill fail me not.   [*Exit* MEGRA *above.*]

King. Sir, I must dearly chide you for this looseness;
You have wronged a worthy lady. But no more,   125
Conduct him to my lodging and to bed.

                          [*Exeunt* PHARAMOND *and* Guard.]

Cle. Get him another wench, and you bring him to bed indeed.

Dion. 'Tis strange a man cannot ride a stage
Or two, to breathe himself, without a warrant.
If this gear hold, that lodgings be searched thus,   130

---

126. my] *Q2;* his *Q1.*   128. stage] *Q1;* stagge *Q2.*

---

110. *breaking*] destruction.

117. *fleerings*] jeering attacks; cf. *Othello,* IV. i. 83: 'the fleers, the gibes,
and notable scorns'.

118. *base carriage*] ignoble behaviour.

122. *wring*] cause distress to. Cf. *O.E.D.* v.t.5.a, b.

124. *dearly*] extremely.

128. *stage*] Gentlemen travelling long distances by coach were accus-
tomed to ease themselves ('breathe') by riding on horseback for stretches
of the journey. Q1's word fits this and the sexual connotations much better
than Q2's 'stagge', which is probably a compositor's spelling of the manuscript 'stag' with a curtailed 'e' ending.

129. *warrant*] official licence.

130. *If . . . hold*] if these happenings continue. Cf. *The Spanish Tragedy*
(Revels edn), III. vi. 23, 'Come, come, come on, when shall we to this gear ?'

Pray God we may lie with our own wives in safety,
That they be not by some trick of state mistaken.

Enter [Guard] *with* MEGRA.

King. Now, lady of honour, where's your honour now?
No man can fit your palate but the Prince.
Thou most ill-shrouded rottenness, thou piece   135
Made by a painter and a 'pothecary,
Thou troubled sea of lust, thou wilderness
Inhabited by wild thoughts, thou swollen cloud
Of infection, thou ripe mine of all diseases,
Thou all sin, all hell, and, last, all devils. Tell me,   140
Had you none to pull on with your courtesies
But he that must be mine, and wrong my daughter?
By all the gods, all these, and all the pages,
And all the Court, shall hoot thee through the Court,
Fling rotten oranges, make ribald rhymes,   145
And sear thy name with candles upon walls.
Do ye laugh, Lady Venus?
Meg.   Faith, sir, you must pardon me;
I cannot choose but laugh to see you merry.
If you do this, O King, nay, if you dare do it,
By all those gods you swore by, and as many   150
More of my own, I will have fellows, and such
Fellows in it, as shall make noble mirth.
The Princess your dear daughter shall stand by me

138. swollen] *This ed.;* swolne *Q2.*

---

133. *honour ... honour*] quibbling on the senses of 'official title' and 'virtuous reputation'.

134. *palate*] homonymic with 'pallet', a bed.

135. *ill-shrouded*] inadequately disguised, with the implication of a poorly wrapped corpse and of the pallet she has been lying on.

139. *mine*] source.

141. *pull on*] entice.

146. *sear ... candles*] Writing names with the smoke of burning candles was a simple way of inscribing graffiti. Cf. *The Alchemist* (Revels edn), v. v. 41. Candles themselves were a ribald symbol of lechery.

148. *merry*] making jokes, i.e., not serious.

151. *fellows*] (1) fellow-sinners; (2) lovers.

On walls, and sung in ballads, anything.
Urge me no more; I know her and her haunts,   155
Her lays, leaps, and outlays, and will discover all;
Nay, will dishonour her. I know the boy
She keeps, a handsome boy, about eighteen;
Know what she does with him, where, and when.
Come, sir, you put me to a woman's madness,   160
The glory of a fury; and if I do not
Do it to the height—

King.   What boy is this she raves at?

Meg. Alas, good-minded Prince, you know not these things;
I am loath to reveal 'em. Keep this fault
As you would keep your health from the hot air   165
Of the corrupted people, or by heaven
I will not fall alone. What I have known
Shall be as public as a print; all tongues
Shall speak it as they do the language they
Are born in, as free and commonly; I'll set it   170
Like a prodigious star for all to gaze at,
And so high and glowing that other kingdoms far and foreign
Shall read it there, nay travel with it, till they find
No tongue to make it more, nor no more people;
And then behold the fall of your fair Princess.   175

King. Has she a boy?

Cle. So please your Grace, I have seen a boy wait
On her, a fair boy.

King.   Go get you to your quarter;
For this time I'll study to forget you.

---

162. height—] *Q1;* height! *Q2.*

---

156. *lays, leaps, and outlays*] lodgings, fornications, and places of assignation.

161. *glory*] exaltation.

164. *Keep*] protect, conceal.

165. *air*] breath.

168. *a print*] a printed broadside ballad.

171. *prodigious star*] a meteor, usually taken as a portent of disaster.

173. *travel with it*] i.e., like the three Kings, who followed the star to Bethlehem.

Meg. Do you study to forget me, and I'll study   180
      To forget you.   *Exeunt* KING, MEGRA, Guard.

Cle. Why, here's a male spirit fit for Hercules. If ever there be
      nine Worthies of women, this wench shall ride astride
      and be their Captain.

Dion. Sure, she has a garrison of devils in her tongue, she   185
      uttered such balls of wild-fire. She has so nettled the
      King that all the doctors in the country will scarce cure
      him. That boy was a strange found-out antidote to cure
      her infections; that boy, that Princess' boy; that brave,
      chaste, virtuous lady's boy; and a fair boy, a well-spoken   190
      boy! All these considered, can make nothing else—but
      there I leave you, gentlemen.

Thra. Nay, we'll go wander with you.   *Exeunt.*

180–1. I'll ... you.] *Q2;* i'le forget your— *Q1.*   186. nettled] *Q1;*
metled *Q2.*

---

182. *male ... Hercules*] a masculine spirit worthy of Hercules himself.
183. *nine Worthies*] In the preface to the *Morte D'Arthur* Caxton lists
'three Paynims, three Jews, and three Christian men'. Shakespeare's list
in *Love's Labour's Lost,* unlike Caxton's, included Hercules.
ride astride] i.e., followed by the other Worthies on foot as her inferiors.
To ride astride was unwomanly, and would carry associations of the strad-
dling position for sexual intercourse.
186. *nettled*] irritated, vexed.
193. *wander with*] accompany, possibly with a play on 'wonder', i.e.,
marvel at the turn events have taken. When the three gentlemen re-enter
they are still discussing Megra's claim.

Act III

Enter DION, CLEREMONT, [*and*] THRASILINE.

Cle. Nay, doubtless 'tis true.

Dion.   Ay, and 'tis the gods
That raised this punishment to scourge the King
With his own issue. Is it not a shame
For us that should write 'noble' in the land,
For us that should be free men, to behold   5
A man that is the bravery of his age,
Philaster, pressed down from his royal right
By this regardless King ? And only look
And see the sceptre ready to be cast
Into the hands of that lascivious lady   10
That lives in lust with a smooth boy, now to be
Married to yon strange Prince, who, but that people
Please to let him be a Prince, is born a slave

III. i.] *Actus* 3. *Scœna* I. *Q2.*

III. i. 0.1.] The same three characters who leave the stage at the end of Act II enter to begin Act III. A night, of course, supposedly intervenes between the acts. See Introduction, p. xxxix.

4. *write 'noble'*] rank as nobles. There is some ambiguity in the precise rank at least of Dion, who is sometimes called 'my Lord Dion', but usually referred to with his companions as a 'gentleman'. The terms 'nobles' and 'gentry' are used almost indifferently in the play to signify the aristocracy as against 'the people', or citizens.

6. *bravery*] the model, paragon, (as of clothes) finest adornment. Cf. I. i. 21, II. iv. 28, etc., and Massinger, *City Madam*, II. i. 86–8: 'sitting at the table with / The braveries of the kingdom, you shall hear / Occurrents from all corners of the world'.

8. *regardless*] i.e., unregarding (of right), and probably unregarded (by the people).

12. *strange*] i.e., foreign. Cf. note to I. i. 77–8.

In that which should be his most noble part,
His mind.

Thra.   That man that would not stir with you   15
To aid Philaster, let the gods forget
That such a creature walks upon the earth.

Cle. Philaster is too backward in 't himself;
The gentry do await it, and the people
Against their nature are all bent for him,   20
And like a field of standing corn that's moved
With a stiff gale their heads bow all one way.

Dion. The only cause that draws Philaster back
From this attempt is the fair Princess' love,
Which he admires, and we can now confute.   25

Thra. Perhaps he'll not believe it.

Dion. Why, gentlemen, 'tis without question so.

Cle. Ay, 'tis past speech, she lives dishonestly.
But how shall we, if he be curious, work
Upon his faith ?   30

Thra. We all are satisfied within ourselves.

Dion. Since it is true, and tends to his own good,
I'll make this new report to be my knowledge;
I'll say I know it; nay, I'll swear I saw it.

Cle. It will be best.

Thra.   'Twill move him.   35

Enter PHILASTER.

25. confute] *Q2;* comfort *Q1.*   30. faith] *Q2;* beleefe *Q1.*   35.1. *Enter
Philaster.*] *so Turner; after* 'best' *Q2.*

---

15. *stir*] rise in revolt (*O.E.D.* v.i.14.c).

20. *Against their nature*] Judging by Dion's other comments about the
people (I. i. 11–12, etc.), this means that they are uncharacteristically single-
minded in their loyalty to Philaster.

bent] (1) inclined; (2) aimed (as of a bow).

24. *the fair . . . love*] i.e., her supposed love for Pharamond, now denied
by her supposed lust for Bellario.

25. *admires*] wonders at.

28. *past speech*] (1) beyond question; (2) unspeakable.

dishonestly] unchastely.

29. *curious*] sceptical, and so inquiring about details.

Dion. Here he comes. Good morrow to your Honour.
   We have spent some time in seeking you.
Phi. My worthy friends,
   You that can keep your memories to know
   Your friend in miseries, and cannot frown   40
   On men disgraced for virtue, a good day
   Attend you all. What service may I do
   Worthy your acceptation?
Dion.   My good Lord,
   We come to urge that virtue which we know
   Lives in your breast, forth: rise, and make a head!   45
   The nobles and the people are all dulled
   With this usurping King; and not a man
   That ever heard the word or knows such a thing
   As virtue but will second your attempts.
Phi. How honourable is this love in you   50
   To me that have deserved none! Know, my friends
   (You that were born to shame your poor Philaster
   With too much courtesy), I could afford
   To melt myself to thanks: but my designs
   Are not yet ripe; suffice it, that ere long   55
   I shall employ your loves; but yet the time
   Is short of what I would.
Dion. The time is fuller, sir, than you expect;
   That which hereafter will not perhaps be reached
   By violence may now be caught; as for the King,   60
   You know the people have long hated him;
   But now the Princess, whom they loved—
Phi. Why, what of her?

45. breast, forth: rise,] *Langbaine;* breast, forth, rise *Q2;* breast: forth,
rise, *Q1.*   48. or knows] *This ed. (Daniel conj.);* or knowne *Q2;* knowes
Q1; or knew *Q3.*

39–40. *You . . . miseries*] i.e., who are not merely fair-weather friends.
45. *make a head*] collect an army (for a rebellion).
46. *dulled*] depressed, made miserable.
53. *I could afford*] it is in my nature to (*O.E.D.* v.i.7).
58. *fuller*] more ready. Cf. II. i. 45.
60. *caught*] won easily, taken by surprise.

Dion.   Is loathed as much as he.
Phi. By what strange means ?
Dion.   She's known a whore.
Phi.   Thou liest!
Dion. My Lord—   65
Phi. Thou liest!   *Offers to draw, and is held.*
    And thou shalt feel it! I had thought thy mind
    Had been of honour; thus to rob a lady
    Of her good name is an infectious sin
    Not to be pardoned. Be it false as hell,   70
    'Twill never be redeemed, if it be sown
    Amongst the people, fruitful to increase
    All evil they shall hear. Let me alone,
    That I may cut off falsehood whilst it springs!
    Set hills on hills betwixt me and the man   75
    That utters this, and I will scale them all,
    And from the utmost top fall on his neck
    Like thunder from a cloud.
Dion.   This is most strange!
    Sure, he does love her.
Phi.   I do love fair truth;
    She is my mistress, and who injures her   80
    Draws vengeance from me. Sirs, let go my arms.
Thra. Nay, good my Lord, be patient.
Cle. Sir, remember this is your honoured friend
    That comes to do his service, and will show you
    Why he uttered this.
Phi.   I ask you pardon, sir;   85
    My zeal to truth made me unmannerly.
    Should I have heard dishonour spoke of you
    Behind your back, untruly, I had been
    As much distempered and enraged as now.

64. *Phi.* Thou ...] *Q1; Di.* Thou ... *Q2.*   74. whilst it springs] *Q2;*
where it grows *Q1.*

---

69. *infectious sin*] i.e., a sin which will infect even a virtuous lady.
74. *springs*] lives and grows.
89. *distempered*] disturbed, the balance of humours upset.

Dion. But this, my Lord, is truth.   90

Phi. O, say not so, good sir, forbear to say so;
    'Tis then truth that womankind is false;
    Urge it no more, it is impossible;
    Why should you think the Princess light?

Dion. Why, she was taken at it.   95

Phi. 'Tis false, by heaven, 'tis false! It cannot be,
    Can it? Speak, gentlemen, for God's love speak!
    Is 't possible? Can women all be damned?

Dion. Why no, my Lord.

Phi.   Why then, it cannot be.

Dion. And she was taken with her boy.

Phi.   What boy?   100

Dion. A page, a boy that serves her.

Phi. O, good gods, a little boy?

Dion. Ay, know you him, my Lord?

Phi. [*Aside*] Hell and sin know him! [*To Dion*] Sir, you are deceived;
    I'll reason it a little coldly with you: 105
    If she were lustful, would she take a boy,
    That knows not yet desire? She would have one
    Should meet her thoughts and know the sin he acts,
    Which is the great delight of wickedness.
    You are abused, and so is she, and I.   110

Dion. How you, my Lord?

Phi.   Why all the world's abused
    In an unjust report.

Dion.   O, noble sir, your virtues
    Cannot look into the subtle thoughts of woman.
    In short, my Lord, I took them; I myself.

Phi. Now all the devils thou didst! Fly from my rage!   115
    Would thou hadst ta'en devils engendering plagues
    When thou didst take them; hide thee from mine eyes!

---

94. *light*] unchaste, lecherous.
95. *taken at it*] caught in the act (of fornication). Cf. ll. 99, 114.
108. *meet*] match.
110. *abused*] deceived, with an implication of moral damage.

Would thou hadst ta'en thunder on thy breast
When thou didst take them; or been strucken dumb
For ever, that this foul deed might have slept   120
In silence.

Thra.   Have you known him so ill-tempered?

Cle. Never before.

Phi.   The winds that are let loose
From the four several corners of the earth
And spread themselves all over sea and land
Kiss not a chaste one. What friend bears a sword   125
To run me through?

Dion. Why, my Lord, are you so moved at this?

Phi. When any fall from virtue I am distracted,
I have an interest in 't.

Dion.   But, good my Lord, recall yourself
And think what's best to be done.

Phi.   I thank you, I will do it.
Please you to leave me, I'll consider of it;   131
Tomorrow I will find your lodging forth
And give you answer.

Dion.   All the gods direct you
The readiest way.

Thra.   He was extreme impatient.

Cle. It was his virtue and his noble mind.   135

          Exeunt DION, CLEREMONT, [*and*] THRASILINE.

Phi. I had forgot to ask him where he took them;
I'll follow him. O, that I had a sea
Within my breast to quench the fire I feel!
More circumstances will but fan this fire;
It more afflicts me now to know by whom   140
This deed is done than simply that 'tis done,
And he that tells me this is honourable,

118. thunder] *Q2;* daggers *Q1.*

---

121. *ill-tempered*] choleric, out of his proper humour.
129. *interest*] (1) curiosity; (2) commitment.

As far from lies as she is far from truth.
O that like beasts we could not grieve ourselves
With that we see not; bulls and rams will fight   145
To keep their females, standing in their sight;
But take 'em from them, and you take at once
Their spleens away; and they will fall again
Unto their pastures, growing fresh and fat;
And taste the waters of the springs as sweet   150
As 'twas before, finding no start in sleep.
But miserable man—

                    Enter BELLARIO.

                    See, see, you gods,
He walks still; and the face you let him wear
When he was innocent is still the same,
Not blasted; is this justice? Do you mean   155
To entrap mortality that you allow
Treason so smooth a brow? I cannot now
Think he is guilty.
Bel.   Health to you, my Lord.
The Princess doth commend her love, her life,
And this unto you.   *He gives him a letter.*
Phi.   O Bellario,   160
Now I perceive she loves me; she does show it
In loving thee, my boy; she has made thee brave.
Bel. My Lord, she has attired me past my wish,
Past my desert; more fit for her attendant,
Though far unfit for me who do attend.   165
Phi. Thou art grown courtly, boy. [*Aside*] O, let all women
That love black deeds learn to dissemble here,

160. *He . . . letter*] *Q1; not in Q2.*

143.] i.e., lying is as foreign to his nature as honesty is to hers.
151. *finding . . . sleep*] sleeping undisturbed.
155. *blasted*] struck by lightning, the vengeance of the gods.
156. *mortality*] the mortal world, i.e., to deceive everyone.
162. *brave*] Cf. note to l. 6.

Here, by this paper; she does write to me
As if her heart were mines of adamant
To all the world besides, but unto me   170
A maiden snow that melted with my looks.
[*To Bellario*] Tell me, my boy, how doth the Princess use thee?
For I shall guess her love to me by that.

Bel. Scarce like her servant, but as if I were
Something allied to her or had preserved   175
Her life three times by my fidelity;
As mothers fond do use their only sons;
As I'd use one that's left unto my trust,
For whom my life should pay if he met harm,
So she does use me.

Phi.   Why, this is wondrous well;   180
But what kind language does she feed thee with?

Bel. Why, she does tell me she will trust my youth
With all her loving secrets, and does call me
Her pretty servant, bids me weep no more
For leaving you, she'll see my services   185
Regarded, and such words of that soft strain
That I am nearer weeping when she ends
Than ere she spake.

Phi.   This is much better still.

Bel. Are you not ill, my Lord?

Phi.   Ill? No, Bellario.

Bel. Methinks your words   190
Fall not from off your tongue so evenly,
Nor is there in your looks that quietness
That I was wont to see.

---

183. loving secrets] *Q2;* maiden store *Q1.*

---

169. *mines of adamant*] 'the very source of diamonds'. 'Adamant' was a
term loosely applied to the hardest metals and minerals, including diamonds and loadstones (magnets). The latter was the primary Elizabethan
sense. Cf. *A Midsummer Night's Dream*, II. i. 195: 'You draw me, you hard-
hearted adamant'. Philaster's image carries the senses both of attracting
and yet standing firm.
186. *Regarded*] rewarded.

Phi.   Thou art deceivèd, boy.
    And she strokes thy head?
Bel. Yes.   195
Phi. And she does clap thy cheeks?
Bel. She does, my Lord.
Phi. And she does kiss thee, boy? Ha?
Bel. How, my Lord?
Phi. She kisses thee?   200
Bel. Never, my Lord, by heaven.
Phi. That's strange; I know she does.
Bel. No, by my life.
Phi. Why then she does not love me. Come, she does.
    I bade her do it; I charged her by all charms   205
    Of love between us, by the hope of peace
    We should enjoy, to yield thee all delights
    Naked, as to her bed; I took her oath
    Thou shouldst enjoy her. Tell me, gentle boy,
    Is she not parallelless? Is not her breath   210
    Sweet as Arabian winds when fruits are ripe?
    Are not her breasts two liquid ivory balls?
    Is she not all a lasting mine of joy?
Bel. Ay, now I see why my disturbèd thoughts
    Were so perplexed. When first I went to her   215
    My heart held augury. You are abused;
    Some villain has abused you; I do see
    Whereto you tend; fall rocks upon his head
    That put this to you: 'tis some subtle train
    To bring that noble frame of yours to nought.   220
Phi. Thou think'st I will be angry with thee. Come,
    Thou shalt know all my drift; I hate her more
    Than I love happiness, and placed thee there

210. parallelless] *Q5;* parrallesse *Q2;* paradise *Q1.*

---

    209. *enjoy her*] i.e., sexually.
    210. *parallelless*] Turner adopts Q2's reading, glossing as 'pareil-less', a
nonpareil.
    216. *My ... augury*] I felt a presentiment.
    222. *Thou ... drift*] I shall be honest with you.

To pry with narrow eyes into her deeds.

Hast thou discovered? Is she fall'n to lust,   225

As I would wish her? Speak some comfort to me.

Bel. My Lord, you did mistake the boy you sent.

Had she the lust of sparrows or of goats,

Had she a sin that way, hid from the world,

Beyond the name of lust, I would not aid   230

Her base desires; but what I came to know

As servant to her I would not reveal

To make my life last ages.

Phi.   O, my heart!

This is a salve worse than the main disease.

Tell me thy thoughts; for I will know the least   235

That dwells within thee, or will rip thy heart

To know it; I will see thy thoughts as plain

As I do now thy face.

Bel.   Why, so you do.

She is (for aught I know), by all the gods,

As chaste as ice; but were she foul as hell,   240

And I did know it, thus: the breath of kings,

The points of swords, tortures, nor bulls of brass,

Should draw it from me.

Phi. Then 'tis no time to dally with thee;

I will take thy life, for I do hate thee.   245

I could curse thee now.

Bel. If you do hate, you could not curse me worse;

The gods have not a punishment in store

Greater for me than is your hate.

---

224. *with narrow eyes*] closely, intently.

228. *sparrows*] as Venus' birds, noted for lechery. Cf. Thomas Cogan, *The Haven of Health* (1589), p. 242: 'such as vse immoderate *Venus*, be short liued, and as the Sparowes, through incontinencie consume themselues'.

234. *salve*] ointment, cure.

the main disease] the disease itself.

242. *bulls of brass*] more or less proverbial torture instruments, named from the brazen bull of Phalaris of Acragas in which victims were roasted alive.

Phi. Fie, fie, so young and so dissembling!   250
    Tell me when and where thou didst enjoy her,
    Or let plagues fall on me, if I destroy thee not.
                              He draws his sword.

Bel. By heaven, I never did; and when I lie
    To save my life, may I live long and loathed;
    Hew me asunder, and whilst I can think   255
    I'll love those pieces you have cut away
    Better than those that grow, and kiss those limbs
    Because you made 'em so.

Phi.   Fear'st thou not death?
    Can boys contemn that?

Bel.   O, what boy is he
    Can be content to live to be a man,   260
    That sees the best of men thus passionate,
    Thus without reason?

Phi.   O, but thou dost not know
    What 'tis to die.

Bel.   Yes, I do know, my Lord:
    'Tis less than to be born; a lasting sleep,
    A quiet resting from all jealousy,   265
    A thing we all pursue; I know besides
    It is but giving over of a game
    That must be lost.

Phi.   But there are pains, false boy,
    For perjured souls; think but on those, and then
    Thy heart will melt, and thou wilt utter all.   270

Bel. May they fall all upon me whilst I live,
    If I be perjured, or have ever thought
    Of that you charge me with; if I be false,
    Send me to suffer in those punishments
    You speak of: kill me.   *[Bellario kneels.]*

Phi.   O, what should I do?   275
    Why, who can but believe him? He does swear

252.1. *He draws his sword*] *Q1; not in Q2.*   275. *Phi.*] *Q1; not in Q2.*

---

259. *contemn*] be contemptuous of.

K

So earnestly that if it were not true
The gods would not endure him. [*Sheathes his sword.*]
   Rise, Bellario.
Thy protestations are so deep, and thou
Dost look so truly when thou utter'st them   280
That though I know 'em false as were my hopes
I cannot urge thee further. But thou wert
To blame to injure me, for I must love
Thy honest looks, and take no revenge upon
Thy tender youth; a love from me to thee   285
Is firm, whate'er thou dost; it troubles me
That I have called the blood out of thy cheeks,
That did so well become thee. But, good boy,
Let me not see thee more. Something is done
That will distract me, that will make me mad,   290
If I behold thee. If thou tender'st me,
Let me not see thee.

Bel.   I will fly as far
As there is morning, ere I give distaste
To that most honoured mind. But through these tears
Shed at my hopeless parting, I can see   295
A world of treason practisèd upon you,
And her, and me. Farewell for evermore;
If you shall hear that sorrow struck me dead,
And after find me loyal, let there be
A tear shed from you in my memory,   300
And I shall rest at peace.

Phi.   Blessing be with thee,
Whatever thou deservest.   *Exit* BELLARIO.
            O, where shall I

---

285. tender youth] *Q2;* honest lookes *Q1.*   296. practisèd] *This ed.;* prac-
tisde *Q2.*   302. *Exit Bellario*] *so Dyce; after* 'peace' (*l. 301*) *Q2.*

---

    282. *urge*] press, put pressure on.
    291. *tender'st*] have a tender regard for.
    293. *distaste*] displeasure. Cf. Bacon, Essay *Of Adversity*: 'Prosperity is
not without many feares and distastes'.

Go bathe this body ? Nature too unkind,
That made no medicine for a troubled mind.   *Exit.*

[III. ii]

Enter ARETHUSA.

Are. I marvel my boy comes not back again,
But that I know my love will question him
Over and over; how I slept, waked, talked,
How I remembered him when his dear name
Was last spoke, and how when I sighed, wept, sung,   5
And ten thousand such. I should be angry
At his stay.

Enter KING.

King. What, at your meditations ? Who attends you ?
Are. None but my single self, I need no guard;
I do no wrong, nor fear none.   10
King. Tell me, have you not a boy ?
Are. Yes, sir.
King. What kind of boy ?
Are. A page, a waiting boy.
King. A handsome boy ?   15
Are. I think he be not ugly;
Well qualified and dutiful I know him;
I took him not for beauty.
King. He speaks and sings and plays ?
Are. Yes, sir.   20
King. About eighteen ?
Are. I never asked his age.
King. Is he full of service ?
Are. By your pardon, why do you ask ?
King. Put him away.   25

303–4. *Nature ... mind*] Cf. *Macbeth*, v. iii. 40–5.

III. ii. 23.] See Introduction, p. lxiv.
25. *Put him away*] get rid of him.

Are. Sir.

King. Put him away, I say, 'has done you that good service
 Shames me to speak of.

Are. Good sir, let me understand you.

King. If you fear me,   30
 Show it in duty; put away that boy.

Are. Let me have reason for it, sir, and then
 Your will is my command.

King. Do not you blush to ask it? Cast him off,
 Or I shall do the same to you. Y' are one   35
 Shame with me, and so near unto myself,
 That by my life, I dare not tell myself
 What you, my self, have done.

Are.   What I have done, my Lord?

King. 'Tis a new language, that all love to learn;
 The common people speak it well already,   40
 They need no grammar; understand me well,
 There be foul whispers stirring. Cast him off,
 And suddenly; do it; farewell.   *Exit.*

Are. Where may a maiden live securely free.
 Keeping her honour fair? Not with the living;   45
 They feed upon opinions, errors, dreams,
 And make 'em truths; they draw a nourishment
 Out of defamings, grow upon disgraces;
 And, when they see a virtue fortified
 Strongly above the battery of their tongues,   50
 O, how they cast to sink it; and defeated
 (Soul-sick with poison) strike the monuments

---

35. the same] *Q2;* that shame *Q1.*   37. my life] *Q2;* the gods *Q1.*
38. I have] *Q2;* haue I *Q3.*

35–6. *Y' are ... with me*] Your disgrace is mine.

37. *my life*] Turner suggests that this is an expurgation in Q2; the instances of expurgation, however, are so few that other explanations, such
as authorial second thoughts, are equally possible.

38.] Q2's puzzled echo of the King's words is more like Arethusa's
character than Q3's direct question, which some editors adopt.

51. *cast*] (1) cast about for ideas; (2) cast shot for their battery.

Where noble names lie sleeping, till they sweat,
And the cold marble melt.   [*She weeps.*]

Enter PHILASTER.

Phi. Peace to your fairest thoughts, dearest mistress.   55
Are. O, my dearest servant, I have a war within me.
Phi. He must be more than man that makes these crystals
    Run into rivers. Sweetest fair, the cause;
    And as I am your slave, tied to your goodness,
    Your creature, made again from what I was   60
    And newly-spirited, I'll right your honour.
Are. O, my best love, that boy!
Phi. What boy?
Are. The pretty boy you gave me—
Phi. What of him?   65
Are. Must be no more mine.
Phi. Why?
Are. They are jealous of him.
Phi. Jealous, who?
Are. The King.   70
Phi. [*Aside*] O, my misfortune!
    Then 'tis no idle jealousy. [*To her*] Let him go.
Are. O cruel; are you hard-hearted too?
    Who shall now tell you how much I loved you?
    Who shall swear it to you, and weep the tears I send?   75
    Who shall now bring you letters, rings, bracelets?
    Lose his health in service? Wake tedious nights
    In stories of your praise? Who shall sing
    Your crying elegies, and strike a sad soul
    Into senseless pictures, and make them mourn?   80
    Who shall take up his lute, and touch it till

74. loved] *Q2;* love *Turner conj.*   80. mourn] *Q2;* warme *Q1.*

---

57. *these crystals*] 'Crystal' was a name variously given to rock-crystal,
fine cut glass, and ice, the sense exploited here.
   77. *Wake*] stay awake through.
   79. *elegies*] i.e., love-poems, technically verses in elegiac metre.
   79–80. *strike . . . pictures*] make inanimate pictures come to life.

He crown a silent sleep upon my eyelids,
Making me dream, and cry, 'O, my dear,
Dear Philaster'?

Phi. [*Aside*] O, my heart!   85
Would he had broken thee that made thee know
This lady was not loyal. [*To her*] Mistress,
Forget the boy; I'll get thee a far better.

Are. O, never, never such a boy again
As my Bellario.

Phi.   'Tis but your fond affection.   90

Are. With thee, my boy, farewell for ever
All secrecy in servants; farewell faith,
And all desire to do well for itself;
Let all that shall succeed thee for thy wrongs
Sell and betray chaste love.

Phi.   And all this passion for a boy? 95

Are. He was your boy, and you put him to me,
And the loss of such must have a mourning for.

Phi. O, thou forgetful woman!

Are.   How, my Lord?

Phi. False Arethusa!
Hast thou a medicine to restore my wits,   100
When I have lost 'em? If not, leave to talk,
And do thus.

Are.   Do what, sir? Would you sleep?

Phi. For ever, Arethusa. O, you gods,
Give me a worthy patience! Have I stood
Naked, alone, the shock of many fortunes?   105
Have I seen mischiefs numberless and mighty
Grow like a sea upon me? Have I taken

86. thee know] *Q2;* me know *Boas conj.*   92. secrecy] *Q2;* seruice *Q1.*

94–5. *Let . . . love*] 'Let all servants who may come to replace Bellario because of the wrongs done to him be betrayers of chaste love.'

102.] Presumably Philaster closes his eyes to simulate death. Arethusa's bewildered misunderstanding is a typical piece of tragicomic pathos which differs from its Shakespearean model in Desdemona by its effect of making Philaster slightly ridiculous.

Danger as stern as death into my bosom,
And laughed upon it, made it but a mirth,
And flung it by ? Do I live now like him,   110
Under this tyrant King, that languishing
Hears his sad bell and sees his mourners ? Do I
Bear all this bravely, and must sink at length
Under a woman's falsehood ? O, that boy,
That cursèd boy! None but a villain boy   115
To ease your lust ?

Are.   Nay, then I am betrayed;
I feel the plot cast for my overthrow.
O, I am wretched.

Phi. Now you may take that little right I have
To this poor kingdom; give it to your Joy,   120
For I have no joy in it. Some far place,
Where never womankind durst set her foot
For bursting with her poisons, must I seek,
And live to curse you;
There dig a cave, and preach to birds and beasts   125
What woman is, and help to save them from you;
How heaven is in your eyes, but in your hearts
More hell than hell has; how your tongues, like scorpions,
Both heal and poison; how your thoughts are woven
With thousand changes in one subtle web,   130
And worn so by you; how that foolish man,
That reads the story of a woman's face

---

112. *his sad bell*] his solemn funeral bell; i.e., 'do I continue living under
this tyranny like one resigned to death ?'

117. *cast*] designed, set.

120. *your Joy*] i.e., Bellario.

123. *For bursting*] for fear of bursting.

128–9. *like scorpions | Both . . . poison*] Scorpions were believed to serve
as antidotes to their own stings. Cf. T. Moufet, *The History of Four-footed
Beasts and Serpents* (1658), Sss6ᵛ: 'The application or use of Scorpions in
medicine, is either by powder or by Oyl, or by applying them bruised to
their own wounds'.

130. *subtle*] ingenious, delicate (Lat. *subtilis*, finely woven). Marvell uses
the same adjective of a net in the *Horatian Ode*, 48–9.

And dies believing it, is lost for ever;
How all the good you have is but a shadow,
I' th' morning with you, and at night behind you   135
Past and forgotten; how your vows are frosts,
Fast for a night, and with the next sun gone;
How you are, being taken all together,
A mere confusion, and so dead a chaos,
That love cannot distinguish. These sad texts   140
Till my last hour I am bound to utter of you.
So farewell all my woe, all my delight.   *Exit.*

Are. Be merciful, ye gods, and strike me dead.
What way have I deserved this ? Make my breast
Transparent as pure crystal, that the world,   145
Jealous of me, may see the foulest thought
My heart holds. Where shall a woman turn her eyes
To find out constancy ?

Enter BELLARIO.

                    Save me, how black
And guiltily, methinks, that boy looks now.
O, thou dissembler, that before thou spakest   150
Wert in thy cradle false, sent to make lies
And betray innocents; thy lord and thou
May glory in the ashes of a maid
Fooled by her passion; but the conquest is
Nothing so great as wicked. Fly away;   155
Let my command force thee to that which shame
Would do without it. If thou understood'st
The loathèd office thou hast undergone,
Why, thou wouldst hide thee under heaps of hills,
Lest men should dig and find thee.

Bel.   O, what god   160
Angry with men hath sent this strange disease

---

137. *Fast*] firm.
140. *distinguish*] i.e., amongst the changeable faces of woman.
158. *undergone*] performed.

Into the noblest minds? Madam, this grief
You add unto me is no more than drops
To seas, for which they are not seen to swell;
My Lord hath struck his anger through my heart,   165
And let out all the hope of future joys.
You need not bid me fly; I came to part,
To take my latest leave. Farewell for ever.
I durst not run away in honesty
From such a lady, like a boy that stole   170
Or made some grievous fault; the power of gods
Assist you in your sufferings; hasty time
Reveal the truth to your abusèd lord
And mine, that he may know your worth; whilst I
Go seek out some forgotten place to die.   *Exit.* 175
Are. Peace guide thee. Th' 'ast overthrown me once;
Yet if I had another Troy to lose,
Thou, or another villain with thy looks,
Might talk me out of it, and send me naked,
My hair dishevelled, through the fiery streets.   180

Enter a Lady.

Lady. Madam, the King would hunt, and calls for you
With earnestness.
Are.   I am in tune to hunt.
Diana, if thou canst rage with a maid
As with a man, let me discover thee

174. mine, that] *Q3;* mine: That *Q2;* mine, / That *Q1.*   177. Troy] *Q2;*
time *Q1.*

168. *latest*] last.
172. *hasty time*] Cf. I. ii. 99.
176–80. *Th' ... streets*] Arethusa apparently sees Bellario as the wooden
horse which has breached her defences through guile, and is admitting that
he 'or another villain with thy looks' could do so again. Arethusa is both
Troy and its Hecuba. Cf. *Hamlet*, II. ii. 499–503.
182. *in tune*] in the right mood.
183–4. *with a maid / As ... man*] Actaeon while hunting saw Diana
(patron goddess of hunting) bathing. In revenge she turned him into a stag
and his own hounds killed him.

Bathing, and turn me to a fearful hind,   185
That I may die pursued by cruel hounds,
And have my story written in my wounds.   *Exeunt.*

Act IV

[IV. i]

Enter KING, PHARAMOND, ARETHUSA, GALATEA, MEGRA, DION,
    CLEREMONT, THRASILINE, *and* Attendants.

King. What, are the hounds before and all the woodmen?
    Our horses ready and our bows bent?
Dion.   All, sir.
King. [*To Pharamond*] Y' are cloudy, sir. Come, we have forgotten
    Your venial trespass; let not that sit heavy
    Upon your spirit; here's none dare utter it.   5
Dion. He looks like an old surfeited stallion after his leaping,
    dull as a dormouse. See how he sinks; the wench has shot
    him between wind and water and I hope sprung a leak.
Thra. He needs no teaching, he strikes sure enough; his great-
    est fault is he hunts too much in the purlieus; would he   10
    would leave off poaching.
Dion. And for his horn, 'has left it at the lodge where he lay

IV. i.] *Actus 4. Scœna 1. Q2.*

IV. i. 1. *woodmen*] huntsmen who went with the hounds to raise the
quarry.

3. *cloudy*] frowning, gloomy.

7. *dull ... dormouse*] proverbial. Cf. M. P. Tilley, *A Dictionary of Proverbs in England in the Sixteenth and Seventeenth Centuries*, Ann Arbor,
1950, D.568.

10. *purlieus*] the borders of a forest, a region which, though largely only
undergrowth, was still subject to the forest laws of hunting. It was the
most convenient region for poachers and lechery; it also lacked the natural
hazards involved in hunting among trees. The same name was used of the
less reputable suburbs of London; *O.E.D.* cites the phrase in the play as
meaning 'to pursue illicit love'.

12. *horn*] (1) hunting-horn; (2) phallus.

71

late. O, he's a precious lyam-hound; turn him loose upon
the persue of a lady, and if he lose her hang him up i' th'
slip. When my fox-bitch Beauty grows proud I'll borrow   15
him.

King. [*To Arethusa*] Is your boy turned away?

Are. You did command, sir, and I obeyed you.

King. 'Tis well done. Hark ye further.   [*They talk apart.*]

Cle. Is 't possible this fellow should repent? Methinks that   20
were not noble in him; and yet he looks like a mortified
member, as if he had a sick man's salve in 's mouth. If a
worse man had done this fault now, some physical Justice
or other would presently (without the help of an almanack) have opened the obstructions of his liver, and let   25
him blood with a dog-whip.

Dion. See, see how modestly yon lady looks, as if she
came from churching with her neighbours. Why, what

---

14. persue] *Q2* (pursue); persuite *Q4.*

13. *lyam-hound*] a leashed hunting-dog, used to scent the quarry. Cf.
Bartholomew Fair (Revels edn), I. iii. 12: 'all the lyam-hounds o' the City
should have drawn after you by the scent'.

14. *persue*] the blood trail of a hunted quarry, from Fr. 'perçu'. Cf. *The
Faerie Queene*, III. v. 28: 'By the great persue, which she there perceau'd, /
Well hoped she the beast engor'd had beene'.

15. *slip*] a slip-leash; roughly comparable to a noose.

proud] sexually excited, a term frequently used punningly. Cf. *Venus and
Adonis*, 299–300: 'Look what a horse should have he did not lack, / Save
a proud rider on so proud a back.'

22. *sick man's salve*] Thomas Becon's *Sycke Mans Salve* was a religious
tract which went through many editions from its first printing in 1561.
Pharamond looks like a sour Puritan, a 'member' whose flesh has been
'mortified'; penitence would be 'not noble' in him (l. 21) because Puritans
were almost always commoners.

23. *physical*] good for the health, medicinal. The sanguine humour was
characteristically the most lustful; hence blood-letting was a cure for
lechery. A 'physical' Justice who ordered whipping for lechery would
therefore provide a medicinal cure as well as a punishment.

24. *presently*] immediately.

24–5. *almanack*] Compendiums of the kind parodied in Dekker's *Owles
Almanacke* (1618) contained amongst other things directives as to the most
favourable times for blood-letting.

27. *yon lady*] i.e., Megra.

28. *churching*] attending a service of thanksgiving for childbirth.

a devil can a man see in her face but that she's honest?

Thra. Faith, no great matter to speak of: a foolish twinkling   30
    with the eye, that spoils her coat; but he must be a cun-
    ning herald that finds it.

Dion. See how they muster one another! O, there's a rank
    regiment, where the devil carries the colours and his dam
    drum-major. Now the world and the flesh come behind   35
    with the carriage.

Cle. Sure this lady has a good turn done her against her will;
    before she was common talk, now none dare say canthari-
    des can stir her. Her face looks like a warrant, willing and
    commanding all tongues, as they will answer it, to be tied   40
    up and bolted when this lady means to let herself loose.
    As I live, she has got her a goodly protection and a graci-
    ous; and may use her body discreetly for her health sake
    once a week, excepting Lent and dog-days. O, if they
    were to be got for money, what a large sum would come   45
    out of the city for these licences.

King. To horse, to horse, we lose the morning, gentlemen.

                                                          Exeunt.

30–1. *twinkling . . . coat*] Mullets or stars in a coat of arms signified cadet
branches of a family. Coats with stars were therefore heraldically inferior.
(Dyce.)

33. *muster*] take a (military) roll-call, probably with a quibble on a
'muster' of peacocks.

33–4. *rank regiment . . . colours*] a proverbial phrase. John Clarke, *Proverbs English and Latin*, 1639, quotes the version ''Tis an ill company
where the devil bears the banner.'

36. *carriage*] the baggage.

38–9. *cantharides*] Spanish fly, the most popular aphrodisiac after eringo.

44. *dog-days*] the days when the dog-star (Sirius) reigns, in high summer;
hence hot and feverish days, i.e., during her periods.

46. *licences*] Cf. 'warrant', l. 39; Megra's reputation is now under the
King's care. The granting of 'licences', patents or monopolies, to courtiers
was a controversial subject in the City and in Parliament. Cf. *The Parliamentary Diary of Robert Bowyer, 1606–1607*, ed. D. H. Willson, Minnea-
polis, 1931, pp. 112, 144, 176, etc.

[IV. ii]

Enter two Woodmen.

1 Wood. What, have you lodged the deer?

2 Wood. Yes, they are ready for the bow.

1 Wood. Who shoots?

2 Wood. The Princess.

1 Wood. No, she'll hunt.   5

2 Wood. She'll take a stand, I say.

1 Wood. Who else?

2 Wood. Why, the young stranger Prince.

1 Wood. He shall shoot in a stone bow for me. I never loved his
beyond-sea-ship since he forsook the say, for paying ten   10
shillings. He was there at the fall of a deer, and would
needs (out of his mightiness) give ten groats for the dowcets; marry, his steward would have the velvet head into
the bargain, to turf his hat withal. I think he should love
venery; he is an old Sir Tristram; for if you be remem-   15

IV. ii. 13. his] *Q1;* the *Q2.*   14. turf] *Q2;* tuft *Theobald conj.*

IV. ii. 1. *lodged*] brought to bay or covert within bowshot of the
butts.

6. *stand*] a butt, or place for shooting from in hunting.

9. *stone bow*] a child's crossbow designed to shoot stones, a toy catapult.
for me] for all I care.

10. *say*] the assay of the quarry, or checking of the entrails. It was custom-
ary for the most highly ranked member of the hunt to assay the deer's
quality as game. The keeper would offer his knife to slice open its belly,
receiving a gratuity of a crown or ten shillings in return. Pharamond passed
up his right as senior member in order to save his money.

12. *groats*] fourpenny pieces.

12–13. *dowcets*] testicles.

13. *velvet head*] The down on growing antlers is called 'velvet'; the term
was sometimes used of velvet caps, with a hint of cuckold's horns. Cf. *The
Knight of the Burning Pestle*, v. v. 50, 'lift aloft your velvet heads'.

14. *turf*] i.e., cover with fur, used contemptuously of clumsy milli-
nery.

15. *venery*] (1) hunting; (2) sexual pleasure.
Sir Tristram] Cf. *Morte D'Arthur*, ed. Vinaver, I, 375: 'Tristrams . . .
began good mesures of blowynge of beestes of venery and beestes of chaace
and all maner of vermaynes, and all the termys we have yet of hawkynge
and huntynge. And therefore the book of venery . . . is called the Booke
of Sir Trystrams'.

bered, he forsook the stag once to strike a rascal milking
in a meadow, and her he killed in the eye. Who shoots
else?

2 Wood. The Lady Galatea.

1 Wood. That's a good wench, an she would not chide us for   20
tumbling of her women in the brakes. She's liberal, and
by the gods they say she's honest, and whether that be a
fault I have nothing to do. There's all?

2 Wood. No, one more: Megra.

1 Wood. That's a firker i'faith, boy; there's a wench will ride   25
her haunches as hard after a kennel of hounds as a hunt-
ing-saddle, and when she comes home, get 'em clapped
and all is well again. I have known her lose herself three
times in one afternoon (if the woods have been answerable), and it has been work enough for one man to find   30
her, and he has sweat for it. She rides well and she pays
well. Hark, let's go.   *Exeunt.*

[IV. iii]

Enter PHILASTER.

Phi. O that I had been nourished in these woods
With milk of goats and acorns, and not known

16. milking] *Q2;* mitching *Theobald conj.*

16–17. *a rascal ... meadow*] a lone hind suckling her calf, or possibly,
as Turner suggests, an undersized deer taking milk from a cow, in a water-
meadow; 'her he killed in the eye' means that he shot accurately at a sitting
target.

21. *tumbling ... brakes*] copulating with her maidservants in the undergrowth.

23. *I have ... do*] it is not for me to say.

25. *firker*] one who goes hard at things; by implication a sexually ener-
getic person.

26. *kennel*] pack.

27. *clapped*] have a poultice applied, with secondary associations of pat-
ting, as at III. i. 196, and possibly of venereal disease.

29–30. *answerable*] responsible; the implication being that Megra deliberately lost herself in order to be alone with the man who found her.

30. *find*] with a sexual innuendo.

IV. iii. 1–13.] a paraphrase of the first lines from Juvenal's sixth satire:

The right of crowns nor the dissembling trains
Of women's looks, but digged myself a cave
Where I, my fire, my cattle, and my bed,   5
Might have been shut together in one shed;
And then had taken me some mountain girl,
Beaten with winds, chaste as the hardened rocks
Whereon she dwelt, that might have strewed my bed
With leaves and reeds, and with the skins of beasts,   10
Our neighbours, and have borne at her big breasts
My large coarse issue. This had been a life
Free from vexation.

Enter BELLARIO.

Bel.   O, wicked men!
An innocent may walk safe among beasts;
Nothing assaults me here. See, my grieved lord   15
Sits as his soul were searching out a way
To leave his body. [*To Philaster*] Pardon me that must
Break thy last commandment, for I must speak.
You that are grieved can pity; hear, my Lord.
Phi. Is there a creature yet so miserable,   20
That I can pity?
Bel.   O, my noble Lord,
View my strange fortune and bestow on me
According to your bounty (if my service
Can merit nothing) so much as may serve

4. women's looks] *Q2;* cruell loue *Q1.*   9. dwelt] *Q1;* dwells *Q2.*

Credo Pudicitiam Saturno rege moratum
in terris visamque diu, cum frigida parvas
praeberet spelunca domos, ignemque Laremque
et pecus et dominos communi clauderet umbra,
silvestrem montana torum cum sterneret uxor
frondibus et culmo vicinarumque ferarum
pellibus ...

Juvenal goes on to ask his friend why he intends to marry when there are
so many other ways of putting an end to one's existence.

   5. *cattle*] i.e., chattels, not only livestock.
   16. *as*] as if.

    To keep that little piece I hold of life   25
    From cold and hunger.
Phi.   Is it thou ? Be gone;
    Go, sell those misbeseeming clothes thou wearest,
    And feed thyself with them.
Bel. Alas, my Lord, I can get nothing for them;
    The silly country people think 'tis treason   30
    To touch such gay things.
Phi.   Now by the gods, this is
    Unkindly done, to vex me with thy sight;
    Th' art fall'n again to thy dissembling trade.
    How shouldst thou think to cozen me again ?
    Remains there yet a plague untried for me ?   35
    Even so thou weptst, and lookedst, and spokest when first
    I took thee up; curse on the time! If thy
    Commanding tears can work on any other,
    Use thy art, I'll not betray it. Which way
    Wilt thou take, that I may shun thee,   40
    For thine eyes are poison to mine, and I
    Am loath to grow in rage; this way, or that way ?
Bel. Any will serve; but I will choose to have
    That path in chase that leads unto my grave.

                                   Exeunt severally.

26–31. Is it ... gay things] *Q2; not in Q1.*

   26–31. *Is it ... gay things*] a late insertion in the text: Philaster's words
at ll. 31–2 are a more direct and relevant response to his first sight of
Bellario than ll. 26–8, which are curiously off-hand. The omission of the
lines from Q1 suggests that they were added to the text from the Q2 manuscript, which was copied out some time after the Q1 manuscript. All that
can be said of the insertion is that it makes an oblique comment on the
'bravery' theme, and stresses the distance between court and country.
   27. *misbeseeming*] i.e., inappropriately 'brave'.
   30. *silly*] innocent, unsophisticated.
   34. *cozen*] deceive, trick.
   44. *in chase*] i.e., to follow.

L

[IV. iv]

Enter DION *and the* Woodmen.

Dion. This is the strangest sudden chance! You, woodman.

1 Wood. My Lord Dion?

Dion. Saw you a lady come this way on a sable horse studded
with stars of white?

2 Wood. Was she not young and tall?   5

Dion. Yes. Rode she to the wood or to the plain?

2 Wood. Faith, my Lord, we saw none.   *Exeunt* Woodmen.

Dion. Pox of your questions then.

Enter CLEREMONT.

What, is she found?

Cle. Nor will be, I think.   10

Dion. Let him seek his daughter himself; she cannot stray
about a little necessary natural business but the whole
Court must be in arms. When she has done, we shall have
peace.

Cle. There's already a thousand fatherless tales amongst us: 15
some say her horse ran away with her; some a wolf pursued her; others 'twas a plot to kill her, and that armed
men were seen in the wood; but questionless she rode
away willingly.

Enter KING *and* THRASILINE.

King. Where is she?   20

Cle. Sir, I cannot tell.

King. How's that? Answer me so again.

Cle. Sir, shall I lie?

King. Yes, lie and damn, rather than tell me that.
I say again, where is she? Mutter not!   25

IV. iv. 12. *a little . . . business*] i.e., urinating.
15. *fatherless*] i.e., of no known origin.
18. *questionless*] undoubtedly.
22. *Answer . . . again*] 'Do you dare give me that reply again?'
24. *damn*] be damned.

Sir, speak you, where is she?

Dion. Sir, I do not know.

King. Speak that again so boldly, and by heaven
It is thy last. You fellows, answer me,
Where is she? Mark me, all, I am your King,   30
I wish to see my daughter, show her me!
I do command you all, as you are subjects,
To show her me! What, am I not your King?
If ay, then am I not to be obeyed?

Dion. Yes, if you command things possible and honest.   35

King. Things possible and honest? Hear me, thou,
Thou traitor, thou darest confine thy King to things
Possible and honest! Show her me,
Or let me perish if I cover not
All Sicily with blood.   40

Dion. Faith, I cannot, unless you tell me where she is.

King. You have betrayed me; y' have let me lose
The jewel of my life. Go, bring her me,
And set her here before me. 'Tis the King
Will have it so, whose breath can still the winds,   45
Uncloud the sun, charm down the swelling sea,
And stop the floods of heaven. Speak, can it not?

Dion. No.

King. No? Cannot the breath of kings do this?

Dion. No, nor smell sweet itself, if once the lungs   50
Be but corrupted.

King.   Is it so? Take heed.

Dion. Sir, take you heed how you dare the powers
That must be just.

King.   Alas, what are we kings?
Why do you gods place us above the rest,
To be served, flattered, and adored till we   55

35.] See Introduction, p. lvi.

44–7.] Davison ('The Serious Concerns of *Philaster*', *op. cit.*, p. 3) sees
this and the succeeding speeches of the King in this scene as a burlesque
of the arguments of King James in *The Trew Law of Free Monarchies*. See
Introduction, pp. lv–lvii.

Believe we hold within our hands your thunder,
And when we come to try the power we have,
There's not a leaf shakes at our threatenings?
I have sinned, 'tis true, and here stand to be punished;
Yet would not thus be punished; let me choose   60
My way, and lay it on.

Dion. [*Aside*] He articles with the gods; would somebody
would draw bonds for the performance of covenants
betwixt them.

Enter PHARAMOND, GALATEA, *and* MEGRA.

King. What, is she found?

Pha.   No; we have ta'en her horse,   65
He galloped empty by. There's some treason.
You, Galatea, rode with her into the wood;
Why left you her?

Gal.   She did command me.

King. Command! You should not.

Gal. 'Twould ill become my fortunes and my birth   70
To disobey the daughter of my King.

King. Y' are all cunning to obey us for our hurts;
But I will have her.

Pha.   If I have her not,
By this hand, there shall be no more Sicily.

Dion. [*Aside*] What, will he carry it to Spain in 's pocket?   75

Pha. I will not leave one man alive, but the King,
A cook, and a tailor.

72. hurts] *Q2;* hurt *Q3.*   74. hand] *Q2;* sword *Q1.*

---

61. *lay it on*] strike hard.
62. *articles*] negotiates a legal contract.
62–4.] Davison (*op. cit.*, p. 4) notes 'The inference of [this] is that if a
bond for the *performance* of a contract between God and king might be
drawn up, the king could not break his part of the contract yet demand
that his people, nevertheless, adhere to their part of the contract'. This, of
course, is precisely what James did demand.
72. *for our hurts*] to our disadvantage.
77. *A cook . . . tailor*] i.e., for the necessities of Pharamond's life. He has

Dion. [*Aside*] Yes, you may do well to spare your lady bed-
    fellow, and her you may keep for a spawner.
King. [*Aside*] I see the injuries I have done must be revenged.   80
Dion. Sir, this is not the way to find her out.
King. Run all, disperse yourselves; the man that finds her,
    Or (if she be killed) the traitor, I'll make him great.
Dion. [*Aside*] I know some would give five thousand pounds
    to find her.   85
Pha. Come, let us seek.
King. Each man a several way; here I myself.
Dion. Come, gentlemen, we here.
Cle. Lady, you must go search too.
Meg. I had rather be searched myself.   *Exeunt omnes.*   90

[IV. v]

Enter ARETHUSA.

Are. Where am I now? Feet, find me out a way
    Without the counsel of my troubled head;
    I'll follow you boldly about these woods,
    O'er mountains, through brambles, pits, and floods.
    Heaven I hope will ease me; I am sick.   *She sits down.*   5

Enter BELLARIO.

Bel. Yonder's my lady. God knows I want nothing,
    Because I do not wish to live; yet I
    Will try her charity. [*To Arethusa*] O hear, you that have
        plenty,

IV. v. 5. *She sits down.*] *Q1; not in Q2.*

---

been already described as fat and 'bravely' dressed. Dion (ll. 78–9) adds
his third necessity to the list.

79. *spawner*] (1) an edible female fish; (2) a fertile woman.

83. *traitor*] The murder of Arethusa, as heiress to the crown, would be
an offence against the state.

90. *searched*] probed (as of a wound), penetrated, i.e., entered sexually.
Cf. *O.E.D.* v.t.8.

IV. v. 8. *try*] test.

From that flowing store drop some on dry ground. See,
The lively red is gone to guard her heart! [*Catches her.*] 10
I fear she faints. Madam, look up! She breathes not.
Open once more those rosy twins, and send
Unto my lord your latest farewell. O, she stirs.
How is it, madam? Speak comfort.

Are.   'Tis not gently done
To put me in a miserable life,   15
And hold me there. I prithee let me go,
I shall do best without thee; I am well.

Enter PHILASTER.

Phi. I am to blame to be so much in rage.
I'll tell her coolly when and where I heard
This killing truth. I will be temperate   20
In speaking, and as just in hearing— [*Sees them.*]
O monstrous! Tempt me not, you gods! Good gods,
Tempt not a frail man! What's he that has a heart
But he must ease it here?

Bel. My Lord, help, help the Princess!   25
Are. I am well; forbear.
Phi. Let me love lightning, let me be embraced
And kissed by scorpions, or adore the eyes
Of basilisks, rather than trust the tongues
Of hell-bred woman. Some good god look down   30
And shrink these veins up; stick me here a stone,
Lasting to ages in the memory
Of this damned act. Hear me, you wicked ones,
You have put hills of fire into this breast,
Not to be quenched with tears, for which may guilt   35
Sit on your bosoms! At your meals and beds

---

30. woman] *Q2;* women *Q1.*

10.] i.e., she has turned pale.
12. *those rosy twins*] her lips.
24. *ease it*] let it melt; weep.
31. *stick ... stone*] turn me into a stone monument.

Despair await you! What, before my face?
Poison of asps between your lips! Diseases
Be your best issues! Nature make a curse,
And throw it on you!
Are.   Dear Philaster, leave   40
To be enraged, and hear me.
Phi.   I have done;
Forgive my passion. Not the calmèd sea,
When Aeolus locks up his windy brood,
Is less disturbed than I. I'll make you know 't.
Dear Arethusa, do but take this sword, [*Offers his sword*]   45
And search how temperate a heart I have;
Then you and this your boy may live and reign
In lust without control. Wilt thou, Bellario?
I prithee kill me; thou art poor and mayst
Nourish ambitious thoughts; when I am dead   50
Thy way were freer. Am I raging now?
If I were mad I should desire to live;
Sirs, feel my pulse, whether have you known
A man in a more equal tune to die?
Bel. Alas, my Lord, your pulse keeps madman's time;   55
So does your tongue.
Phi.   You will not kill me, then?
Are. Kill you?
Bel.   Not for the world.
Phi.   I blame not thee,
Bellario; thou hast done but that which gods
Would have transformed themselves to do; be gone,

40. throw] *Q1;* through *Q2.*   51. Thy] *Q1;* This *Q2.*

___

40. *leave*] cease.
43. *Aeolus*] god of the winds.
46. *search*] seek out by probing.
53. *Sirs*] used indifferently of male and female.
whether] i.e., think whether or not.
59. *transformed themselves*] Mortals could not look on the gods in their
proper shape; the gods therefore disguised themselves when mating with
mortals.

Leave me without reply; this is the last   60
Of all our meeting.   *Exit* BELLARIO.
               Kill me with this sword;
Be wise, or worse will follow; we are two
Earth cannot bear at once. Resolve to do,
Or suffer.

Are. If my fortune be so good to let me fall   65
Upon thy hand, I shall have peace in death.
Yet tell me this, there will be no slanders,
No jealousy in the other world, no ill there?

Phi. No.

Are.   Show me then the way.

Phi.   Then guide
My feeble hand, you that have power to do it,   70
For I must perform a piece of justice. If your youth
Have any way offended heaven, let prayers
Short and effectual reconcile you to it.

Are. I am prepared.

                Enter a Country Fellow.

C. Fell. I'll see the King, if he be in the forest; I have hunted   75
him these two hours; if I should come home and not see
him my sisters would laugh at me. I can see nothing but
people better horsed than myself, that outride me; I can
hear nothing but shouting. These Kings had need of good
brains, this whooping is able to put a mean man out of his   80
wits. There's a courtier with his sword drawn; by this
hand, upon a woman, I think.

---

61. meeting] *Q2;* meetings *Q1.*   *Exit Bellario.*] *so Weber; at end of l. 60*
Q2.   69. then the way] *Q2;* the way to ioy *Q1.*

---

66. *Upon thy hand*] i.e., 'by thy hand', or 'upon thy sword', signifying
her willingness to die.

71–3.] Cf. *Othello,* v. ii. 27–9.

74.1. *Country Fellow*] Turner notes that Q1 depicts a 'Countrey Gallant'
both in the text and in the woodcut of the title-page, in place of Q2's more
rustic 'Fellow'. The difference may be due either to what the Q1 scribe
saw on stage or to an attempt noticeable in the Q2 text to extend the distance between country and court. See Introduction, p. lxxviii.

Phi. Are you at peace?

Are. With heaven and earth.

Phi. May they divide thy soul and body.   *Philaster wounds her.*

C. Fell. Hold, dastard, strike a woman? Th' art a craven I   86
    warrant thee; thou wouldst be loath to play half a dozen
    venies at wasters with a good fellow for a broken head.

Phi. Leave us, good friend.

Are. What ill-bred man art thou, to intrude thyself   90
    Upon our private sports, our recreations?

C. Fell. God 'uds me, I understand you not; but I know the
    rogue has hurt you.

Phi. Pursue thy own affairs; it will be ill
    To multiply blood upon my head,   95
    Which thou wilt force me to.

C. Fell. I know not your rhetoric, but I can lay it on if you
    touch the woman.

Phi. Slave, take what thou deservest.   *They fight.*

Are. Gods guard my lord!   100

C. Fell. O, do you breathe?

Phi. I hear the tread of people. I am hurt,
    The gods take part against me, could this boor

85.1. *Philaster* ... *her*] *Q1; not in Q2.*   86–7. craven ... thee;] *Q2;*
craven, ... thee, *Q1.*   99. *They fight*] so *Q1; at l.* 98 *Q2.*   100. Gods]
Q1; Heauen *Q2.*

---

85. *divide*] share; i.e., may your soul go to heaven while your body remains on earth.

88. *venies at wasters*] bouts or rounds with cudgels. Cudgel-fighting had strict rules governing the length of bouts and fair and unfair blows.

for ... head] to see which of us gets his head broken.

92. *'uds*] a minced form of 'God save' (*O.E.D.* s.v.2).

95. *To multiply blood*] to take responsibility for shedding the Country Fellow's blood as well as Arethusa's.

100. *Gods*] At IV. vi. 12 Philaster quotes Arethusa as having said 'gods'. Also, Q2 by expurgating loses the implication that the gods here show their justice by, in the event, not guarding Arethusa's lord.

101. *do you breathe?*] 'Are you having a rest?' The fight was evidently not meant to be short, or at least not stopping at the first injury, since the Country Fellow is himself wounded (cf. l. 142) before he defeats Philaster.

103–4.] See Introduction, p. xlvi.

Have held me thus else ? I must shift for life,
Though I do loathe it. I would find a course   105
To lose it rather by my will than force.   *Exit.*
C. Fell. I cannot follow the rogue. I prithee wench, come
and kiss me now.

Enter PHARAMOND, DION, CLEREMONT, THRASILINE,
and Woodmen.

Pha. What art thou ?
C. Fell. Almost killed I am for a foolish woman; a knave has   110
hurt her.
Pha. The Princess, gentlemen! Where's the wound,
madam ? Is it dangerous ?
Are. He has not hurt me.
C. Fell. By God, she lies; 'has hurt her in the breast, look   115
else.
Pha. O sacred spring of innocent blood!
Dion. 'Tis above wonder. Who should dare this ?
Are. I felt it not.
Pha. Speak, villain, who has hurt the Princess ?   120
C. Fell. Is it the Princess ?
Dion. Ay.
C. Fell. Then I have seen something yet.
Pha. But who has hurt her ?
C. Fell. I told you, a rogue; I ne'er saw him before, I.   125
Pha. Madam, who did it ?
Are. Some dishonest wretch; alas, I know him not,
And do forgive him.
C. Fell. He's hurt too, he cannot go far; I made my father's
old fox fly about his ears.   130
Pha. How will you have me kill him ?
Are. Not at all, 'tis some distracted fellow.

---

104. *shift*] adopt expedients (*O.E.D.* v.i.1.6).
115–16. *look else*] look and see if you don't believe me.
130. *fox*] an old-fashioned broadsword. In *Henry V* it is Pistol's weapon
('O Signieur Dew, thou diest on point of fox', IV. iv. 9).

Pha. By this hand, I'll leave never a piece of him bigger
  than a nut, and bring him all to you in my hat.
Are. Nay, good sir,   135
  If you do take him, bring him quick to me,
  And I will study for a punishment
  Great as his fault.
Pha. I will.
Are. But swear.   140
Pha. By all my love I will. Woodman, conduct the Princess
  to the King, and bear that wounded fellow to dressing.
  Come, gentlemen, we'll follow the chase close.

> *Exeunt* ARETHUSA, PHARAMOND, DION, CLEREMONT,
>   THRASILINE, *and* 1 Woodman.

C. Fell. I pray you, friend, let me see the King.
2 Wood. That you shall, and receive thanks.   145
C. Fell. If I get clear of this, I'll go to see no more gay sights.

> *Exeunt.*

[IV. vi]

Enter BELLARIO.

Bel. A heaviness near death sits on my brow,
  And I must sleep. Bear me, thou gentle bank,
  For ever if thou wilt. [*Lies down*] You sweet ones all,
  Let me unworthy press you; I could wish
  I rather were a corse strewed o'er with you   5
  Than quick above you. Dulness shuts mine eyes,
  And I am giddy; O that I could take
  So sound a sleep that I might never wake.   [*Sleeps.*]

Enter PHILASTER.

Phi. I have done ill; my conscience calls me false,

IV. vi. 1. A ... death] *Q2;* Oh heauens! heauy death *Q1.*

---

136. *quick*] alive.
143. *the chase*] i.e., the new one for the Princess's attacker.

IV. vi. 3. *You sweet ones*] the flowers.

To strike at her that would not strike at me.   10
When I did fight, methought I heard her pray
The gods to guard me. She may be abused,
And I a loathèd villain; if she be,
She will conceal who hurt her. He has wounds
And cannot follow, neither knows he me.   15
Who's this? Bellario sleeping? If thou be'st
Guilty, there is no justice that thy sleep
Should be so sound, and mine whom thou has wronged
So broken. (*Cry within.*) Hark, I am pursued; you gods,
I'll take this offered means of my escape.   20
They have no mark to know me but my wounds,
If she be true; if false, let mischief light
On all the world at once. Sword, print my wounds
Upon this sleeping boy. I ha' none I think
Are mortal, nor would I lay greater on thee. *Wounds him.* 25
Bel. O, death I hope is come. Blessed be that hand,
It meant me well. Again, for pity's sake.
Phi. I have caught myself;   *Philaster falls.*
The loss of blood hath stayed my flight. Here, here
Is he that struck thee; take thy full revenge,   30
Use me as I did mean thee, worse than death;
I'll teach thee to revenge. This luckless hand
Wounded the Princess; tell my followers
Thou didst receive these hurts in staying me,
And I will second thee; get a reward.   35

19. *Cry within.*] *at right margin Q1; after* 'sleep' (*l. 17*) *Q2.*

---

24. *this sleeping boy*] It is a measure of Philaster's being out of his right
mind that he should follow his wounding of a woman with an attack on a
sleeping boy. Either action would be sufficient to underline the effects of
adversity, and prepare for the demonstration of the uses of adversity in the
final act when the hero comes to 'himself' and the realization of the enor-
mities he has committed when not 'himself'.

33. *followers*] i.e., pursuers.

35. *second*] confirm, support. Line 35 completes sheet H and the first compositor's stint in setting Q2. The page ends with a wrong catchword, 'And'
instead of '*Bel.*', which, together with the comma wrongly used in place of
a full stop after 'reward', might imply that a line or more of text may have

Bel. Fly, fly, my Lord, and save yourself.
Phi.   How's this?
   Wouldst thou I should be safe?
Bel.   Else were it vain
   For me to live. These little wounds I have
   Ha' not bled much; reach me that noble hand,
   I'll help to cover you.
Phi.   Art thou true to me?   40
Bel. Or let me perish loathed. Come, my good Lord,
   Creep in among those bushes; who does know
   But that the gods may save your much loved breath?
Phi. Then I shall die for grief, if not for this,
   That I have wounded thee. What wilt thou do?   45
Bel. Shift for myself well; peace, I hear 'em come.
                          [*Philaster creeps into a bush.*]
([*Voices*] *within.*) Follow, follow, follow, that way they went.
Bel. With my own wounds I'll bloody my own sword.
   I need not counterfeit to fall; heaven knows
   That I can stand no longer.   *Falls down.*   50

Enter PHARAMOND, DION, CLEREMONT, *and* THRASILINE.

Pha. To this place we have traced him by his blood.
Cle. Yonder, my Lord, creeps one away.
Dion. Stay, sir, what are you?

---

50. *Falls down.*] *Q1; not in Q2.*   51. traced] *This ed.;* tract *Q2;* track'd
Theobald.

---

been omitted at this point. Q1, however, has substantially the same text
as Q2, and it would be an extraordinary coincidence if both texts were for
different reasons to omit the same line. Turner suggests that the error may
simply have been the wrong reproduction of a catchword from the same
line (35) instead of the one following; the comma would then be a second
error following from the first, since a catchword 'And' would suggest a less
complete punctuation mark than the full stop which the line required.
   40. *cover you*] conceal your flight.
   49. *counterfeit*] the standard term for play-acting or feigning.
   51. *traced*] Most editors modernize as 'tracked'. 'Trace', however, was
the normal word in hunting for the trail or scent left by the quarry. 'Track-
ing' as a term meaning the same thing is not recorded before 1681 (*O.E.D.*
s.v.i.b).

Bel. A wretched creature wounded in these woods
    By beasts; relieve me, if your names be men,   55
    Or I shall perish.
Dion.   This is he, my Lord,
    Upon my soul, that hurt her; 'tis the boy,
    That wicked boy that served her.
Pha. O, thou damned in thy creation!
    What cause couldst thou shape to strike the Princess?   60
Bel. Then I am betrayed.
Dion. Betrayed; no, apprehended.
Bel.   I confess,
    Urge it no more, that big with evil thoughts
    I set upon her, and did make my aim
    Her death. For charity let fall at once   65
    The punishment you mean, and do not load
    This weary flesh with tortures.
Pha. I will know who hired thee to this deed.
Bel. Mine own revenge.
Pha. Revenge, for what?   70
Bel. It pleased her to receive
    Me as her page, and when my fortunes ebbed,
    That men strid o'er them careless, she did shower
    Her welcome graces on me, and did swell
    My fortunes till they overflowed their banks,   75
    Threat'ning the men that crossed 'em; when as swift
    As storms arise at sea she turned her eyes
    To burning suns upon me, and did dry
    The streams she had bestowed, leaving me worse
    And more contemned than other little brooks,   80
    Because I had been great. In short, I knew
    I could not live, and therefore did desire
    To die revenged.

---

60. *cause*] justifiable motive, legal justification. Cf. *Othello*, v. ii. 1.
73. *strid . . . careless*] i.e., the 'river' of his fortunes was so small that men could cross it in a casual stride.
76. *crossed*] (1) stepped over; (2) thwarted.

Pha.   If tortures can be found
          Long as thy natural life, resolve to feel
          The utmost rigour.

                    PHILASTER *creeps out of a bush.*

Cle.   Help to lead him hence.   85
Phi. Turn back, you ravishers of innocence;
          Know ye the price of that you bear away
          So rudely?
Pha. Who's that?
Dion. 'Tis the Lord Philaster.   90
Phi. 'Tis not the treasure of all kings in one,
          The wealth of Tagus, nor the rocks of pearl
          That pave the court of Neptune, can weigh down
          That virtue. It was I that hurt the Princess.
          Place me, some god, upon a pyramis   95
          Higher than hills of earth, and lend a voice
          Loud as your thunder to me, that from thence
          I may discourse to all the under-world
          The worth that dwells in him.
Pha. How's this?   100
Bel. My Lord, some man
          Weary of life, that would be glad to die.
Phi. Leave these untimely courtesies, Bellario.
Bel. Alas, he's mad. Come, will you lead me on?
Phi. By all the oaths that men ought most to keep   105
          And gods do punish most when men do break,
          He touched her not. Take heed, Bellario,
          How thou dost drown the virtues thou hast shown
          With perjury. By all the gods, 'twas I;

104. lead me on] *Q2;* bear me hence *Q1.*

---

92. *Tagus*] a river in central Spain, running from Toledo through Portugal to Lisbon; an apt metaphor to use in Pharamond's presence. It was proverbially associated with gold.

95. *pyramis*] an obelisk. The Egyptian pyramids were widely known from the mid-sixteenth century.

98. *under-world*] the world lying around the obelisk.

You know she stood betwixt me and my right.   110
Pha. Thy own tongue be thy judge.
Cle. It was Philaster.
Dion. Is 't not a brave boy?
     Well, sirs, I fear me we were all deceived.
Phi. Have I no friend here?   115
Dion. Yes.
Phi. Then show it:
     Some good body lend a hand to draw us nearer.
     Would you have tears shed for you when you die?
     Then lay me gently on his neck, that there   120
     I may weep floods and breathe forth my spirit.
                              [*Embraces Bellario.*]
     'Tis not the wealth of Plutus nor the gold
     Locked in the heart of earth can buy away
     This armful from me; this had been a ransom
     To have redeemed the great Augustus Caesar,   125
     Had he been taken. You hard-hearted men,
     More stony than these mountains, can you see
     Such clear pure blood drop and not cut your flesh
     To stop his life, to bind whose bitter wounds
     Queens ought to tear their hair, and with their tears   130
     Bathe 'em? Forgive me, thou that art the wealth
     Of poor Philaster.

          Enter KING, ARETHUSA, *and a* Guard.

King. Is the villain ta'en?
Pha.   Sir, here be two
     Confess the deed; but sure it was Philaster.
Phi. Question it no more, it was.   135
King. The fellow that did fight with him will tell us that.
Are. Ay me, I know he will.

134. sure] *Dyce;* say *Q2;* sute *Q1.*

---

     122. *Plutus*] the god of wealth.
     126. *taken*] captured.
     129. *To . . . life*] i.e., to prevent his life flowing away with his blood.

King. Did not you know him ?

Are. Sir, if it was he, he was disguised.

Phi. I was so. O my stars, that I should live still!   140

King. Thou ambitious fool,

　　　　Thou that hast laid a train for thy own life!

　　　　Now I do mean to do I'll leave to talk.

　　　　Bear them to prison.

Are. Sir, they did plot together to take hence   145

　　　　This harmless life; should it pass unrevenged

　　　　I should to earth go weeping. Grant me then

　　　　(By all the love a father bears his child)

　　　　Their custodies, and that I may appoint

　　　　Their tortures and their deaths.   150

Dion. Death ? Soft; our law will not reach that for this fault.

King. 'Tis granted; take 'em to you with a guard.

　　　　Come, princely Pharamond, this business past

　　　　We may with more security go on

　　　　To your intended match.   155

Cle. I pray that this action lose not Philaster the hearts of the
　　　　people.

Dion. Fear it not; their overwise heads will think it but a
　　　　trick.   *Exeunt omnes.*

---

144. them] *Q1;* him *Q2.*   159. S.D.] *Finis Actus quarti. Exeunt omnes.*
Q2.

---

　　140. *I was so*] Philaster is quibbling on the senses of 'disguised': (1) wearing a disguise; (2) not himself; (3) intoxicated. Cf. *The Virgin Martyr*
(*The Dramatic Works of Thomas Dekker*, ed. F. Bowers, III, 428), III. iii.
133–4: '*Harpax.* I am a Prince disguised. / *Hirc.* Disguised! How! Drunk ?'
The third sense may not be intended here.

　　143. *leave to talk*] give up words.

　　158–9. *a trick*] i.e., on the part of the King to entrap Philaster.

M

Act V

[v. i]

Enter DION, CLEREMONT, *and* THRASILINE.

Thra. Has the King sent for him to death?

Dion. Yes, but the King must know 'tis not in his power to
war with heaven.

Cle. We linger time; the King sent for Philaster and the
headsman an hour ago. 5

Thra. Are all his wounds well?

Dion. All; they were but scratches, but the loss of blood
made him faint.

Cle. We dally, gentlemen.

Thra. Away. 10

Dion. We'll scuffle hard before he perish. *Exeunt.*

[v. ii]

Enter PHILASTER, ARETHUSA, *and* BELLARIO *in prison.*

Are. Nay, faith, Philaster, grieve not; we are well.

Bel. Nay, good my Lord, forbear, we're wondrous well.

Phi. O Arethusa, O Bellario, leave to be kind;
I shall be shot from heaven, as now from earth,
If you continue so. I am a man 5
False to a pair of the most trusty ones
That ever earth bore. Can it bear us all?

v. i.] *Actus Quintus. Scena prima. Q2.*   7. All;] *Colman;* All *Q2.*
v. ii. 0.1. *in prison*] *Q1; not in Q2.*   4. shot] *Q2;* shut *Q1.*

---

v. ii. 3. *leave . . . kind*] stop being kind. Cf. IV. vi. 143.
4. *shot*] expelled (Turner).
7. *bore . . . bear*] a play on 'bear' as (1) give birth to; (2) tolerate, carry as
a burden.

94

Forgive, and leave me. But the King hath sent
To call me to my death; O show it me,
And then forget me; and for thee, my boy,   10
I shall deliver words will mollify
The hearts of beasts to spare thy innocence.

Bel. Alas, my Lord, my life is not a thing
Worthy your noble thoughts; 'tis not a life,
'Tis but a piece of childhood thrown away.   15
Should I outlive you I should then outlive
Virtue and honour, and when that day comes,
If ever I shall close these eyes but once
May I live spotted for my perjury,
And waste by limbs to nothing.   20

Are. And I (the woefull'st maid that ever was,
Forced with my hands to bring my lord to death)
Do by the honour of a virgin swear
To tell no hours beyond it.

Phi.   Make me not hated so.

Are. Come from this prison all joyful to our deaths.   25

Phi. People will tear me when they find you true
To such a wretch as I; I shall die loathed.
Enjoy your kingdoms peaceably whilst I
For ever sleep forgotten with my faults.
Every just servant, every maid in love,   30
Will have a piece of me, if you be true.

Are. My dear Lord, say not so.

Bel.   A piece of you?
He was not born of woman that can cut it
And look on.

---

20. by limbs] *Q2;* by time *Q1;* my limbs *Q3.*   33. woman] *Q1;* women *Q2.*

---

20. *by limbs*] Editors variously adopt Q1's or Q3's readings. The reference is probably to leprosy, the wasting disease which eats at the limbs and leaves its victims to 'live spotted' (l. 19), i.e., diseased.

24. *tell*] count.

30. *just servant*] i.e., faithful lover. Lines 30–1 broadly repeat the sense of ll. 26–7.

32–4. *A piece ... on*] i.e., 'Nobody on earth could cut away a piece of you without blenching.'

Phi.   Take me in tears betwixt you,
For my heart will break with shame and sorrow.   35
Are. Why, 'tis well.
Bel. Lament no more.
Phi.   What would you have done
If you had wronged me basely, and had found
Your life no price compared to mine ? For love, sirs,
Deal with me truly.   40
Bel. 'Twas mistaken, sir.
Phi. Why, if it were ?
Bel. Then, sir, we would have asked your pardon.
Phi. And have hope to enjoy it ?
Are. Enjoy it ? Ay.   45
Phi. Would you indeed ? Be plain.
Bel. We would, my Lord.
Phi. Forgive me then.
Are. So, so.
Bel. 'Tis as it should be now ?   50
Phi. Lead to my death.   *Exeunt.*

[v. iii]
                    Enter KING, DION, CLEREMONT, THRASILINE.

King. Gentlemen, who saw the Prince ?
Cle. So please you, sir, he's gone to see the city
And the new platform, with some gentlemen
Attending on him.

39. Your ... mine ?] *Mason; My ... yours: Q2.*   51. *Exeunt] Q2ᶜ; not*
in Q2ᵘ.

v. iii. 0.1.] *Q1 adds: 'and a guard'.*

---

39. *Your ... mine*] Mason's conjecture makes good sense, though it is
possible to read 'no price' as meaning 'valueless', in which case Q2 might
stand.

v. iii. 2. *city*] Although the setting of the play is Sicily, the citizens are
unquestionably Londoners, and the 'city' identifiable as the City of London.

3. *the new platform*] See Introduction, p. xxvii.

King.   Is the Princess ready
     To bring her prisoner out ?
Thra.   She waits your Grace.   5
King. Tell her we stay.   *Exit* THRASILINE.
Dion. (*Aside*)   King, you may be deceived yet.
     The head you aim at cost more setting on
     Than to be lost so lightly. If it must off,
     Like a wild overflow that soops before him
     A golden stack, and with it shakes down bridges,   10
     Cracks the strong hearts of pines, whose cable roots
     Held out a thousand storms, a thousand thunders,
     And so made mightier takes whole villages
     Upon his back, and in that heat of pride
     Charges strong towns, towers, castles, palaces,   15
     And lays them desolate; so shall thy head,
     Thy noble head, bury the lives of thousands
     That must bleed with thee like a sacrifice
     In thy red ruins.

Enter ARETHUSA, PHILASTER, BELLARIO *in a robe and garland*
                    [*and* THRASILINE].

6. *Exit Thrasiline*] *Q1; not in Q2.*   9. overflow] *Q2ᶜ;* ouer-throw *Q2ᵘ.*
soops] *Q2;* swoops *Langbaine conj.*

---

7. *The head . . . at*] i.e., Philaster's.

cost . . . setting on] more went to his making ('setting on' presupposes
that the King's aim is cutting off).

9. *soops*] a dialect word, 'sweeps'.

10. *stack*] a haystack.

11. *cable*] i.e., anchoring; the term was normally applied to the anchor-
rope of a ship. Cf. Drayton, *The Battle of Agincourt*, l. 370: 'Three as tall
Ships, as e'r did Cable tewe'.

16. *thy head*] i.e., Philaster's.

19.1. Bellario . . . garland] The actors in masques wore richly colourful
robes. To judge from Bellario's rôle as presenter of the masque and the
King's response (ll. 53–5), he was dressed in saffron like Hymen, god of
marriages, who 'sings / His holy numbers over marriage-beds' (41–2). In
Jonson's *Hymenaei* the god was dressed 'in a saffron-coloured robe, his
vnder-vestures white, his socks yellow, a yellow veile of silke on his left
arme, his head crowned with *Roses*, and *Marioram*, in his right hand a
torch of *pine tree*' (Jonson, VII, 210–11).

King. How now, what masque is this?

Bel.   Right royal sir, I should   20
    Sing you an epithalamium of these lovers,
    But having lost my best airs with my fortunes
    And wanting a celestial harp to strike
    This blessèd union on, thus in glad story
    I give you all. These two fair cedar branches,   25
    The noblest of the mountain where they grew
    Straightest and tallest, under whose still shades
    The worthier beasts have made their lairs, and slept
    Free from the Sirian star and the fell thunder-stroke,
    Free from the clouds, when they were big with humour,   30
    And delivered in thousand spouts their issues to the earth;
    O, there was none but silent quiet there!
    Till never-pleasèd Fortune shot up shrubs,
    Base underbrambles to divorce these branches;
    And for a while they did so, and did reign   35
    Over the mountain and choke up his beauty
    With brakes, rude thorns and thistles, till the sun
    Scorched them even to the roots and dried them there;
    And now a gentler gale hath blown again,
    That made these branches meet and twine together,   40
    Never to be divided. The god that sings

26. mountain] *Q2ᶜ;* Mountaines *Q2ᵘ.*   28. lairs] *Q2ᶜ;* baytes *Q2ᵘ.*
29. Sirian] *Q2;* firuer of the *Serian Q1.*   31. delivered] *Q4;* deliuer *Q2.*
41. divided] *Q2;* vnarmde *Q1.*   sings] *Q2ᶜ;* slings *Q2ᵘ.*

---

20. *masque*] a celebratory show or pageant.
21. *epithalamium*] poem written in celebration of a wedding.
22. *my best airs*] (1) my best tunes; (2) my social graces.
24. *story*] i.e., narrative, instead of song.
29. *the Sirian star*] Sirius, in the ascendant in the heat of August and thought to rule over passions and fevers. Q1's addition, being extra-metrical, is possibly an actor's clarification.
30. *clouds . . . big with humour*] moisture-laden rain-clouds. Water was the 'humour' of the clouds, its characteristics including a downward tendency as fire had an upward tendency.
37. *brakes*] undergrowth, clumps of bushes.
41. *The god*] See note to l. 19.1. Bellario's function in this scene as presenter of the marriage celebration is a visual symbol of his rôle as inter-

His holy numbers over marriage-beds
Hath knit their noble hearts, and here they stand
Your children, mighty King; and I have done.

King. How, how?

Are. 　　　　　Sir, if you love it in plain truth　　　　45
(For now there is no masquing in 't), this gentleman,
The prisoner that you gave me, is become
My keeper, and through all the bitter throes
Your jealousies and his ill fate have wrought him,
Thus nobly hath he struggled, and at length　　　　50
Arrived here my dear husband.

King. 　　　　　　　　Your dear husband! Call in
The captain of the citadel; there you shall keep
Your wedding! I'll provide a masque shall make
Your Hymen turn his saffron into a sullen coat,
And sing sad requiems to your departing souls;　　　55
Blood shall put out your torches, and instead
Of gaudy flowers about your wanton necks
An axe shall hang like a prodigious meteor,
Ready to crop your loves' sweets. Hear, you gods:
From this time do I shake all title off　　　　60
Of father to this woman, this base woman;
And what there is of vengeance in a lion
Chafed among dogs or robbed of his dear young,

---

42. numbers] *Q4;* number *Q2.*　　　63. Chafed] *Q1;* Chast *Q2.*

---

mediary and creator of the harmonious union of the lovers. His garland
here, as in Philaster's story of their first meeting (I. ii. 111–36), is an ex-
plicit visual suggestion of his more than human rôle in the play.

48. *throes*] agonies, probably with a reference to the 'throws' of dice;
i.e., fortune.

52. *keep*] (1) celebrate; (2) be enclosed with.

54. *saffron*] yellow, the colour of Hymen's robe. 'Sullen' here means
dark, a colour appropriate to a funeral.

57. *gaudy flowers*] i.e., Bellario's garland.

58. *meteor*] a portent of disaster.

59. *crop*] reap, cut the head off.

63. *Chafed*] A long-s/f error in Q2 ('Chast') has been adopted by some
editors. Q1's word, which also occurs at II. iv. 105, is more appropriate to

The same enforced more terrible, more mighty,
Expect from me.   65
Are. Sir,
By that little life I have left to swear by,
There's nothing that can stir me from myself.
What I have done I have done without repentance,
For death can be no bugbear unto me   70
So long as Pharamond is not my headsman.
Dion. [*Aside*] Sweet peace upon thy soul, thou worthy maid,
Whene'er thou diest; for this time I'll excuse thee,
Or be thy prologue.
Phi.   Sir, let me speak next;
And let my dying words be better with you   75
Than my dull living actions. If you aim
At the dear life of this sweet innocent,
Y' are a tyrant and a savage monster
That feeds upon the blood you gave a life to;
Your memory shall be as foul behind you   80
As you are living, all your better deeds
Shall be in water writ, but this in marble;
No chronicle shall speak you, though your own,
But for the shame of men. No monument
(Though high and big as Pelion) shall be able   85
To cover this base murder; make it rich
With brass, with purest gold and shining jasper,
Like the pyramids; lay on epitaphs

79.] *Q1; not in Q2.*

---

a lion, here meaning 'brought to bay and worried by hounds', than flight
and pursuit by dogs, as Q2's word would have it.
    68.] i.e., 'Nothing will make me abandon my purpose, which is a part
of what I am.'
    70–1.] 'I had rather die by the executioner than lose my maidenhead to
Pharamond.'
    73–4. *I'll ... thee | Or ... prologue*] 'I'll save you from death or else go
first (to death) to announce your coming.'
    82. *in water writ*] i.e., quickly forgotten.
    83. *speak you*] celebrate you.
    85. *Pelion*] a mountain in Greece, symbol of immensity.
    88. *pyramids*] See note to IV. vi. 95.

Such as make great men gods; my little marble
(That only clothes my ashes not my faults)   90
Shall far outshine it. And for after-issues
Think not so madly of the heavenly wisdoms
That they will give you more for your mad rage
To cut off, unless it be some snake, or something
Like yourself, that in his birth shall strangle you.   95
Remember my father, King; there was a fault,
But I forgive it. Let that sin persuade you
To love this lady. If you have a soul,
Think, save her, and be saved. For myself
I have so long expected this glad hour,   100
So languished under you and daily withered,
That by the gods it is a joy to die,
I find a recreation in 't.

Enter a Messenger.

Mess. Where's the King?
King.   Here.
Mess.   Get you to your strength
    And rescue the Prince Pharamond from danger,   105
    He's taken prisoner by the citizens,
    Fearing the Lord Philaster.
Dion. [*Aside*] O brave followers!
    Mutiny, my fine dear countrymen, mutiny!
    Now my brave valiant foremen, show your weapons   110
    In honour of your mistresses!

Enter another Messenger.

96. father,] *Theobald;* father *Q2.*

---

89. *little marble*] small burial urn which 'clothes' (i.e., encloses) his ashes.
91. *for after-issues*] so far as future heirs are concerned.
94. *cut off*] i.e., kill. See note to l. 7.
104. *Get ... strength*] collect your military forces.
107. *Fearing*] fearing for the safety of.
110. *foremen*] senior artisans. See note to l. 164.
weapons] with a sexual quibble.

2 Mess. Arm, arm, arm, arm!

King. A thousand devils take 'em.

Dion. A thousand blessings on 'em.

2 Mess. Arm, O King, the city is in mutiny,   115
    Led by an old grey ruffian, who comes on
    In rescue of the Lord Philaster.

King. Away to the citadel.   *Exeunt* [Messengers] *with* ARETHUSA,
                                   PHILASTER, BELLARIO.
                              I'll see them safe,
    And then cope with these burghers. Let the Guard
    And all the gentlemen give strong attendance. *Exit* KING.   120
                Manent Dion, Cleremont, Thrasiline.

Cle. The city up! This was above our wishes.

Dion. Ay, and the marriage too; by my life this noble lady
    has deceived us all; a plague upon myself, a thousand
    plagues for having such unworthy thoughts of her dear
    honour; O, I could beat myself, or do you beat me and   125
    I'll beat you, for we had all one thought.

Cle. No, no, 'twill but lose time.

Dion. You say true. Are your swords sharp? Well, my dear
    countrymen What-ye-lacks, if you continue and fall not
    back upon the first broken shin I'll have ye chronicled   130
    and chronicled, and cut and chronicled, and all to-be-

---

112. *2 Mess.*] *Turner; Mes. Q2.*   115. *2 Mess.*] *Turner; Mes. Q2.*   118.
S.D.] *so Turner; after* 'Philaster' (*l. 117*) *Q2.*   122. my life] *Q2;* all the
gods *Q1.*

---

119. *burghers*] citizens, usually of foreign cities; here used contemptuously.

120. *give strong attendance*] come in attendance on me in large numbers.

122. *my life*] Turner adopts Q1's reading of this oath, taking it as another
of Q2's very unsystematic expurgations.

129. *What-ye-lacks*] the shopkeeper's cry. Cf. John Earle, *Microcosmo-
graphie* (1628), Character No. 34, A Shopkeeper: 'Hee utters to all men,
though he sels but to a few, and intreats for his owne necessities by asking
others what they lacke.'

131. *cut*] depicted in woodcuts as illustrations. Cf. Jonson, *On Shakespeare's Portrait*, in the First Folio: 'This Figure, that thou here seest
put, / It was for gentle Shakespeare cut.'

praised and sung in sonnets and bathed in new brave
ballads that all tongues shall troll you *in saecula saecu-*
lorum, my kind can-carriers.

Thra. What if a toy take 'em i' th' heels now and they run all   135
away and cry the devil take the hindmost ?

Dion. Then the same devil take the foremost too and souse
him for his breakfast; if they all prove cowards my
curses fly among them and be speeding; may they have
murrains reign to keep the gentlemen at home unbound   140
in easy frieze; may the moths branch their velvets and
their silks only be worn before sore eyes; may their false-
lights undo 'em and discover presses, holes, stains, and
oldness in their stuffs, and make them shop-rid; may

132. bathed] *Q2;* grav'd *Theobald conj.;* bawled *Dyce conj.*

---

132. *sonnets*] technically any short song, not necessarily a fourteen-line
love-sonnet. Here it is used, as is 'bathed', partly for the alliteration.

133. *troll*] sing, especially drinking-songs and ballads.

133–4. in saecula saeculorum] 'for ever and ever'; the final phrase of the
doxology to the Lord's Prayer in the Vulgate.

134. *can-carriers*] carriers of (pewter) beer-cans, possibly with an allusion to the pewter armour they would be wearing. See v. iv. 134.

135. *a toy . . . i' th' heels*] they get an impulse to run away.

137. *souse*] (1) to marinade (for cooking) or to pickle (for preserving);
(2) to beat. The word was also used to describe a hawk swooping on its prey.

139. *speeding*] (1) quick; (2) successful.

140. *murrains*] plagues, especially of cattle. The plague was understandably bad for business, keeping the gentry at home for fear of contagion,
and so needing to wear only 'easy frieze', i.e., cheap wool. In *Ram Alley*
(*Dodsley's Old English Plays,* ed. W. C. Hazlitt, 15 vols., London, 1874–6,
x, 357), one character accuses another: 'yourself / Do never wear but
buckram out of sight: / A flannel waist-coat or a canvas truss, / A shift of
thrift.'

141–2. *may . . . sore eyes*] Branched (patterned) velvet was a current
fashion; silk was of course the most popular rich cloth of all. 'May their
velvet be eaten by moths and only enough silk bought as may be worn for
eye-bandages.'

142–3. *false-lights*] obscured windows, sometimes deliberately darkened
to make examination of the goods difficult. Quomodo the draper in *Michaelmas Term* has two assistants, Shortyard and Falselight, who are said to be
his 'familiar spirits'.

143. *presses*] creases.

144. *make them shop-rid*] an obscure phrase. *O.E.D.*, citing this passage,
glosses it 'worn out by lying in a shop'.

they keep whores and horses, and break, and live mewed   145
up with necks of beef and turnips; may they have many
children and none like the father; may they know no
language but that gibberish they prattle to their parcels,
unless it be the goatish Latin they write in their bonds,
and may they write that false and lose their debts.   150

Enter the KING.

King. Now the vengeance of all the gods confound them;
how they swarm together! What a hum they raise!
Devils choke your wild throats; if a man had need to use
their valours he must pay a brokage for it, and then
bring 'em on and they will fight like sheep. 'Tis Phil-   155
aster, none but Philaster must allay this heat; they will
not hear me speak but fling dirt at me and call me
tyrant. O, run dear friend, and bring the Lord Philaster;
speak him fair, call him Prince, do him all the courtesy
you can, commend me to him. O my wits, my wits!   160

Exit CLEREMONT.

Dion. O my brave countrymen! As I live, I will not buy a pin
out of your walls for this; nay, you shall cozen me and
I'll thank you and send you brawn and bacon and soil
you every long vacation a brace of foremen that at

164. every] *Q1;* euer *Q2.*

---

145. *break*] be ruined.
145–6. *mewed up*] locked up, i.e., in debtors' prison.
148. *parcels*] children, with a suggestion that the citizens view their families quantitatively, as commodities.
149. *goatish*] barbarous, with a suggestion of 'Gothic'.
152. *hum*] (1) a clamour of voices; (2) a buzzing, as of bees.
154. *valours*] (1) courage; (2) velours. 'Paying a brokage' means that they are mercenary, demanding a bribe either to be courageous or for their goods. The term originated with the 'broaching' or covert tapping of wine-casks. Cf. Sylvester, *St Lewis the King* (1615), p. 448: 'after-Judges . . . from Bribes and Brokeage might be warned fair'.
161–2. *a pin . . . walls*] 'I will not buy so much as a pin from anyone but the merchants of the City.'
163–4. *soil you*] fatten for you to eat.
164. *a brace of foremen*] a pair of geese fattened for eating.

Michaelmas shall come up fat and kicking.   165

King. What they will do with this poor Prince the gods know,
 and I fear.

Dion. Why, sir, they'll flay him and make church buckets
 on 's skin to quench rebellion, then clap a rivet in 's
 sconce and hang him up for a sign.   170

Enter CLEREMONT *with* PHILASTER.

King. O worthy sir, forgive me, do not make
 Your miseries and my faults meet together
 To bring a greater danger. Be yourself,
 Still sound amongst diseases. I have wronged you,
 And though I find it last, and beaten to it,   175
 Let first your goodness know it. Calm the people
 And be what you were born to; take your love
 And with her my repentance, all my wishes
 And all my prayers. By the gods, my heart speaks this,
 And if the least fall from me not performed   180
 May I be struck with thunder.

Phi.   Mighty sir,
 I will not do your greatness so much wrong
 As not to make your word truth; free the Princess
 And the poor boy, and let me stand the shock
 Of this mad sea-breach, which I'll either turn   185
 Or perish with it.

King.   Let your own word free them.

Phi. Then thus I take my leave, kissing your hand,
 And hanging on your royal word. Be kingly

---

170. a] *Q1; not in Q2.*   182. your] *Q1;* you *Q2.*

---

168. *church buckets*] fire-fighting buckets made from leather. They were
usually stored in the parish church.

170. *sconce*] pate, the top of his head.

sign] (1) display-board or device hung over a shop or tavern; (2) lesson
or portent.

175. *I find it last*] I am the last to find it.

185. *sea-breach*] flood, breach in a sea-wall. Cf. ll. 9–19.

And be not moved, sir, I shall bring you peace
Or never bring myself back.

King.   All the gods go with thee.   190

Exeunt omnes.

[v. iv]

Enter an old Captain *and* Citizens *with* PHARAMOND.

Cap. Come, my brave myrmidons, let's fall on, let your caps
swarm, my boys, and your nimble tongues forget your
mother gibberish of what-do-you-lack, and set your
mouths ope, children, till your palates fall frighted half a
fathom past the cure of bay-salt and gross pepper, and   5
then cry 'Philaster, brave Philaster!' Let Philaster be
deeper in request, my ding-dongs, my pairs of dear indentures, kings of clubs, than your cold water-camlets or
your paintings spitted with copper; let not your hasty
silks or your branched cloth of bodkin or your tissues,   10
dearly beloved of spiced cake and custards, you Robin

189. you] *Q1;* your *Q2.*

v. iv. 1. your] *Q1;* our *Q2.*   4. ope] *Q1;* Vp *Q2.*   11–12. you ...
Johns] *Theobald;* Your Robin-hoods scarlets and Iohns *Q2.*

---

v. iv. 1. *myrmidons*] faithful followers, originally used of Achilles' war-
riors. *O.E.D.* notes that the term was used chiefly comically at this time.

1–2. *let . . . swarm*] fling up your caps till they look like a swarm of bees.

5. *bay-salt*] sea salt, obtained by evaporation.

gross] coarse; the larger grains of sea salt or coarse pepper would be more
readily identified by the palate than finer-grained spices; the captain demands that their palates be numbed until even these should be unrecog-
nizable.

7. *ding-dongs*] Cockneys, born in sound of the bells of St Mary-le-Bow.

7–8. *indentures*] The mob is largely composed of indentured apprentices.

8. *kings of clubs*] in cards, i.e., as distinct from knaves. Clubs were the
standard weapon of the apprentice bands.

8–10.] 'cold water-camlets': a rich moiré (watered) silk or wool; 'paintings spitted with copper': painted cloth broché with copper thread; 'hasty
silks': silks stiffened with gum, a cheap way of giving a temporary shine
to a fabric; 'branched cloth of bodkin': embroidered gold on silk and gold
cloth. Cf. M. C. Linthicum, *Costume in the Drama of Shakespeare and his
Contemporaries*, Oxford, 1936, pp. 74, 115.

11. *dearly beloved*] (1) my beloved congregation; (2) you who love (spiced,
i.e., currant, cake and custards).

Hoods, Scarlets, and Johns, tie your affections in darkness to your shops; no, dainty duckers, up with your
three-piled spirits, your wrought valours, and let your
uncut cholers make the King feel the measure of your　15
mightiness. Philaster! Cry, my rose-nobles, cry!

All. Philaster, Philaster!

Cap. How do you like this, my Lord Prince? These are mad
boys, I tell you, these are things that will not strike their
top-sails to a foist and let a man of war, an argosy, hull　20
and cry cockles.

Pha. Why, you rude slave, do you know what you do?

Cap. My pretty Prince of puppets, we do know, and give your
Greatness warning that you talk no more such bug's

20. foist and] *This ed.;* Foist. And *Q2;* Foist, / And *Q1.*　　　20–1. hull . . .
cockles] *Q2;* stoope to carry coales *Q1.*

---

12. *Scarlets, and Johns*] i.e., Will Scarlet and Little John, companions of
Robin Hood. The legends were popular citizen reading.

12–13. *in darkness*] See note to v. iii. 142–3.

13. *duckers*] (1) servile head-bobbing tradesmen; (2) duck hunters, i.e.,
of Pharamond.

13–15. *your three-piled . . . measure*] a series of quibbles on mercer's
terms. 'Three-piled' velvet or velours was the best of the pile silks: 'wrought
valour' (velours) suggests intricate workmanship and a show of courage;
'cholers' (Q2 'Collers') plays on collars and choler = anger; and 'measure'
refers to tailors' yardsticks, with a bawdy innuendo rather broader than
the other quibbles.

16. *rose-nobles*] a further quibble on commercial language. Rose-nobles
were coins, value 6s. 8d., originally minted in the reign of Edward III, so
called because of the rose with which they were stamped. The apprentices
are 'rose' or commercial nobles, as distinct from the great nobles.

19–21. *will . . . cockles*] 'will not surrender to a sailing-barge and let
their great warship or merchant ship drift by the shore hawking shellfish'.
To 'hull' meant to ride with the sails furled (*O.E.D.* s.v.2.1: cf. *Richard III*,
IV. iv. 433–9). Argosies were the largest kind of merchant ship. Q1's reading for the last phrase has the same general implication of degrading employment. Savage ('The "Gaping Wounds" in the Text of *Philaster*', *op.
cit.*, p. 455) considers the Q2 reading to be a reference to the shipbuilder's
inability to launch the King's new ship, the *Prince Royal*, on 24 September
1610, and that the Q1 reading is an alteration made at the demand of the
censor. Q2's phrase, however, is a very oblique reference, if it is one, to
the launching of a ship. See Introduction, pp. xxvii and lxxvi.

24–5. *bug's words*] bogeyman's threats. Cf. *A New Way to Pay Old Debts*
III. ii. 306–7: 'Give place to a tatterdemalion? / *Mar.* No bug words, sir.'

words or that soldered crown shall be scratched with a   25
musket; dear Prince Pippin, down with your noble blood
or as I live I'll have you coddled. Let him loose, my
spirits; make us a round ring with your bills, my Hectors,
and let me see what this trim man dares do. Now, sir,
have at you; here I lie, and with this washing blow (do   30
you see, sweet Prince?) I could hulk your Grace and
hang you up cross-legged like a hare at a poulter's, and
do this with this wiper.

Pha. You will not see me murdered, wicked villains?

1 Cit. Yes, indeed will we, sir, we have not seen one for a great   35
while.

Cap. He would have weapons, would he? Give him a broadside, my brave boys, with your pikes, branch me his skin
in flowers like a satin, and between every flower a mortal
cut; your royalty shall ravel; jag him, gentlemen, I'll   40

---

35. for] *Weber;* foe *Q2.*

---

25. *soldered crown*] (1) patched-up emblem of royalty; (2) poulticed head.
26. *musket*] (1) gun; (2) male sparrowhawk.
Pippin] (1) apple grown from seed; (2) Spanish 'pepita', a grain of gold.
27. *coddled*] parboiled or stewed, a term used especially of apples.
28. *make . . . bills*] 'use the hafts of your pikes to clear a circle for fighting
in'. The pike was the weapon of the City Watch.
Hectors] like the hero of Troy. The sense of 'swashbuckling' (cf. 'washing', l. 30) did not clearly develop until after this date. Cf. *O.E.D.* s.v.2.
29. *trim*] an ironic term, 'prettily dressed' (*O.E.D.* s.v.3).
30. *washing*] i.e., swashing, slashing. Cf. *The Staple of News*, v. v. 15:
'I doe confesse a washing blow' (Jonson, v, 377).
31. *hulk*] disembowel, a term from venery. Cf. Turbervile, *Booke of
Venerie* (1575), p. 175: 'Hulke hir (which is to open hir and take out hyr
garbage)'.
32. *poulter's*] i.e., poulterer's.
33. *wiper*] a steel rod for cleaning musket barrels, a pull-through. It bore
a superficial resemblance to a rapier.
34.] The divergence between Q1 and Q2 is almost complete by this line
(see Appendix A), except for occasional resemblances of single words such
as 'golls' (l. 93).
35. *seen one*] i.e., murdered.
37-8. *broadside*] simultaneous attack.
38. *branch*] See note to v. iii. 141-2.
40. *ravel*] become frayed, unstitched.
jag] slash raggedly.

have him cut to the kell, then down the seams. O for a
whip to make him galloon-laces! I'll have a coach-whip.

Pha. O, spare me, gentlemen.

Cap. Hold, hold; the man begins to fear and know himself;
he shall, for this time, only be seeled up with a feather   45
through his nose that he may only see heaven and think
whither he's going. Nay, my beyond-sea sir, we will proclaim you. You would be King: thou tender heir-apparent
to a church-ale, thou slight Prince of single sarcenet,
thou royal ring-tail fit to fly at nothing but poor men's   50
poultry and have every boy beat thee from that too with
his bread and butter.

Pha. Gods keep me from these hell-hounds.

1 Cit. Shall 's geld him, Captain?

Cap. No, you shall spare his dowcets, my dear donsels; as you   55
respect the ladies let them flourish. The curses of a long-
ing woman kills as speedy as a plague, boys.

1 Cit. I'll have a leg, that's certain.

2 Cit. I'll have an arm.

---

41. *kell*] a Northern dialect form, cognate with M.E. 'calla', a caul: the
omentum or membrane covering the intestines. In hunting the 'kell' of a
deer was the part slit open for the assay (see note to IV. ii. 10).

42. *galloon-laces*] binding or trimming tape; lace edging.

I'll have] i.e., give me.

45. *seeled up*] sewn, as in falconry, when a bird would have its eyelids
stitched with a thread or feather so that its range of vision was limited to
downwards, a device employed both to get it used to being hooded and to
ensure that it did not fly out of sight of its handler. The image of Pharamond being tamed like a hawk is picked up again in ll. 118–22.

48–9. *heir-apparent ... church-ale*] Church-ales (see *O.E.D.*) or parish
malt-festivals had a notoriously licentious reputation. The captain is calling Pharamond a bastard.

49. *single sarcenet*] a very light taffeta silk. Sarcenet was usually worn
doubled, since single sarcenet was one of the lightest materials made.

50. *ring-tail*] a minor bird of prey, a kind of buzzard. Latham's *Falconry*
(1618) does not consider it a bird for hawking with.

51–2. *with ... butter*] i.e., by pelting him with scraps.

55. *donsels*] esquires (Spanish), a common name for would-be chivalric
heroes; the name of the hero of a Peninsula romance popular with citizens
and apprentices, part of which was translated by Anthony Mundy as *The
Mirror of Knighthood*. It was burlesqued in *The Knight of the Burning Pestle*.

N

3 Cit. I'll have his nose and at mine own charge build a college   60
and clap 't upon the gate.

4 Cit. I'll have his little gut to string a kit with, for certainly a
royal gut will sound like silver.

Pha. Would they were in thy belly and I past my pain once.

5 Cit. Good Captain, let me have his liver to feed ferrets.   65

Cap. Who will have parcels else ? Speak.

Pha. Good gods consider me, I shall be tortured.

1 Cit. Captain, I'll give you the trimming of your two-hand
sword and let me have his skin to make false scabbards.

2 Cit. He had no horns, sir, had he ?   70

Cap. No, sir, he's a pollard; what wouldst thou do with horns ?

2 Cit. O, if he had had, I would have made rare hafts and
whistles of 'em; but his shin-bones if they be sound shall
serve me.

Enter PHILASTER.

All. Long live Philaster, the brave Prince Philaster!   75

Phi. I thank you, gentlemen. But why are these
Rude weapons brought abroad, to teach your hands
Uncivil trades ?

Cap.   My royal Rosicleer,
We are thy myrmidons, thy Guard, thy roarers,
And when thy noble body is in durance   80
Thus do we clap our musty morions on

60–1.] a reference to Brasenose College, Oxford, the name of which was
the occasion of several jokes.

62. *kit*] cittern, a kind of small guitar.

66. *parcels*] portions. See v. iii. 148.

69. *and*] i.e., if you will. The trimming on the captain's sword will be
provided from Pharamond's skin.

71. *pollard*] a polled or hornless stag.

78. *Rosicleer*] hero of the Peninsula romance known in English as *The
Mirror of Knighthood*, brother of donsel del Phebo, its eponymous hero.
See note to l. 55.

79. *myrmidons*] See note to v. iv. 1.

roarers] rioters; cf. Massinger, *The Renegado*, I. iii. 286: 'O strange! /
A lady to turn roarer and break glasses!'

81. *morions*] round iron helmets, the headgear of the ordinary soldier
through the sixteenth century.

And trace the streets in terror. Is it peace,
Thou Mars of men ? Is the King sociable
And bids thee live ? Art thou above thy foemen
And free as Phoebus ? Speak. If not, this stand   85
Of royal blood shall be a-broach, a-tilt, and run
Even to the lees of honour.

Phi. Hold and be satisfied. I am myself,
Free as my thoughts are; by the gods I am.

Cap. Art thou the dainty darling of the King ?   90
Art thou the Hylas to our Hercules ?
Do the lords bow and the regarded scarlets
Kiss their gummed golls and cry 'We are your servants' ?
Is the Court navigable and the presence stuck
With flags of friendship ? If not, we are thy castle,   95
And this man sleeps.

Phi. I am what I do desire to be, your friend;
I am what I was born to be, your Prince.

Pha. Sir, there is some humanity in you,
You have a noble soul. Forget my name   100
And know my misery, set me safe aboard
From these wild cannibals and as I live
I'll quit this land for ever. There is nothing,
Perpetual prisonment, cold, hunger, sickness

---

82. *trace*] hunt, pursue the quarry.

83. *sociable*] disposed to be friendly (*O.E.D.* s.v.2).

85. *Phoebus*] i.e., the sun; probably a confusion for donsel del Phebo. See notes to ll. 55 and 78.

stand] a cask set on its end, or its contents.

86–7. *a-broach ... honour*] 'opened, tipped up, and emptied to the dregs of his honour'.

91. *the Hylas ... Hercules*] a phrase in apposition to the preceding line, the King being described sarcastically as the archetypal man of action.

92–3.] Scarlet was the colour worn by court officials. 'Golls' is a slang term for fists. 'Do the respected officers of the Crown kiss their perfumed fists in allegiance ?'

94–5.] The image is of the court as a harbour, with the King ('the presence') as the welcoming flagship. 'Castle' in this context probably means 'warship'. Cf. *O.E.D.* 'castle', s.v.II.5.

96. *sleeps*] i.e., will be killed.

Of all sorts, of all dangers, and all together,   105
The worst company of the worst men, madness, age,
To be as many creatures as a woman,
And do as all they do, nay to despair,
But I would rather make it a new nature
And live with all these than endure one hour   110
Amongst these wild dogs.

Phi. I do pity you. Friends, discharge your fears,
Deliver me the Prince. I'll warrant you
I shall be old enough to find my safety.

3 Cit. Good sir, take heed he does not hurt you; he's a fierce   115
man, I can tell you, sir.

Cap. Prince, by your leave I'll have a surcingle
And make you like a hawk.   [*Pharamond*] *strives.*

Phi. Away, away, there is no danger in him.
Alas, he had rather sleep to shake his fit off;   120
Look you, friends, how gently he leads. Upon my word
He's tame enough, he needs no further watching.
Good my friends, go to your houses,
And by me have your pardons and my love,
And know there shall be nothing in my power   125
You may deserve but you shall have your wishes.
To give you more thanks were to flatter you.
Continue still your love, and for an earnest

---

105. Of ... dangers] *Q2;* All dangers of all sorts *Theobald conj.*   118.
make] *Q2;* male *Dyce.*   *Pharamond*] *This ed.; He Q2.*   strives] *Q7;*
strires Q2; stirres Q3.   122. needs] *Q9;* neede *Q2.*

---

114. *old enough*] presumably to win his inheritance.
117. *surcingle*] a girth on a horse, reaching under the belly to fasten the
saddle. It was also used of a strap fastening a package and of the belt-strap
for a cassock. The general sense of a strap around a large body is clear.
118. *make*] train or tame. Dyce adopted the Q8 misprint 'male', which
happens also to be a term from falconry, meaning to pinion or wrap a bird
in cloth, a practice used when it needed quietening for an operation or any
sort of handling; but the Q2 text is perfectly sound. Turbervile writes of
the pleasure it gives 'To make and man ... a haggard Hawke'.
121. *how ... leads*] (1) how tamely he is led; (2) what a noble leader he is.
122. *watching*] keeping awake, a technique used in training hawks.
128. *an earnest*] a part-payment.

Drink this.   *Gives 'em his purse.*

All. Long mayst thou live, brave Prince, brave Prince, brave   130
    Prince!   *Exeunt* PHILASTER *and* PHARAMOND.

Cap. Go thy ways, thou art the King of courtesy. Fall off
    again, my sweet youths, come, and every man trace to his
    house again and hang his pewter up, then to the tavern
    and bring your wives in muffs; we will have music, and   135
    the red grape shall make us dance and rise, boys.   *Exeunt.*

[V. v]

Enter KING, ARETHUSA, GALATEA, MEGRA, CLEREMONT,
    DION, THRASILINE, BELLARIO, *and* Attendants.

King. Is it appeased?
Dion. Sir, all is quiet as the dead of night,
    As peaceable as sleep. My Lord Philaster
    Brings on the Prince himself.
King.   Kind gentlemen,
    I will not break the least word I have given   5
    In promise to him; I have heaped a world

---

129. *Gives ... purse*] *Q1; not in Q2.*

v. v. 0.2. Attendants] *Q4; attendance Q2.*   2. the] *Theobald; this Q2.*
4. gentlemen] *Q2; gentleman Theobald conj.*

---

129. Gives 'em his purse] Q1's text is widely variant from Q2's at this
point, but the stage direction at the conclusion of its version of the citizen
scene is appropriate.
    132. *Fall off*] i.e., fall out, dismiss.
    134. *pewter*] cheap armour. The best armour was of course made of steel.
See note to v. iii. 134.
    135. *muffs*] Muffs were a winter fashion only recently imported from
Holland. Jonson refers to them in *Cynthia's Revels* (1599), II. ii. 47.

    v. v. 2. *the*] There is no indication besides Q2's 'this' that the final
scene is played at night, and there seems to be no reason why it should be.
    4. *Brings on ... himself*] accompanies the Prince in person.
    gentlemen] I see no reason to adopt Theobald's conjecture, which would
make the King refer to Philaster. He is in conversation with the gentlemen
led by Dion, who were witnesses of the promise he made to Philaster, and
who are 'kind' in the reassuring news they bring.

Of grief upon his head which yet I hope
To wash away.

Enter PHILASTER *and* PHARAMOND.

Cle.   My Lord is come.
King. [*embraces Philaster*]   My son,
Blessed be the time that I have leave to call
Such virtue mine; now thou art in mine arms   10
Methinks I have a salve unto my breast
For all the stings that dwell there. Streams of grief
That I have wronged thee and as much of joy
That I repent it issue from mine eyes.
Let them appease thee. Take thy right, take her;   15
She is thy right too; and forget to urge
My vexèd soul with that I did before.
Phi. Sir, it is blotted from my memory,
Past and forgotten. For you, Prince of Spain,
Whom I have thus redeemed, you have full leave   20
To make an honourable voyage home.
And if you would go furnished to your realm
With fair provision, I do see a lady
Methinks would gladly bear you company;
How like you this piece?
Meg.   Sir, he likes it well,   25
For he hath tried it and hath found it worth
His princely liking. We were ta'en abed;
I know your meaning. I am not the first
That nature taught to seek a fellow forth;
Can shame remain perpetually in me   30
And not in others? Or have princes salves
To cure ill names, that meaner people want?
Phi. What mean you?

13. wronged] *Theobald;* wrought *Q2.*

---

15. *thy right*] i.e., to the kingdom of Sicily.
16. *urge*] prompt, remind.
31-2. *salves / To . . . names*] Cleremont (IV. i. 37-46) claimed that Megra
herself had such salves from the King.

Meg.   You must get another ship
        To bear the Princess and her boy together.
Dion. How now?   35
Meg. Others took me and I took her and him.
        At that, all women may be ta'en some time.
        Ship us all four, my Lord, we can endure
        Weather and wind alike.
King. Clear thou thyself, or know not me for father.   40
Are. This earth,
        How false it is! What means is left for me
        To clear myself? It lies in your belief.
        My lords, believe me and let all things else
        Struggle together to dishonour me.   45
Bel. O, stop your ears, great King, that I may speak
        As freedom would: then I will call this lady
        As base as are her actions. Hear me, sir;
        Believe your heated blood when it rebels
        Against your reason sooner than this lady.   50
Meg. By this good light, he bears it handsomely.
Phi. This lady! I will sooner trust the wind
        With feathers or the troubled sea with pearl
        Than her with anything. Believe her not!
        Why, think you if I did believe her words   55
        I would outlive 'em? Honour cannot take
        Revenge on you; then what were to be known
        But death?
King.   Forget her, sir, since all is knit
        Between us. But I must request of you
        One favour, and will sadly be denied.   60
Phi. Command whate'er it be.
King. Swear to be true to what you promise.
Phi. By the powers above,

42-3. me / ... myself?] *Q3;* me? / ... my selfe: *Q2.*

---

37. *At that*] i.e., at fornication.
51. *bears it handsomely*] puts a bold face on his deceit.
60. *will ... denied*] It will be a serious matter if it is not granted.

Let it not be the death of her or him
And it is granted.
King.   Bear away that boy   65
To torture. I will have her cleared or buried.
Phi. O, let me call my word back; worthy sir,
Ask something else; bury my life and right
In one poor grave, but do not take away
My life and fame at once.   70
King. Away with him; it stands irrevocable.
Phi. Turn all your eyes on me! Here stands a man,
The falsest and the basest of this world.
Set swords against this breast, some honest man,
For I have lived till I am pitièd.   75
My former deeds were hateful, but this last
Is pitiful, for I unwillingly
Have given the dear preserver of my life
Unto his torture. Is it in the power
Of flesh and blood to carry this, and live?   80
                                  Offers to kill himself.
Are. Dear sir, be patient yet. O, stay that hand!
King. Sirs, strip that boy.
Dion. Come, sir, your tender flesh will tire your constancy.
Bel. O, kill me, gentlemen!
Dion. No. Help, sirs.   85
Bel. Will you torture me?
King. Haste there, why stay you?
Bel. Then I shall not break my vow,

83. tire] *Q2;* trie *Q3.*

77. *pitiful*] i.e., because this cruelty, unlike the others, is performed against his will.
81. *patient yet*] See Introduction, p. xxxiv.
83. *tire*] (1) be sufficient clothing for; (2) make weary (and bring to an end). Most editors, missing the quibble, adopt Q3's 'trie'. Cf. Marston, *The Dutch Courtesan,* v. iii. 47–8: 'with her own vain strivings / See here she's tired', and *Cymbeline,* III. vi. 2.
85. *Help, sirs*] It is theatrically necessary to the dénouement that Dion should be the most officious in manhandling Bellario.

You know, just gods, though I discover all.
King. How's that ? Will he confess ?   90
Dion. Sir, so he says.
King. Speak then.
Bel.   Great King, if you command
  This lord to talk with me alone, my tongue,
  Urged by my heart, shall utter all the thoughts
  My youth hath known, and stranger thing than these   95
  You hear not often.
King.   Walk aside with him.

  [Dion and Bellario walk apart.]

Dion. Why speak'st thou not ?
Bel. Know you this face, my Lord ?
Dion. No.
Bel. Have you not seen it, nor the like ?   100
Dion. Yes, I have seen the like, but readily I know not where.
Bel. I have been often told
  In Court of one Euphasia, a lady
  And daughter to you, betwixt whom and me
  They that would flatter my bad face would swear   105
  There was such strange resemblance that we two
  Could not be known asunder, dressed alike.
Dion. By heaven, and so there is.
Bel.   For her fair sake
  Who now doth spend the spring-time of her life
  In holy pilgrimage, move to the King   110
  That I may scape this torture.
Dion.   But thou speak'st
  As like Euphrasia as thou dost look.
  How came it to thy knowledge that she lives
  In pilgrimage ?

105.] *Theobald;* (They ... sweare) *Q2.*

---

89. *discover*] disclose; probably with a visual connotation. See note to
l. 119.
110. *holy pilgrimage*] See I. i. 322.
move to] urge it upon.

Bel.   I know it not, my Lord;
         But I have heard it and do scarce believe it.   115
Dion. O, my shame, is 't possible ? Draw near
         That I may gaze upon thee. Art thou she,
         Or else her murderer ? Where wert thou born ?
Bel. In Syracusa.
Dion.   What's thy name ?
Bel.   Euphrasia.
Dion. O, 'tis just, 'tis she.   120
         Now I do know thee. O that thou hadst died
         And I had never seen thee nor my shame.
         How shall I own thee ? Shall this tongue of mine
         E'er call thee daughter more ?
Bel. Would I had died indeed. I wish it too,   125
         And so must have done by vow, ere published
         What I have told, but that there was no means
         To hide it longer. Yet I joy in this,
         The Princess is all clear.
King.   What, have you done ?
Dion. All's discovered.
Phi.   Why then hold you me ?   130
         All is discovered. Pray you let me go.
                                    He offers to stab himself.
King. Stay him.
Are.   What is discovered ?

---

118. *her murderer*] 'It was the received opinion, in some barbarous coun-
tries, that the murderer was to inherit the qualities and shape of the person
he destroyed' (Mason).

119. *Syracusa*] Syracuse, the coastal city in Sicily near which is Arethusa's well. Q1 at the comparable point in its version of the last scene adds
a stage direction: '*Kneeles to* LEON *and discovers her haire*', which may
have been derived from a memory of the play as performed.

Euphrasia] the Greek meaning of this name is, appropriately, 'mind-
gladdening'.

120. *just*] exactly right, with an echo of the 'secret justice of the gods'
(I. ii. 103).

123. *own*] admit parenthood to.

129. *clear*] innocent. Cf. l. 66.

Dion.   Why, my shame.
It is a woman; let her speak the rest.
Phi. How? That again.
Dion.   It is a woman.
Phi. Blessed be you powers that favour innocence!   135
King. Lay hold upon that lady.   [*Megra is seized.*]
Phi. It is a woman, sir! Hark, gentlemen,
It is a woman! Arethusa, take
My soul into thy breast that would be gone
With joy. It is a woman! Thou art fair   140
And virtuous still to ages in despite of malice.
King. Speak you, where lies his shame?
Bel. I am his daughter.
Phi. The gods are just.
Dion. I dare accuse none, but before you two,   145
The virtue of our age, I bend my knee
For mercy.   [*Kneels.*]
Phi.   [*Raising him*] Take it freely, for I know
Though what thou didst were undiscreetly done
'Twas meant well.
Are.   And for me,
I have a power to pardon sins as oft   150
As any man has power to wrong me.
Cle. Noble and worthy.
Phi.   But, Bellario
(For I must call thee still so), tell me why
Thou didst conceal thy sex. It was a fault,
A fault, Bellario, though thy other deeds   155
Of truth outweighed it; all these jealousies
Had flown to nothing if thou hadst discovered
What now we know.
Bel.   My father oft would speak
Your worth and virtue, and I as did grow
More and more apprehensive I did thirst   160

---

141. *to ages*] i.e., for all ages to come.
160. *apprehensive*] capable of comprehending.

To see the man so raised. But yet all this
Was but a maiden-longing, to be lost
As soon as found; till sitting in my window,
Printing my thoughts in lawn, I saw a god,
I thought (but it was you), enter our gates.   165
My blood flew out and back again as fast
As I had puffed it forth and sucked it in
Like breath; then was I called away in haste
To entertain you. Never was a man,
Heaved from a sheep-cote to a sceptre, raised   170
So high in thoughts as I; you left a kiss
Upon these lips then which I mean to keep
From you for ever; I did hear you talk
Far above singing. After you were gone
I grew acquainted with my heart, and searched   175
What stirred it so; alas, I found it love,
Yet far from lust, for could I but have lived
In presence of you I had had my end.
For this I did delude my noble father
With a feigned pilgrimage, and dressed myself   180
In habit of a boy; and for I knew
My birth no match for you I was past hope
Of having you; and understanding well
That when I made discovery of my sex
I could not stay with you, I made a vow,   185
By all the most religious things a maid
Could call together, never to be known

---

161. raised] *Q2;* prais'd *Langbaine conj.*   170. sheep-cote ... sceptre,]
Langbaine; sheepe-coate, ... Scepter *Q2.*   177. could I] *Q3;* I could
Q2.

---

164. *Printing ... lawn*] embroidering. In *The Maid's Tragedy,* II. ii.
39–78, the forlorn Aspatia spends some time commenting on her maids'
versions in tapestry of her lost love.

170. *from ... sceptre*] Tamburlaine rose from being a Scythian shepherd
till his rule stretched through Turkey as far as North Africa.

174. *Far above singing*] i.e., 'your speaking voice was far superior to any
singing.'

178. *my end*] all I could wish for.

Whilst there was hope to hide me from men's eyes
For other than I seemed, that I might ever
Abide with you. Then sat I by the fount,   190
Where first you took me up.

King.   Search out a match
Within our kingdom, where and when thou wilt,
And I will pay thy dowry; and thyself
Wilt well deserve him.

Bel.   Never, sir, will I
Marry; it is a thing within my vow;   195
But if I may have leave to serve the Princess,
To see the virtues of her lord and her,
I shall have hope to live.

Are.   I, Philaster,
Cannot be jealous, though you had a lady
Dressed like a page to serve you; nor will I   200
Suspect her living here. Come, live with me;
Live free as I do. She that loves my lord,
Cursed be the wife that hates her.

Phi. I grieve such virtue should be laid in earth
Without an heir. Hear me, my royal father: 205
Wrong not the freedom of our souls so much
To think to take revenge of that base woman;
Her malice cannot hurt us. Set her free
As she was born, saving from shame and sin.

King. Set her at liberty. But leave the Court;   210
This is no place for such. You, Pharamond,
Shall have free passage, and a conduct home
Worthy so great a Prince. When you come there
Remember 'twas your faults that lost you her
And not my purposed will.

194–5. *Never . . . I | Marry*] In Q1 Bellario is married to Thrasiline and
Galatea to Cleremont.

198. *I, Philaster*] i.e., unlike her husband.

201. *Suspect her living here*] be suspicious of her in the future when she
continues in her service (cf. l. 196).

209. *saving*] except.

Pha.   I do confess,   215
     Renownèd sir.
King. Last, join your hands in one. Enjoy, Philaster,
     This kingdom, which is yours, and after me
     Whatever I call mine. My blessing on you;
     All happy hours be at your marriage-joys   220
     That you may grow yourselves over all lands
     And live to see your plenteous branches spring
     Wherever there is sun. Let Princes learn
     By this to rule the passions of their blood,
     For what heaven wills can never be withstood.   225
                                        [*Exeunt omnes.*]

222. live] *Q6;* like *Q2.*

221-3.] an extension of Bellario's cedar image of v. iii. 25-41. The cedar
was the king of trees. A similar use of the same image is in *Cymbeline,*
v. v. 451-6.
221. *yourselves*] i.e., your qualities.
224. *blood*] See note to II. ii. 104.

The Variant Sections of QI

The text that follows reprints the variant sections at the beginning and end of QI *Philaster*. It follows the line arrangements of the QI text even in sections of prose; the Elizabethan traditions of using initial v and medial u for u and v, and of using i for j, have been retained, but long s has been silently replaced by the short form. A few minor compositorial errors have been silently corrected. Line-numbering follows the lineation of QI, counting stage directions as well as the text itself. Each section is numbered separately from the beginning of the passage quoted.

The Actors Names.

KING of Cecely
ARATHVSA, the Princesse.
PHYLASTER.
PHARAMONT, a Spanish Prince,
LEON, a Lord.
GLEREMON ⎫
TRASILIN ⎭ Two Noble Gentlemen.
BELLARIO a Page, LEONS daughter.
CALLATEA, a Lady of Honor.
MEGRA, another Lady.
A Waiting Gentlewoman.
Two Woodmen.
A Countrey Gallant.
An old Captaine.
And Souldiers.
A Messenger.

Actus I. *Scœn*. I.

Enter at seuerall doores Lord LYON, TRASILINE *followes him,*
                    CLERIMON *meetes them.*

TRASILINE. Well ore tane my Lord.
LYON. Noble friend welcome, and see who encoun-   [5]
    ters vs, honourable good *Clerimon.*
CLE. My good Lord *Lyon,* most happily met wor-
    thy *Trasiline,*
    Come gallants, whats the newes,
    the season affoords vs variety,   [10]
    the nouilsts of our time runnes on heapes,
    to glut their itching eares with airie sounds,
    trotting to'th burse; and in the Temple walke
    with greater zeale to heare a nouall lye,
    then a pyous Anthum tho chanted by Cherubins.   [15]
TRAS. True Sir:
    and holds set counsels, to vent their braine sicke opinions
    with presagements what all states shall designe.
CLE. Thats as their intelligence serues.
LYON. And that shall serue as long as inuention lastes,   [20]
    there dreames they relate, as spoke from Oracles,
    or if the gods should hold a synod, and make them their secritaries,
    they will diuine and prophecie too: but come and speake your
    thoughts of the intended marriage with the Spanish Prince,   [B1v]
    He is come you see, and brauely entertainde.   [25]
TRAS. Hee is so, but not married yet.
CLE. But like to be, and shall haue in dowry with the Princesse
    this Kingdome of *Cycele.*
LEON. Soft and faire, there is more will forbid the baines, then
    say amen to the marriage: though the King vsurped the Kingdome,   [30]
    during the non-age of the Prince *Phylaster,* hee must not thinke to
    bereaue him of it quite; hee is now come to yeares to claime the
    Crowne.
TRA. And lose his head i'the asking.
LEON. A diadem worn by a headlesse King wold be wonderous,   [35]
    Phylaster is too weake in power.
CLE. He hath many friends.
LEON. And few helpers.
TRA. The people loue him.
LEON. I grant it, that the King knowes too well,   [40]
    And makes this Contract to make his faction strong:
    Whats a giddy-headed multitude,

125

That's not Disciplinde nor trainde vp in Armes,
To be trusted vnto ? No, he that will
Bandy for a Monarchie, must prouide   [45]
Braue marshall troopes with resolution armde,
To stand the shock of bloudy doubtfull warre,
Not danted though disastrous Fate doth frowne,
And spit all spightfull fury in their face :
Defying horror in her vgliest forme,   [50]
And growes more valiant, the more danger threats ;
Or let leane famine her affliction send,
Whose pining plagues a second hel doth bring,
Thei'le hold their courage in her height of spleene,
Till valour win plenty to supply them,   [55]
What thinke ye, would yer feast-hunting Citizens
Indure this ?
TRA. No sir, a faire march a mile out of town that their wiues may
     bring them their dinners, is the hottest seruice that they
     are trained vp to.   [60]
CLE. I could wish their experience answered their loues,   [B2ʳ]
     Then should the much too much wrongd *Phylaster*,
     Possesse his right in spight of Don and the diuell.
TRA. My heart is with your wishes.
LEON. And so is mine,   [65]
     And so should all that loues their true borne Prince,
     Then let vs ioyne our Forces with our mindes,
     In whats our power to right this wronged Lord,
     And watch aduantage as best may fit the time
     To stir the murmuring people vp,   [70]
     Who is already possest with his wrongs,
     And easily would in rebellion rise,
     Which full well the King doth both know and feare,
     But first our seruice wee'le proffer to the Prince,
     And set our proiects as he accepts of vs ;   [75]
     But husht, the King is comming.
                              sound musicke within.

Enter the King, PHARAMONT, *the Princesse, the Lady* GALLA-
TEA, *the Lady* MEGRA, *a Gentlewoman, with Lords attending,*
the King takes his seate.   [80]

KING. Faire Prince,
     Since heauens great guider furthers our intents,
     And brought you with safety here to arriue
     Within our Kingdome and Court of *Cycele*,
     We bid you most welcome, Princely *Pharamont*,   [85]
     And that our Kingly bounty shall confirme,
     Euen whilst the Heauens hold so propitious aspect
     Wee'le crowne your wisht desires (with our owne)
     Lend me your hand sweet Prince, hereby enioy
     A full fruition of your best contents,   [90]

The interest I hold I doe possesse you with,
Onely a fathers care, and prayers retaine,
That heauen may heape on blessings, take her Prince,
A sweeter Mistrisse then the offered Language of any dame,

[*The texts begin to correspond with this line, the last of B2ʳ in Q1, the
eleventh of B2ᵛ (I. i. 105) in Q2.*
The texts diverge again increasingly from the beginning of v. iv *(I2ᵛ in
Q1, K2ᵛ in Q2). From* v. iv. 18, *the line in the text proper which corresponds with the first line below, the Q1 text diverges rapidly from Q2, until
there are only occasional words echoing the substantive text in* v. iv, *and no
correspondences in* v. v.]

CAP. How doe you like this, my Lord prisoner ?   [I2ᵛ]
    These are mad boyes I can tell you,
    These bee things that will not strike top-sayle to a Foyst,
    And let a Man of warre, an Argosea,
    Stoope to carry coales.   [5]
PHAR. Why, you damn'd slaues, doe you know who I am ?
CAP. Yes, my pretie Prince of puppits, we do know, and giue you
    gentle warning, you talke no more such bugs words, lest that sod-
    den Crowne should be scracht with a musket; deare Prince pip-   [I3ʳ]
    pin, I'le haue you codled, let him loose my spirits, and make a ring [10]
    with your bils my hearts: Now let mee see what this braue man
    dares doe: note sir, haue at you with this washing blow, here I lie,
    doe you huffe sweete Prince ? I could hock your grace, and hang
    you crosse leg'd, like a Hare at a Poulters stall; and do thus.
PHAR. Gentlemen, honest Gentlemen—   [15]
1 SOVL. A speakes treason Captaine, shal's knock him downe ?
CAP. Hold, I say.
2 SOVL. Good Captaine let me haue one mal at's mazard, I feele
    my stomacke strangely prouoked to bee at his Spanish pot-nowle,
    shal's kill him ?   [20]
OMNES. I, kill him, kill him.
CAP. Againe I say hold.
3 SOVL. O how ranke he lookes, sweete Captaine let's geld him,
    and send his dowsets for a dish to the Burdello.
4 SOVL. No, let's rather sell them to some woman Chymist, that   [25]
    extractions, shee might draw an excellent prouocative oyle from
    vseth them, that might be very vsefull.

CAP. You see, my scuruy Don, how precious you are in esteem a-
mongst vs, had you not beene better kept at home, I thinke you
had: must you needes come amongst us, to haue your saffron hide   [30]
taw'd as wee intend it: My Don, *Phylaster* must suffer death to
satisfie your melancholly spleene, he must my Don, he must; but we
your Physitians, hold it fit that you bleede for it: Come my robu-
sticks, my braue regiment of rattle makers, let's cal a common cor-
nuted counsell, and like graue Senators, beare vp our brancht   [35]
crests, in sitting upon the seuerall tortures we shall put him to, and
with as little sense as may be, put your wils in execution.

SOME CRIES. Burne him, burne him.

OTHERS. Hang him, hang him.   *Enter* PHYLASTER.

CAP. No, rather let's carbinade his cods-head, and cut him to col-   [40]
lops: shall I begin?

PHI. Stay your furies my louing Countrimen.

OMNES. *Phylaster is come, Phylaster, Phylaster.*

CAP. My porcupines of spite, make roome I say, that I may salute
my braue Prince: and is Prince *Phylaster* at liberty?   [45]

PHI. I am, most louing countrimen.   [I3ᵛ]

CAP. Then giue me thy Princely goll, which thus I kisse, to whom
I crouch and bow; But see my royall sparke, this head-strong
swarme that follow me humming like a master Bee, haue I led forth
their Hiues, and being on wing, and in our heady flight, haue seazed   [50]
him shall suffer for thy wrongs.

OMNES. I, I, let's kill him, kill him.

PHI. But heare me, Countrimen.

CAP. Heare the Prince, I say, heare *Phylaster.*

OMNES. I, I, heare the Prince, heare the Prince.   [55]

PHIL. My comming is to giue you thankes, my deere Countrimen,
whose powerfull sway hath curb'd the prossecuting fury of my
foes.

OMNES. We will curb vm, we will curb vm.

PHI. I finde you will,   [60]
But if my intrest in your loues be such,
As the world takes notice of, Let me craue
You would deliuer *Pharamont* to my hand,
And from me accept this   *Giues vm his purse.*
Testimonie of my loue.   [65]
Which is but a pittance of those ample thankes,
Which shall redowne with showred courtesies.

CAP. Take him to thee braue Prince, and we thy bounty thanke-
fully accept, and will drinke thy health, thy perpetuall health my
Prince, whilst memory lasts amongst vs, we are thy Mermidons, my   [70]
Achillis: we are those will follow thee, and in thy seruice will scowre
our rusty murins and our bill-bow-blades, most noble *Phylaster*,
we will: Come my rowtists let's retyer till occasion calls vs to attend the noble *Phylaster.*

OMNES. *Phylaster, Phylaster, Phylaster.*   [75]

Exit CAPTAINE, *and Citizens.*

PHAR. Worthy sir, I owe you a life,
For but your selfe theres nought could haue preuail'd.
PHI. Tis the least of seruice that I owe the King,
Who was carefull to preserue ye.   *Exit.* [80]

Enter LEON, TRASILINE, *and* CLERIMON.

TRA. I euer thought the boy was honest.
LEON. Well, tis a braue boy Gentlemen.   [I4ʳ]
CLE. Yet you'ld not beleeue this.
LEON. A plague on my forwardnesse, what a villaine was I, to [85]
wrong vm so; a mischiefe on my muddy braines, was I mad?
TRA. A little frantick in your rash attempt, but that was your loue
to *Phylaster,* sir.
LEON. A pox on such loue, haue you any hope my countinance
will ere serue me to looke on them?   [90]
CLE. O very well Sir.
LEON. Very ill Sir, vds death, I could beate out my braines, or
hang my selfe in reuenge.
CLE. There would be little gotten by it, ene keepe you as ye are.
LEON. An excellent boy, Gentlemen beleeue it, harke the King [95]
is comming,   *Cornets sounds.*

Enter the King, Princesse, GALLATEA, MEGRA, BELLARIO,
a Gentlewoman, and other attendants.

K. No newes of his returne,
Will not this rable multitude be appeas'd?   [100]
I feare their outrage, lest it should extend
With dangering of *Pharamonts* life.

Enter PHILASTER *with* PHARAMONT.

LEON. See Sir, *Phylaster* is return'd.
PHI. Royall Sir,   [105]
Receiue into your bosome your desired peace,
Those discontented mutineares be appeasde,
And this forraigne Prince in safety.
K. How happie am I in thee *Phylaster*?
Whose excellent vertues begets a world of loue,   [110]
I am indebted to thee for a Kingdome.
I here surrender vp all Soueraignetie,
Raigne peacefully with thy espoused Bride,   *Deliuers his Crowne*
Ashume my Son to take what is thy due.   *to him.*
PHA. How Sir, yer son, what am I then, your Daughter you gaue [115]
to me.
KIN. But heauen hath made asignement vnto him,   [I4ᵛ]
And brought your contract to anullity:
Sir, your entertainment hath beene most faire,

O

Had not your hell-bred lust dride vp the spring,   [120]
From whence flow'd forth those fauours that you found:
I am glad to see you safe, let this suffice,
Your selfe hath crost your selfe.

LEON. They are married sir.

PHAR. How married? I hope your highnesse will not vse me so,   [125]
I came not to be disgraced, and returne alone.

KING. I cannot helpe it sir.

LEON. To returne alone, you neede not sir,
Here is one will beare you company,
You know this Ladies proofe, if you   [130]
Fail'd not in the say-taging.

ME. I hold your scoffes in vildest base contempt,
Or is there said or done, ought I repent,
But can retort euen to your grinning teeths,
Your worst of spights, tho Princesse lofty steps   [135]
May not be tract, yet may they tread awry,
That boy there—

BEL. If to me ye speake Lady,
I must tell you, you haue lost your selfe
In your too much forwardnesse, and hath forgot   [140]
Both modesty and truth, with what impudence
You haue throwne most damnable aspertions
On that noble Princesse and my selfe: witnesse the world;
Behold me sir.   *Kneeles to* LEON, *and discouers her haire.*

LEON. I should know this face; my daughter.   [145]

BEL. The same sir.

PRIN. How, our sometime Page, *Bellario*, turn'd woman?

BEL. Madame, the cause induc't me to transforme my selfe,
Proceeded from a respectiue modest
Affection I bare to my Lord,   [150]
The Prince *Phylaster*, to do him seruice,
As farre from any laciuious thought,
As that Lady is farre from goodnesse,
And if my true intents may be beleeued,   [K1r]
And from your Highnesse Madame, pardon finde,   [155]
You haue the truth.

PRIN. I doe beleeue thee, *Bellario* I shall call thee still.

PHI. The faithfullest seruant that euer gaue attendance.

LEON. Now Lady lust, what say you to'th boy now;
Doe you hang the head, do ye, shame would steale   [160]
Into your face, if ye had grace to entertaine it,
Do ye slinke away?
                                        Exit MEGRA *hiding her face.*

KING. Giue present order she be banisht the Court,
And straightly confinde till our further   [165]
Pleasure is knowne.

PHAR. Heres such an age of transformation, that I doe not know
how to trust my selfe, I'le get me gone to: Sir, the disparagement

you haue done, must be cald in question. I haue power to right my
selfe, and will.   [170]

Exit PHARAMONT.

KING. We feare ye not sir.

PHI. Let a strong conuoy guard him through the Kingdome,
With him, let's part with all our cares and feare,
And Crowne with ioy our happy loues successe.   [175]

KING. Which to make more full, Lady *Gallatea*,
Let honour'd *Clerimont* acceptance finde
In your chast thoughts.

PHI. Tis my sute too.

PRIN. Such royall spokes-men must not be deni'd.   [180]

GAL. Nor shall not, Madame.

KING. Then thus I ioyne your hands.

GAL. Our hearts were knit before.   *They kisse.*

PHI. But tis you Lady, must make all compleat,
And giues a full period to content,   [185]
Let your loues cordiall againe reuiue,
The drooping spirits of noble *Trasiline*.   [K1ᵛ]
What saies Lord *Leon* to it ?

LEON. Marry my Lord I say, I know she once lou'd him.
At least made shew she did,   [190]
But since tis my Lord *Phylasters* desire,
I'le make a surrender of all the right
A father has in her; here take her sir,
With all my heart, and heauen giue you ioy.

KING. Then let vs in these nuptuall feastes to hold,   [195]
Heauen hath decreed, and Fate stands vncontrold.

FINIS.

APPENDIX B

Lineation

The following list of variants in lineation collates the chief passages where editors have questioned the arrangement of Q2, or where this edition has adopted an arrangement different from that of Q2. The Q1 reading is also cited in each instance where it differs from Q2, except in the beginning and end (reproduced in Appendix A), where its text differs substantially from Q2's. Not all rearrangements of the lineation by editors have followed the same pattern, and not all editors have followed their predecessors' rearrangements. In this collation only the lineation of the first editor to rearrange the text is given, unless the rearrangement has been adopted for this edition, in which case the editor whose arrangement has been followed is noted.

I. i

117–18. When . . . off] *Q1;* When . . . done, / Whilst . . . off *Q2.*

121–2. I fear . . . more] *Q1 (with break at* too: / well); I fear . . . too: / Well . . . more *Q2.*

158–65. I . . . judgment] *Q1, 2;* I . . . certainly / He'll . . . shape: / But . . . speeches, / Than . . . them; / Let . . . find, / In . . . virtues, / One . . . him, / He . . . sun, / He'll . . . trifles / In . . . judgment *Langbaine.*

169–70. Mark . . . us] *Q1 (with break at* feares / and); Mark . . . feares. / O . . . us *Q2.*

194–5. Here's . . . tooth-drawer] *Q1 (with break at* vaines, / the); Here's . . . vaines: / The . . . tooth-drawer *Q2.*

196–7. Sir . . . mad] *Dyce;* I . . . appeare / to . . . mad *Q1;* Sir . . . appeare / To . . . mad *Q2.*

200–1. A faint . . . nothing] *Weber;* A faint . . . ouer, / And . . . nothing *Q2;* . . . a faint shaddow: / That . . . ouer, / And . . . nothing *Q1.*

204–7. Has . . . kingdom] *Q2; prose of irregular line-lengths in Q1;* Has . . . already, / For . . . means / To . . . gentlemen, / By . . . hazard / Although . . . kingdom *Weber.*

258–60. That . . . gods] *Dyce;* That . . . we / Will . . . gods *Q2; prose in Q1.*

291–6. See . . . dew] *Q2; prose in Q1;* See . . . not / Spoke home
. . . *(rest as Q2) Theobald.*

I. ii

2–3. Dear . . . me / At first] *Weber; one line in Q1;* Deare . . .
wont / To . . . first *Q2.*

163–4. If . . . gone] *Q2; one line in Q1.*

171–9. Good . . . Pharamond] *Q2;* Good . . . gods — / Peace . . .
Philaster. / I . . . back. / You . . . Pharamond *Boas.*

192–3. 'Tis . . . married] *Q1;* 'Tis . . . stop / His . . . married *Q2.*

202–5. If . . . elsewhere] *Q1;* If . . . thoughts, / I . . . honour / *rest
as prose Q2.*

II. i

6–10. Sir . . . Perhaps] *Q2;* Sir . . . nothing, / And . . . yours, / *rest
as prose on new page Q1;* Sir . . . up / When . . . something / By . . .
unknown, / And . . . conster / A . . . perhaps / *Theobald.*

II. ii

31–4. No . . . being] *Q2;* No . . . though / I . . . you. / Do . . .
give / No . . . being *Dyce.*

69–70. talk an hour / Out quickly] *Q1, 2;* talk / An hour out
quickly *Dyce.*

92–7. By . . . me] *This ed.;* By . . . not: / I'le . . . now ? / Me thinkes
. . . before: / But . . . it. / Sticke . . . to morrow, / I'le . . . time; /
Can . . . me ? *Q2.*

112–13. By . . . sir] *Q2;* By . . . indeed, / But . . . sir *Dyce.*

134–6. bashful . . . you] *Q2; prose of irregular line-lengths in Q1;*
bashful; / Speak . . . this, / And . . . you *Dyce.*

II. iii

33–4. Sir . . . so] *Boas; one line Q1, 2.*

II. iv

21–4. Why . . . herself] *Q2; prose of irregular line-lengths in Q1;*
Why . . . he / That must . . . pillow / Like . . . voice / Binding . . .
princess / Does . . . herself *Boas.*

31–2. All . . . bed] *Q1;* All . . . rest, / Come . . . bed *Q2.*

108–9. Let . . . business] *Theobald;* Let . . . vp, / *rest as prose Q1;*
Let . . . Prince, / Let . . . businesse *Q2.*

177–8. So . . . wait / On . . . boy] *Q2; prose in Q1.*

III. i

27–30. Why . . . faith] *Q1, 2;* Why, gentlemen, / 'Tis . . . speech. /
She . . . we, / If . . . faith *Theobald.*

36–7. Here . . . you] *Q1, 2;* Here . . . comes. / Good . . . spent /
Some . . . you *Theobald.*

91–4. O . . . light] *Q2;* O . . . not so, / *rest as prose Q1;* O . . . not
so, / Good . . . truth / That . . . more, / It . . . think / The . . . light
Weber.

102. O . . . boy] *Q1, 2;* O . . . gods, / A . . . boy *Theobald.*

127–9. Why . . . in 't] *Q1, 2;* Why . . . you / So . . . this ? / When
. . . virtue, / I . . . in 't *Dyce.*

190–3. Methinks . . . to see] *Q2; prose in Q1;* Me thinkes . . .
tongue / So . . . lookes / That . . . see *Turner.*

244–6. Then . . . now] *Q2;* Then . . . life, / For . . . now *Q1;* Then
. . . time / To . . . life, / For . . . now *Theobald.*

250–2. Fie . . . not] *Q2;* Fie . . . where, / Thou . . . me, / If . . .
not *Q1;* Fie, fie, / So . . . when / And . . . plagues / Fall . . . not *Theobald.*

262–3. O . . . die] *Theobald; one line Q1, 2.*

III. ii

9–10. None . . . none] *Q1, 2;* None . . . self, / I . . . none *Turner.*

24. By . . . ask] *Q1, 2;* By . . . pardon, / Why . . . ask *Turner.*

27–8. Put . . . of] *Q1, 2;* Put . . . that / Good . . . of *Turner.*

73–84. O cruel . . . Philaster] *Q2; Q1 similar except l. 82* . . . it /
Till he . . .; O cruel! / Are . . . tell you / How . . . to you, / And . . .
bring you / Letters . . . service ? / Wake . . . praise ? / Who . . .
elegies, / And . . . pictures, / And . . . lute, / And . . . sleep / Upon
. . . cry, / O . . . Philaster *Theobald.*

85–8. O . . . better] *Dyce; so Q2 except ll. 87–8* . . . forget / The . . . ;
O . . . thee, / That . . . loyall. / Mistresse . . . better *Q1.*

IV. i

18. You . . . you] *Q1, 2;* You . . . sir, / And . . . you *Dyce.*

IV. iv

22. How's . . . again] *Q1, 2;* How's that ? / Answer . . . again *Weber.*

41. Faith . . . is] *Q1, 2;* Faith, I cannot / Unless . . . is *Dyce.*

76–7. I will . . . tailor] *Q2;* I will . . . aliue, / But . . . Taylor *Q1;
lined as prose in Turner.*

87. Each . . . myself] *Q1, 2;* Each . . . way; / Here . . . myself
Weber.

IV. v

95–6. To multiply . . . to] *Q2; prose in Q1;* To multiply . . . thou /
Wilt . . . to *Dyce.*

127–8. Some . . . him] *Q1, 2;* Some . . . wretch; / Alas . . . him
Theobald.

141-3. By all . . . close] *Q1, 2;* By . . . will. / Woodman . . . King, / And . . . dressing. / Come . . . close *Dyce.*

iv. vi
59-60. O . . . Princess] *Q2; prose in Q1;* O . . . damned / In . . . shape / To . . . Princess *Theobald.*
68. I . . . deed] *Q1, 2;* I . . . know / Who . . . deed *Theobald.*
133-4. Sir . . . Philaster] *Q2; prose in Q1;* Sir . . . sure / It . . . Philaster *Weber.*
135. Question . . . was] *Q1, 2;* Question . . . more, / It was *Dyce.*
136. The . . . that] *Q1, 2;* The . . . him, / Will . . . that *Dyce.*
139. Sir . . . disguised] *Q1, 2;* Sir . . . he, / He . . . disguised *Weber.*
140. I . . . still] *Q1, 2;* I . . . stars, / That . . . still *Weber.*

v. ii
34-5. Take . . . sorrow] *Q1, 2;* Take . . . heart / Will . . . sorrow *Dyce.*
40-51. Deal . . . death] *Q1, 2;* Deal . . . sir. / Why . . . asked / Your . . . it? / Enjoy . . . plain. / We . . . so. / 'Tis . . . death *Boas.*

v. iii
29-31. Free . . . earth] *Q2; prose in Q1;* Free from the fervour of the . . . star / And . . . clouds, / When . . . delivered / In . . . earth *Dyce.*
51-4. Your . . . coat] *Q2; prose in Q1;* Your . . . husband! / Call . . . citadel; / There . . . provide / A . . . saffron / Into . . . coat *Weber.*
66-7. Sir . . . swear by] *Q2; one line Q1, Weber.*
122-6. Ay . . . thought] *Q1;* Ay . . . life, / This . . . *rest as prose Q2;* Ay . . . life, / This . . . all; / A . . . plagues / For . . . honour; / O . . . me / And . . . thought *Colman.*

v. iv
1-16.] *Q1;* Come . . . caps / Swarm . . . mother / Gibberish . . . mouthes / Vp . . . halfe a / Fathome . . . Pepper, / And . . . *Philaster,* / Let . . . dongs, / My . . . Clubs, / Then . . . paintings; / Spitted . . . silkes, / Or . . . Tishues, / Dearely . . . Custards, / Your . . . affections / In . . . duckers, / Vp . . . valors, / And . . . feele / The . . . *Philaster,* / Cry . . . cry *Q2;* Come . . . fall on, / Let . . . Boys, / And . . . mother / Gibberish . . . *(rest as Q2) Theobald.*
18-21.] *This ed.;* How . . . boyes; / I . . . -sailes / To . . . Argosie / Hull . . . Cockles *Q2;* How . . . Lord prisoner? / These . . . you, / These . . . Foyst, / And . . . Argosea, / Stoope . . . coales *Q1. Q1 ceases to correspond closely with Q2 after this passage.*
23-33.] *This ed.;* My . . . know / And . . . talke / No . . . Crowne / Shall . . . Pippen, / Downe . . . liue, / Ile . . . spirits, / Make . . .

Hectors, / And . . . do, / Now . . . lye, / And . . . Prince, / I . . . -legd, /
Like . . . wiper Q2.

37–42. He would . . . coach-whip] This ed.; in prose, then . . . /
downe . . . whip / To . . . galoone-laces, / Ile . . . Coach-whip Q2;
He . . . he ? / Give . . . pikes ; / Branch . . . satin, / And . . . cut. / Your
. . . gentlemen: / I'll . . . seams. / Oh . . . galloon-laces! / I'll . . .
coach-whip Weber.

44–52. Hold . . . butter] This ed.; Hold . . . himselfe, / He . . .
seald vp / With . . . see / Heauen . . . going, / Nay . . . you, / You . . .
King. / Thou . . . Church-ale, / Thou . . . scarcenet, / Thou . . . nothing / But . . . Boy / Beate . . . Butter Q2; Hold, hold, / The . . .
himself; / He . . . seeled up / With . . . only / See . . . rest as Q2, Dyce.

55–7. No . . . boys] This ed.; No . . . Donsels, / As . . . flourish, /
The . . . kils / As . . . Boyes Q2.

60–1.] Q2; I'll . . . build / A . . . gate Theobald.

62–3. I'll . . . silver] This ed.; Ile . . . with, / For . . . siluer Q2.

68–9.] Q2; Captain . . . sword, / And . . . scabbards Theobald.

71–4.] Q2; No . . . do / With . . . made / Rare . . . bones, / If . . .
me Weber.

86–7. Of . . . honour] Q2; Of . . . a-tilt, / And . . . honour Theobald.

115–16. Good . . . sir] Turner; Good . . . you, / Hee's . . . Sir Q2.

123–4. Good . . . love] Colman; prose in Q2.

130–1.] Q2; one verse-line Dyce.

132–6. Go . . . boys] This ed.; Go . . . Curtesie. / Fall . . . man /
Trace . . . to / The . . . haue / Musicke . . . Boyes Q2; Go . . . courtesy. / Fall . . . come, / And . . . again / And . . . tavern / And . . .
music, / And . . . boys Weber.

v. v

62. Swear . . . promise] Q2; Swear . . . true / To . . . promise Theobald.

83. Come . . . constancy] Q2; Come . . . flesh / Will . . . constancy
Weber.

87. Haste . . . you] Q2; Haste there, / Why . . . you Weber.

101. Yes . . . where] This ed.; Yes . . . readily / I . . . where Q2.

141. And . . . malice] Q2; And . . . despite / Of malice Weber.

Index to Annotations

An asterisk before a word indicates information which supplements that given in *O.E.D.* The index usually lists the form of a word which appears in the text, but the basic form is occasionally given for the grouping together of more than one occurrence of a word.

137